MS. facsimile: *Child Harold*, stanzas 12, 13 and 14
(MS. 8, page 56)

THE LATER POEMS
OF JOHN CLARE

The Later Poems

of

John Clare

edited by

ERIC ROBINSON

and

GEOFFREY SUMMERFIELD

MANCHESTER UNIVERSITY PRESS

171257

1

Published by the University of Manchester at
THE UNIVERSITY PRESS
316–324 Oxford Road, Manchester 13

Printed in Great Britain by Butler & Tanner Ltd, Frome and London

Contents

INTRODUCTION   1

THE MANUSCRIPTS AND THE LONGER POEMS   12

NOTES ON THE LONGER POEMS   21

CHILD HAROLD   33

DON JUAN   81

MS. 110   95

SHORTER POEMS   153

POEMS FROM THE KNIGHT TRANSCRIPTS   163

GLOSSARY   278

INDEX OF FIRST LINES   281

PLATES

Facsimile of MS. 8, page 56, *Child Harold*, stanzas 12, 13, 14 *frontispiece*

I Facsimile of MS. 8, pages 46–7, *Child Harold*   *facing page* 47

II Facsimile of MS. 10, pages 96–7   157

All three plates are by courtesy of Northampton Public Library Committee.
The photographs were taken by Mr. Bruce A. Bailey.

Acknowledgments

THE editors wish to thank most warmly the Committee of the Northampton Public Library, and Mr. Halliday and his staff; the Peterborough Museum Society and their secretary, Dr. Bell; and the Delegates of the Bodleian Library. We are also very grateful to Mr. A. J. V. Chapple, of the University of Manchester, who so kindly read through our manuscript and advised us on editorial method.

The Delegates of the Clarendon Press have kindly extended to us their copyright of John Clare's unpublished works.

Introduction

I

THE various protestations of Clare's editors that they have at last done justice to his poetry must make the critical reader wary of them. What the reader cannot appreciate, if he has not looked at Clare's manuscripts for himself, is the immense difficulties that every editor of Clare encounters: the sheer bulk of the material, the intricacies of much of the handwriting, the state of the manuscripts which are often mere scraps of paper pasted into a larger book, the apparent disorder of Clare's creative processes which produced notes, poems, letters, and anagrams all mixed together in a furious welter. Moreover, as Clare manuscripts leave the sale-rooms from time to time for America, further editorial problems occur, and it must be a grief to all lovers of Clare's poetry to watch his autograph manuscripts being so widely dispersed over the Western hemisphere. In the face of these difficulties, any editor of Clare may make mistakes, but it is important that the search to establish true texts of Clare's poems should go on, and it is also true that Clare has not been altogether fortunate in his editors—from John Taylor, his first publisher,[1] down to the present day. First of all, they have all corrected his spelling, altered his punctuation, and have generally felt themselves entitled to adjust his texts wherever they have thought fit. Even Mr. Geoffrey Grigson, who, in his introduction to *Poems of John Clare's Madness*, made the same complaint about 'the condescension of those who can spell and insert semicolons', frequently made alterations to Clare's text without saying what he had done, and in addition hit an all-time low for inaccuracy in his readings of Clare's poetry. The occasional mistake is forgivable but Grigson's inaccuracy is persistent. Remarks like this make us vulnerable also. So what claims do we make to greater accuracy?

[1] See E. Robinson and G. Summerfield, 'John Taylor's editing of Clare's "The Shepherd's Calendar" ', in *Review of English Studies*, N.S. XIV, 56, 1963.

When we are working from a Clare text, not as in the Knight transcripts from an already edited version, we have published Clare exactly as he wrote, preserving his punctuation or lack of it, his capitalization and his spelling. The only alterations we have made are first, to expand ampersands into the word 'and', capitalizing the word when it comes at the beginning of a line, and second, if it appears to us that a word has been omitted, we have inserted it in square brackets [ ] in the text. One other, rather more important qualification has to be made to the phrase 'exactly as he wrote'. In the manuscripts of the High Beech period and the years that followed at Northborough, and in the Northampton General Lunatic Asylum, Clare intermingled all sorts of material on the pages. The poems *Child Harold* and *Don Juan*, closely related in subject matter, are woven in with each other on the pages, together with a long series of scripture paraphases, notes, letters, and the journal of his escape from High Beech. Such confusions occur in his earlier manuscripts also, but not to the same extent. They may have been caused partly by his shortage of writing paper, but even in the earlier papers the habit is nearer to the tradition of the eighteenth-century commonplace book with its jottings of all that might occur to the writer as thoughts pass through his mind. For that reason to talk about 'confusions' is misleading. What we have before us in Clare's manuscripts is a mass of material all conditioned by a dominant mood or emotion, further complicated by Clare's need to use every scrap of paper in the book. Oftentimes the juxtaposition of material in the manuscripts is illuminating. One gets an idea of how Clare's mind was working, but we found it difficult to believe that the reader would be prepared to read Clare in the order presented by the manuscripts. It must also be remembered that Clare himself has indicated in these rough books what was the order that he himself intended in his longer poems, by numbering stanzas, making insertions with asterisks, and generally clarifying his own mind. We have disentangled *Child Harold* and *Don Juan* from the other material but in doing so we have produced a very different result from Mr. Grigson, especially for *Child Harold*, a point to which we return later in the introduction. For the moment it suffices to say that we have done the minimum of rearrangement, and that for the rest we have not altered Clare's text, so that the reader may be assured that he is reading John Clare in his natural state and not John Clare scrubbed and spruced up for inspection by the Board of Guardians.

In MSS. 6 and 8 at Northampton Public Library,[1] Clare has drawn up one or two drafts of advertisements for the books that he was then writing. One refers to the poem he called *Don Juan*:

Speedily will be published

The Sale of Old Wigs and sundries
A Poem By Lord Byron

In Quarto 8vo and twelves[2]

Another suggests that Clare himself envisaged all the varied contents of these manuscripts as material for one volume:

In a short time will be Published

A New Vol of Poems by Lord Byron
Not yet collected in his works
Containing. Songs New Cantos of Child Harold
And ~~Scripture Paraphrases~~ additional Hebrew Mel[o]dies
~~Letters etc~~ Fragments etc[3]

In his letters of this time there are also references to his Byronic creations, as in the following to Mary Joyce:

I have been rather poorly I might say ill for 8 or 9 days before haymakeing and to get my self better I went a few evenings on Fern hill and wrote a new Canto of 'Child Harold' and now I am better I sat under the Elm trees in old Mathews Homestead Leppits Hill where I now am—2 or 3 evenings and wrote a new canto of Don Juan— merely to pass the time away but nothing seems to shorten it in the

---

[1] See below, pp.12, 13-14.   [2] MS. 8, p.32; MS. 6 p.37.
[3] MS. 8, p.39.

least and I fear I shall not be able to wear it away—nature seems dead
and her very pulse seems frozen to an icicle in the summer sun . . .[1]
Byron occupied his mind, and for very understandable reasons.
Clare believed that he had been 'imprisoned' at High Beech because he had committed bigamy with Mary Joyce and Patty
Turner. Byron's own flouting of the sexual *mores* of the time,
together with the worship which he drew to himself from many
women, young and old, his championship of radical political
causes and the great success of his poetry, all led Clare to have an
intense interest in him and then, in his mental disorder, to identify
himself with him. Cyrus Redding, after visiting Clare at High
Beech, wrote:

I found Clare in a field cutting up thistles, a small man and slender
rather than stout. He was pleased to see me. We entered at once upon
the subject of poetry. He was in his conversation as simple as in his
verse. He had nothing of the clown about him but his dress. He leaned
upon the tool he was using, and spoke of Byron and his poetry in
perfect good taste.[2]

Clare also asked Redding to send him Byron's works.[3] Redding does not comment on Clare's self-identification with Byron
as G. J. de Wilde did in a letter to F. Martin, many years later,
25 February 1865,[4] but presumably he had not seen Clare's own
manuscript of *Don Juan* where that identification is explicit (see
below, p.92). It was, of course, only one of many illusions
experienced by Clare—that he was Jack Randall, the prizefighter,
or Robert Burns, or Shakespeare, etc. The volumes of Byron
owned by Clare at High Beech, presumably including those sent
him by Redding, are mentioned in Clare's letter to Dr. Allen
(27 August 1841):

I had Eleven Books sent me from How & Parsons Book sellers some
lent and some given me—out of the Eleven I only brought 5 vols

---

[1] *Letters*, p.290. (See below, pp.19-20, for list of expanded titles.) Cf. also,
the letter to Eliza Phillips, *Letters*, p.291.
[2] Letter quoted in *Sketches*, p.37.
[3] Cyrus Redding, 'Clare, the Poet', in *The English Journal*, 15 May 1841, p.306.
[4] *Sketches*, p.39.

here & as I dont want any part of Essex in Northamptonshire agen I wish you would have the kindness to send a servant to get them for me I should be very thankfull not that I care about the books altogether only it may be an excuse to see me & get me into company that I do not want to be acquainted with—one of your Labourers Pratts wife borrowed Childe Harold & [　　　　]¹ & Mrs Fishers Daughter has two or three or perhaps more all Lord Byrons Poems & Mrs King late of the Owl Public house Leppit Hill & now of Endfield High Way has two or three all Lord Byrons Poems and one is the 'Hours of Idleness'.²

The dating of *Child Harold* and *Don Juan* is not altogether simple. MS. 8 has inscribed at the front, 'John Clares Poems Feby 1841'. It contains parts of *Don Juan*, *Child Harold*, and a first draft of Clare's account of his journey from Essex when he escaped on 20 July 1841. MS. 6 is later than MS. 8, containing a fair copy of much of the contents of MS. 8, MS. Don C. 64 (Bodleian Library) and MS. 49 (Peterborough Museum Society). MS. 6 was still in use after 11 November 1841. Clare's letter to Eliza Phillips, in which he says that he is writing a new canto of *Don Juan* and that he has written a new canto of *Child Harold*, was written between 11 July and 20 July 1841 when he ran away. The day, Sunday, 11 July 1841, is established by internal evidence from *Don Juan* itself:

> Now this day is the eleventh of July
> & being sunday——³

One of Clare's *Hebrew Melodies*, which immediately precedes stanza 24 of *Child Harold*, is dated by Clare, 30 April 1841.⁴ Certain drafts of stanzas of *Child Harold* appear in a copy book, Peterborough MS. 57, inscribed 'Wm Clare 19 April 1841'. Just exactly when Clare began his Byronic creations therefore cannot be established, but it is certain that they were not completed by the time he left High Beech; and probably not until December 1841. The newspapers, *The Lincolnshire Chronicle & General Advertiser* and *The Lincoln Rutland & Stamford Mercury*, in the Bodleian

¹ Word illegible.
² Bodleian MS. Don. a. 8. Note discrepancies with *Letters*, pp.294–5.
³ See below, p.91.　　　　⁴ MS. 8, p.64.

Library, in the margins of which stanzas of *Child Harold* appear, are dated 27 August 1841 and 3 September 1841 respectively. What is more important than the precise dating is the evidence provided by these manuscripts of Clare's persistent endeavour over several months to write two long poems and to revise them according to his creative light, and this at a time when his mind was severely disordered and when, after his journey back from Essex, he was physically exhausted. Though it is true that he never wrote another long poem after this period to compare with *Child Harold*, the impulse to do so remained with him, as MS. 110 shows. There the combination of nine-line stanzas and songs continues, together with the Byronic influence, even to eulogies of Greece. Out of this turmoil, then, came *Don Juan* and *Child Harold*—bone of each other's bone, flesh of each other's flesh, and yet so very different from each other both in style and quality.

Don Juan is not Clare at his best. It is more extensively coarse than anything else that he wrote and cannot be said even by the most indulgent critic to represent good satirical writing. But it would be wrong to suppose that its coarseness is quite unprecedented in Clare's verse. His long poem *The Parish*, several epigrams, and many scraps about doctors and lawyers to be found among his unpublished verse, anticipate *Don Juan*. Mrs. Emmerson, Lord Radstock and John Taylor all tried to restrain his outspokenness in sexual matters and when that failed John Taylor suppressed or bowdlerized his poems. James Reeves's excellent anthology, *The Idiom of the People*, has shown in recent times the sort of sexual imagery in folk poetry from which Clare's own poems sprang. Yet there is still a difference between the sort of writing represented on the one hand by *The Foggy Dew* and several of Clare's love ballads, and on the other by the four-ale-bar jokes of Clare's 'satirical' writings. The latter may not be poetically satisfying but they are at least a testimony to the poet's lack of mawkishness. As Clare had said to Taylor when he omitted *My Mary* and *Dolly's Mistake* from the second edition of *Poems Descriptive*:

... those frumpt up misses brought up in those seminaries of mysterious wickedness (Boarding Schools) what will please em? Why we well know—but while their heart and soul loves to extravagance (what we dare not mention) false delicacy's seriousness muscles up the mouth and condemns it.[1]

Don Juan also reveals Clare the avid reader of newspapers, in which also a great deal of his verse was published.[2] The style of Clare's *Don Juan*, though nowhere near so finished as Byron's, does show affinities with the more famous poem. Its racy colloquialism, its nine-line stanza, its conversational order, and the habit of inventing ridiculous rhymes in order to complete the stanza remind us of Byron. So does the habit of inserting songs to amplify a theme or underline a mood:

> —Bricklayers want lime as I want ryhme for fillups
> —So here's a health to sweet Eliza Phillips

> *Song*
> Eliza now the summer tells . . .[3]

This only happens once in Clare's *Don Juan* but that it does so provides us with one of our arguments for publishing *Child Harold* in a quite different form from Mr. Grigson's two attempts.[4] Mr. Grigson has been quite arbitrary in his editing of *Child Harold*. One or two songs he has included but the bulk of them he has omitted. Yet they are clearly an integral part of the poem. Songs to Mary follow some mention of her name in the nine-line stanzas;[5] a word is caught up in the first line of a song, as when a song begins:

> Dying gales of sweet even
> How can you *sigh*[6] so

where the word 'sigh' is taken up from the last line of the previous nine-line stanza: 'I *sigh*[6] a poet and a lover still'; or on another

---

[1] *Letters*, p.58.

[2] No adequate survey of Clare's fugitive verse has been made, but Mr. D. Powell of Northampton Public Library is engaged on this task.

[3] See below, p.88.

[4] See *Poems of John Clare's Madness* (1949) and *Selected Poems of John Clare* (1950), both edited by Geoffrey Grigson.

[5] See below, pp.3–78, 39.   [6] Our italics.

occasion the general subject matter conditions stanzas and songs. One stanza begins:

> The autumn morn looks mellow as the fruit
> And ripe as harvest . . .

Then comes the song, 'Tis autumn now and natures scenes'. After the song, Clare continues the theme with 'Sweet comes the misty mornings in September'. To remove these songs from their contexts is to destroy the poem as Clare conceived it.

While he was at High Beech, and in the years immediately subsequent, Clare thought hard about many things. First about his own identity, since he so often became confused about it; secondly about love and marriage, and his relationships with Woman; thirdly about the conflict between the individual and society; and fourthly, about the educative force of Nature. In the midst of his mental turmoil, therefore, he began work on a poem which is more sustained in thought than anything else he ever attempted. *Child Harold* is not a complete success—it is not in the first place a unity—but it represents a real advance for Clare. The theme of Eden and the Fall is particularly interestingly handled in it.

MS. 110, which follows *Child Harold*, has moments of illumination but holds together much less well. It continues the pattern of nine-line stanzas and songs, but the songs are generally inferior to those in *Child Harold* and to many in the Knight transcripts, though the apocalyptic furor of 'There is a day a dredfull day' is quite terrifying.[1] As in *Don Juan* and *Child Harold*, the Eden image occurs with its connected preoccupations, but Clare seems to alternate in his *persona* between Byron and Burns, so that Scots dialect words occur more frequently. Needless to say, the Scots songs are not always the best things in MS. 110. As examples of the best things we should like to refer the reader to the sequence beginning:

> The healthfull mind that muses and inhales;[2]

to the songs, *March Violet*[3] and *The North Star*, and to several of the nine-line stanzas.

[1] See below, pp.104-5, 108-9.   [2] See below. p.151.   [3] See below, p.148.

No lover of Clare's poetry can fail to be grateful to W. F. Knight, the enlightened Superintendent of the Northampton Asylum, for transcribing so much of Clare's poetry and thus preserving it for posterity. At the same time, it must be confessed that he was not a perfect copyist and was rather inconsistent in his methods. Thus he sometimes preserves Clare's spelling and punctuation but more often corrects them. Occasionally when he cannot read a word he leaves a blank, but at other times he put in what he thinks the word must be. By and large it is probably true that he gives us a good picture of what Clare wrote, but he was unfamiliar with Clare's dialect words as he shows by underlining even those he has correctly transcribed.[1] The extent of his alterations can be seen in the following poem which occurs in Clare's own hand in MS. 110 at Northampton[2] and also in the Knight transcripts:

Song

1

'Twas just when early spring began
To open daiseys eyes again
And show the golden light within
Upon a sunny morning

2

Twas just when buds will swell to shoot
And budding primrose at the root
Begins to shew its sulphur suit
All on the dewy morning

3

When violets peep afore the dawn
On sweet moss-banks beneath the thorn
Ere yet a single leaf is born
To shield the chilly morning

[1] Unless these words were underlined by A. E. Baker when compiling her *Glossary*.
[2] See below, pp.135-6.

4

I saw a maid that morning grey
Upon her misty milking way
When dead grass tufts and naked spray
Bent with the wet that morning

5

As any flower her face was fair
And had the rose of June been there
There'd been nought in it to compare
With her I met that morning
Feby 15th/45

One does not know how much trust to put in Knight's observation that 'Clare will seldom turn his attention to pieces he has been interrupted in while writing—and in no instance has he ever rewritten a single line'. If the statement is true of his years at Northampton, it is certainly not true of his earlier years, when he was a most assiduous reviser and correcter of his own work. Clare may have been a little impatient with Knight's failure to understand his idiom and with the tendency he encountered in Knight, as he had with others in earlier days, to think that they knew better than he did.

The poems in the Knight transcripts are uneven, and we have taken only a selection. A third of those printed here have been previously published by Cherry, J. W. Tibble or Grigson, but there are many interesting variants. Almost every poem has at least one of Clare's insights, one of his moments of personal vision. At times there is a resemblance to Van Gogh, and the same assurance in an idiom peculiar to himself:

You see naught in shape but hear a deep song
That lasts through the sunshine the whole summer long
That pierces the ear as the heat gathers strong
And the lake like a burning fire glitters[1]

or:

How hot the sun rushes
Like fire in the bushes[2]

[1] See below, p.168.   [2] See below, p.180.

or:

> I love to see the breeze at eve
> Go winnowing oer the land[1]

His sense of stillness and movement is very acute, but it is not mere accuracy of observation that gives him his power. It is rather his ability to create his own universe of calm and storm, intense sunlight and misty shade, privacy and exposure. Though his lyrical gift was sometimes diffuse, he often compressed into a few lines the characteristic features of what he was describing:

> With the jackdaw that nauntles among the molehills
> In their grey powdered wigs, and bright yellow bills[2]

> Where high the brown hawk herries
> As if he'd gone to sleep i the marble coloured sky's[3]

> See the spinners lace work shine
> On the bents among the heather
> On the gorse from spine to spine
> Beaded with the dewy weather[4]

But it is unnecessary to make further selections. The reader will constantly encounter them for himself.

In these later lyrics, as in the other poems printed in this volume, Clare's interest in the theme of Eden is very clear. It is a symbolic pattern to which he continually returns in his poetry and his prose. Without examining the theme here in detail, it suffices to say that Clare lived with Eden always before him, a vision of perpetual freshness and innocence against which he tested, so to speak, the society in which he lived. He does right to claim for himself that:

> To him the dismal storm appeared
> The very voice of God
> And where the Evening rock was reared
> Stood Moses with his rod

---

[1] See below, p.185. [2] See below, p.171.
[3] See below, p.231. [4] See below, p.232.

B

This interest in the innocence of First Love which represents Paradise before the Fall links the poems of the Knight transcripts with *Child Harold*, *Don Juan* and MS. 110. Consequently they should not be labelled merely 'nature lyrics' and consigned to the primary-school anthology. Not all of the last songs are superb poetry—simplicity sometimes deteriorates into obviousness, emotion into sentimentality, provincial energy into eccentricity—but most of the songs we have printed here have excellent touches of observation, some have delicacy of feeling, and the best of them are hardly equalled except by the songs of the seventeenth century.

II

THE MANUSCRIPTS AND THE LONGER POEMS

MS. 6, Northampton Public Library

A folio volume, $10'' \times 14\frac{1}{2}''$, with 58 unlined pages. It contains numerous Biblical paraphrases (or Hebrew Melodies, as Clare preferred to call them), Clare's account of his escape from Essex, one or two short passages of descriptive prose, and fair copies of *Don Juan* and *Child Harold*, the latter remaining unfinished. Clare began to use this volume immediately after his return to Northborough from Essex, and it was still in use on or after 11 November 1841, since the stanza of *Child Harold*, 'Tis winter and the fields are bare . . .' is found in draft form in MS. Don. C. 64, following two stanzas written at Martinmass, 'Tis martinmass from rig to rig . . .'

MS. 7, Northampton Public Library

This is a scrap-book, $12'' \times 15''$, of 152 pages. Letters and scraps of paper carrying drafts of verse are pasted on alternate pages.

Page 15: one scrap of paper with Biblical paraphrases, quotation, and drafts of four stanzas of *Child Harold*.

Page 27: one page of a notebook, which contains drafts of three stanzas of *Don Juan*, and part of Chapter 38 of the Book of Job, following the words 'My dear Mary Joyce Clare' which suggest that he had proposed to write a letter and had then changed his mind. There are a significant number of unfinished letters in the Asylum MSS.: they suggest either a mind unable to see anything through or a mind facing a reality which proved intolerable.

Page 47: part of a catalogue for an auction-sale of furniture, addressed to Mrs. Clare, Northborough. On this Clare has written drafts of two of the songs from *Child Harold*.

Page 49: a fragment of what is presumably the same catalogue, which gives the address of the auction as Postland, Lincolnshire. On this are drafts of two stanzas of *Child Harold*.

Page 55: the margins of *The Morning Chronicle*, Friday, 18 June 1841. On these are written drafts of two songs from *Child Harold*, and a memorandum about the loan of books of poetry by Byron to various people living in the vicinity of Dr. Allen's Asylum. These are the same volumes as Cyrus Redding had lent to Clare and which Clare later asked Dr. Allen to send on to Northborough (see MS. Don. a. 8).

MS. 8, Northampton Public Library

A notebook, $4\frac{1}{4}'' \times 6\frac{1}{2}''$, containing 68 pages. It is inscribed: *John Clares Poems Feby 1841*, and contains drafts of *Don Juan* and *Child Harold*, many scriptural paraphrases and quotations, an attempt—such as recurs throughout Clare's MSS.—to keep an account of his finances, and a draft of the narrative of his escape from Dr. Allen's Asylum. It seems likely that he actually made entries in this notebook while on the journey, for on page 25 we find the following, written in a very disordered hand:

The man whose daughter is the queen of England is now sitting on a stone heap on the highway to bugden without a farthing in his pocket and without eating a bit of food ever since yesterday morning—when he was offered a bit of bread and cheese at Enfield—he has not had any since but if I put a little fresh speed on hope too may speed tomorrow —O Mary mary If you knew how anxious I am to see you and dear Patty with the childern I think you would come and meet me.[1]

Odd jottings in this notebook give us some idea of the sense of

---

[1] Cf. *Prose*, p.249, footnote, which reads *I rest near* for *I am to see.*

impotent grievance that he suffered or thought he suffered under Dr. Allen's regime:

Jack Randalls Challange To All The World

Jack Randall The Champion Of The Prize Ring Begs Leave To Inform The Sporting World That He Is Ready To Meet Any Customer In The Ring Or On The Stage To Fight For The Sum Of £500 Or £1000 Aside A Fair Stand Up Fight half Minute Time Win Or Loose he Is Not Particular As to Weight Colour Or Country All He Wishes Is To Meet With a Customer Who Has Pluck Enough To Come To The Scratch

Jack Randall

May 1st 1841 (p.42)

The source of such aggressiveness as he showed through the *persona* of the pugilist may well be implicit in the following:

April 21st 1841

		s	d		s	s	d

1 Weeks Labour—2 / 6—Drawn 1 – 1 left 6
April 27th Received 1s &
Ap 30 Received 6

s d

May 1st Do 6 2 / 6 left
May 3rd Do 6
Matthew Gammons over 5^d a day—
worked all the week and received only
6^d – due or left 2^s

(p.46)

Many stanzas of *Child Harold* were never transcribed from the draft of MS. 8 to the fair copy of MS. 6. This may have been due to his removal to St. Andrew's Asylum, Northampton, but there is no clear evidence for it.

MS. 9, Northampton Public Library

A small notebook of 16 pages, with an Almanack for 1850 inside the covers, containing three letters in code,[1] women's

[1] See E. Robinson and G. Summerfield, 'John Clare: An Interpretation of Certain Asylum Letters', *Review of English Studies*, N.S., XII, 50, May 1962.

names and addresses, some verse, and two characteristic notes:

1850 May 12th. Plumbs Pears and Apple Trees are in bloom and the Orchards are all blossoms. (p.12)

I think while I'm shut up of ID and her I cannot hear I silent seem and DI (p.14)

The second note is typical of Clare's use of code at this period, a pathetic attempt to pay homage to a sacred object without giving the game away. ID may be an anagram of Haidee or, more probably, the concealed name of a real girl.

MS. 10 (Halfpenny Ballad Book), Northampton Public Library

This is a pocket-book entitled *The Daily Journal, or Gentleman's, Merchant's, and Tradesman's Complete Annual Accompt-Book for the Pocket or Desk, 1827*. Inside the front cover, Clare has written: *John Clare Northborough near M Deeping Decr 26th 1849*; then, by way of advertisement, *Halfpenny Ballads by John Clare 1 Vol. 8s.* Thus, the name, *Halfpenny Ballad Book*, by which this volume is normally known, is a misnomer, for the volume contains very little verse, but many lists of women's names, some with addresses, lists of book-titles, a few letters and accounts of delusions:

Lord Nelson (John Clare) on Board the 'L'Orient' Flag Ship recieving the Sword of the Enemy—Blown up by the Spanish Admirals son— Lord Nelson. (p.118)

Child Harold began in 1809

1793

..16 and finished in 1818

1793

25 Jany 10 1850

Lord Byron was 16 yrs old when he began to write 'Child Harold' and finished it in 1818 when he was 25 when he wrote the 4th Canto he was Courting one Martha Turner the Daughter of Mr Willm Turner Walk Lodge he began it one Sunday and finished it in three or four hours under an Ash Tree in her Fathers Home Clare Byron. (p.93)

The letters in this pocket-book give us some inkling of the intensity of Clare's sense of deracination: two have been published by Professor and Mrs. Tibble; of the one to Elizabeth Dadford (*Letters*, p.305) they observe: 'Eliza Dadford exists only as a name'; but the fact that she is remembered in a particular locality, The Snow, i.e. part of Helpstone Common before enclosure, would suggest that, in common with many of the other women in the Asylum MSS., she inhabited the real world, the world with which Clare was still trying to maintain contact. The pathos of his attempt comes out in the following letter to his son, John:

My Dear John

I have not heard from you so long—how do you get on—I wrote to your brother Fred a few Days after Christmass and supposed that he was with You keeping the Holiday—'Love one another'—and be a happy Family and I will be as usual when I get oppertunity—for there is no oppertunity for it here there is neither room nor time for pleasure or common sense we are always wrongways—and may we all be wrongways for ever

Amen

(pp.55-6: early 1850)

MS. *110*, Northampton Public Library

This is a notebook, $4\frac{1}{2}'' \times 6\frac{3}{4}''$, covered in dark green leather, and inscribed: *John Clare Northborough Northamptonshire Novr 1845*. In addition to poetry, this volume contains some crude drawings, book-titles, lists of women's names, quotations from Cowper and Burns, names with comment attached and names turned into riddles:

Eliz^bth Newbon
'These two had been friends in Youth
'But slanderous tongues will poison truth'
Now oceans roll between them twain
That never can heal up again

(p.16)

Ass I eye knee's

(p.93)

In Fir Mary

(p.27)

May Rye Ann Pease Good

(p.33)

NO JOY C

(p.67)

Another riddle is the numeral, 49, which occurs at least sixteen times in the volume: since it refers neither to 1849 nor to Clare's age, it seems probable that it is intended as a record of Mary Joyce's forty-ninth birthday, which would have fallen in January 1846, had she lived. Support for an earlier dating of MS. 110 is perhaps found in the references to Queen Victoria, which may have been stimulated by her visit to Northampton in November 1844 and in the song 'Twas just when early springs begin . . .' which appears in Knight's transcripts with the date, February 15th 1845.

Knight Transcripts, Northampton Public Library

We have used the two volumes initiated by W. F. Knight himself, in preference to the two transcripts of these volumes. Knight admits that he experienced difficulties in reading Clare's manuscripts and it is also clear that Knight emended Clare in order to produce a more acceptable and tidier text.[1] It is illuminating, in this respect, to compare Knight with Baker. Knight's transcript of *The Wind* begins thus:

> The frolicksome wind the trees and the bushes
> Keep sueing and sobbing and waiving all day . . .

Baker (*Glossary*, II, p.308) reads:

> The frolicsome wind through the trees and the bushes
> Keeps sueing and sobbing and roaring all day . . .

Knight first wrote 'Keeps' and then amended it to 'Keep' to agree grammatically with the first line where he had omitted, presumably through oversight, 'through'; his misreading of 'roaring' as 'waiving' will be forgiven by anyone who has struggled with Clare's MSS. but this comparison does serve to suggest that, though Knight was remarkably pertinacious, it is perhaps sanguine to assume 'that most of them represent the poems as well as was ever possible' (*G.P.*, p.228).

MS. Don. a. 8, Bodleian=MS. Da8.

A copy of *The Lincolnshire Chronicle and General Advertiser*, Friday, 27 August 1841. In the margins and between the columns

[1] See Introduction, p.9.

of print Clare has written a draft of his letter to Dr. Allen, of High Beech Asylum, Epping, in which he gives an account of his escape and his reasons for escaping, and asks Allen to send his books on. This letter is published, with many errors, in *Letters*, pp.294–5.

A copy of *The Lincoln Rutland and Stamford Mercury*, Friday, 3 September 1841. In the margins are drafts of the Biblical paraphrases, *The New Jerusalem* and *The Last Judgment*, and of six stanzas of *Child Harold*, including a defective and cancelled eight-line draft of the stanza, 'What mellowness these harvest days unfold . . .' which Grigson uses in preference to the later version of MS. 6 (see *G.S.*, p.199).

A copy of *The Lincolnshire Chronicle and General Advertiser*, Friday, 27 August 1841. In the margins are drafts of six stanzas of *Child Harold* and of part of Clare's paraphrase of *Job*.

MS. Don. C. 64, Bodleian=*MS. DC 64*

A collection of manuscripts which include an exercise-book containing drafts of several Biblical paraphrases and of five stanzas of *Child Harold*, following the poem written at Martinmass (11 November 1841). These manuscripts also contain a collection of proverbs, which begins with the following characteristic definition:

Proverbs may be compared to a safe and beautiful arch of the simplest orders thrown over the blackest and most dangerous eddies and precipices that abound in the checkered landscape of life—over which we may walk in safety

MS. 49, Peterborough Museum

A notebook which contains Biblical paraphrases, a draft of the prose on Autumn (see *Prose*, p.241),[1] and drafts of fourteen stanzas from *Child Harold*. This notebook clearly belongs to the autumn and winter of 1841 and as in other notebooks Clare has made entries both at the front and at the back of the book: the latter pages we have numbered R1, R2, etc.

---

[1] In MS. 49, the description of the larks reads: 'a couple often fluskers and fights'.

On 19 October, Clare recorded: William found a Cowslip in flower.

On 4 November: a immense flock of sturnels settled on an ash tree in the orchard and when they took wing it was like a large roll of thunder.

On 12 December: Found a Cowslip in flower.

This notebook also contains a touch of that coarseness which characterizes *Don Juan*:

> His face is like a dragon
> His a–se is like a frog
> At heart a mere piegon
> In manner quite a hog　　　　　(p.R5)

But it speaks more emphatically of Clare's delight to be in Northborough once again:

The starnels flock in the fields and make a loud chattering wether quarreling or playing I cannot tell but the harmony of nature is seldom interupted by bad feelings the sparrows too flock and chitter in the neighbourhood of corn stacks which shepherds and other living almanacks say tokens bad weather.　　　　　(p.R7)

And even more emphatically of his abiding love for Mary Joyce:

> My heart my dear Mary from thee cannot part
> But the sweetest of pleasure that joy can impart
> Is nought to the memory of thee　　　　　(p.8)

MS. 57, Peterborough Museum

This consists of the cover only of an exercise or copy book, inscribed: *Wm Clare 19 April 1841*. It contains drafts of twelve stanzas of *Child Harold* and was presumably used by Clare after his return to Northborough.

The Books

CL—J. L. Cherry (ed.), *Life and Remains of John Clare*, London and Northampton, 1873.

GP—G. Grigson (ed.), *Poems of John Clare's Madness*, London, 1949.

GS—G. Grigson (ed.), *Selected Poems of John Clare*, London, 1950.

TP1 and *TP2*—J. W. Tibble (ed.), *The Poems of John Clare*, 2 vols., London, 1935.

Glossary—A. E. Baker, *Glossary of Northamptonshire Words and Phrases*, 2 vols., London, 1845.

Letters—J. W. and Anne Tibble (ed.), *The Letters of John Clare*, London, 1951.

Prose— J. W. and Anne Tibble (ed.), *The Prose of John Clare*, London, 1951.

Sketches—E. Blunden (ed.), *Sketches in the Life of John Clare written by himself*, London, 1931.

Burns—*The Poetical Works of Robert Burns*, Edinburgh, 1816.

The Editorial Conventions

Square brackets [ ] are used *in the notes* for variants rejected by Clare himself. The actual words are printed in Roman. If Clare has rejected more than one variant, they are placed in order, *a*, *b*, *c*, etc., as they appear to have occurred to him. Thus in *Child Harold*, note 1, p.55 below, the manuscript appears like this:

> Turns night into
> ~~Is still all the~~ day

and is represented in our note as:

> *a* [Is still all the] day *b* Turns night into

We have also used square brackets [ ] *in the text* on those few occasions where we have thought it necessary to interpolate a missing word or letter.

Curly brackets { } are used *in the notes* for Clare's alternative readings, either in the same manuscript or from another. The appropriate manuscript symbol is given after the curly brackets thus:

> {lifes sojourning} *MS.8, p.23*

Clare's own words are given in the footnotes in Roman. Editorial observations are given in Italic.

Sometimes we have given the correct spelling of a word in a footnote, where we have felt that the reader might have difficulty in identifying the word for himself. These corrected spellings are given in Italic in accordance with our convention. Similarly, any speculation of ours about the word or words intended by Clare is given in Italic and followed by a question mark.

Divergent readings by other editors are given in Italic between single quotation marks. Thus in the footnotes to the Knight Transcripts, Knight's readings are given in Italic between single quotation marks as they cannot be taken without question to represent Clare's own words.

Glossary

Clare's poetry is very rich in dialect words, many of which will be unfamiliar to the average reader. The glossary does not pretend to be exhaustive but includes all words not to be found in *The Shorter Oxford English Dictionary*. Simple vocabulary difficulties are therefore not dealt with in the footnotes and the reader is advised to consult the glossary whenever he encounters a difficulty in meaning.

III

NOTES ON THE LONGER POEMS

Don Juan

Our text is that of MS. 6, which contains the latest extant version of the poem. This version is clearly derived in part from both MS. 8 and MS. 7, p.27. Stanzas 2, 3, 4 and 5 are the fruit of later thought: they do not appear in MS. 8 at all, but a draft of three of them, 2, 3, and 4, appears on p.27 of MS. 7, while all four stanzas are appended to the fair copy of the poem in MS. 6 with this instruction: *To be inserted between the first and second verses at the beginning of the Poem.*

The form of the poem shows the influence of Byron, and, as in Clare's *Child Harold*, song forms an integral part of the poem's sequence. The one song in *Don Juan* is addressed to Eliza Phillips, and it is to her that he explicitly dedicates the poem in a letter which is found in MS. 8, p.13, following immediately after the draft of *Don Juan*:

My dear Eliza Phillips
Having been cooped up in this Hell of a Madhouse till I seem to be disowned by my friends and even forgot by my enemies for there is none to accept my challanges which I have from time to time given to the public I am almost mad in waiting for a better place and better company and all to no purpose It is well known that I am a prize fighter by profession and a man that never feared anybody in my life either in the ring or out of it—I do not much like to write love letters but this which I am now writing to you is a true one—you know that we have met before and the first oppertunity that offers we will meet again—I am now writing a New Canto of Don Juan which I have taken the liberty to dedicate to you in remembrance of Days gone bye and when I have finished it I would send you the vol if I knew how in which is a new Canto of Child Harold also—I am my dear Elize
yours sincerely
John Clare
(MS. 8, p.13)

Although we have so far failed to trace Elizabeth Phillips, there seems to us to be no good *prima facie* case for writing her off as a product of Clare's fantasies.

When the full range of Clare's poetry is eventually published, it seems likely that *Don Juan* will be regarded as less of a 'sport' than it is as present. Byronic idiosyncrasies of style apart, the themes of the poem are very much Clare's own, although some of its elements may have been stimulated by passing events of a transient kind. The company, for example, that he was keeping in Dr. Allen's Asylum certainly seems to have provoked in him a coarseness such as one meets only occasionally in the rest of his work:

Nigh Leopards hill stand All–ns hells
The public know the same
Where lady sods and buggers dwell
To play the dirty game

A man there is a prisoner there
Locked up from week to week
He's very fond they do declare
To play at hide and seek

With sweethearts so they seem to say
And such like sort of stuff
Well—one did come the other day
With half a pound of snuff

The snuff went here the snuff went there
And is not that a bad house
To cheat a prisoner of his fare
In a well ordered madhouse

Theyll cheat you of your money friend
By takeing too much care o't
And if your wives their cun–ys send
They're sure to have a share o't

Now where this snuff could chance to stop
Perhaps gifts hurded are up
Till Mat and steward open shop
And have a jolly flare up

Madhouses they must shut up shop
And tramp to fairs and races
Master and men as madmen stop
Life lives by changing places

(MS. 8, pp.21–2)

Similarly the preoccupation with Victoria and Albert may be traced in part to the news-worthiness of the recent marriage, but must also stem more deeply from Clare's recurrent and desperate concern with marriage and love-relationships, and also with the problem of patronage. In his letter to Dr. Allen, following his escape, he wrote:

You told me somthing before haytime about the Queen alowing me a yearly sallery of £100 . . . the first quarter had then commenced or else I dreamed so—if I have the mistake is not of much consequence to any one save myself and if true I wish you would get the Quarter

for me if due as I want to be independant and pay for board and
lodging while I remain here—I look upon myself as a widow or
bachellor I dont know which—I care nothing about the women now
for they are faithless and decietfull . . .   (MS. Da. 8)

When one considers the poem in the light of Clare's predica-
ments, one can perhaps most appropriately read it as a stylized
joke, one of the means whereby life is rendered tolerable. As for
the choice of *Don Juan* for his medium, it must be remembered
that one of the favourite literary exercises of the later 1820's and
the 1830's was to write a continuation of *Don Juan*,[1] and that
Clare had an example of this in his own library: *Continuation of
Don Juan*, Cantos XVII and XVIII, London, 1825 (presented to
Clare by C. F. Pitman). What more natural than that Clare should
do likewise?

Child Harold

The main sources for the text of *Child Harold* are MS. 6 and
MS. 8; other preparatory drafts are also found in MSS. 7, 49, 57,
Don. a. 8 and Don. C. 64. It is in our editing of this poem that we
differ most radically from Mr. Grigson, and our main differences
are, firstly, in the reading of particular words or phrases in the
MSS., second in the precedence given to one version rather than
another, and, third, in the organization of the sequence of the
parts. To dispose of these in the same order, Mr. Grigson's reading
of *Child Harold*, and of many other poems, seems to us seriously
inaccurate, in that it often presents a piece of nonsense where Clare
had in fact written good sense. In one case he prints an incomplete
stanza (*GS*, p.192) where Clare wrote a complete stanza, and in
another case he prints an incomplete draft (*GS*, p.199) in preference to the completed final version which is equally accessible.
The sequence of the parts is a more debatable matter, but the
evidence of the MSS. shows that Clare himself regarded the songs
as an integral part of the total poem, for in both MS. 6 and MS. 8
the nine-line stanzas and the songs are very clearly set out as parts
of a continuous sequence: there is ample evidence to show that
Clare was consciously following the Byronic precedent.

[1] See *Cambridge Bibliography of English Literature*, Vol. III, p.198.

It is clear, however, that the final draft of the poem in MS. 6 was never completed: the evidence of the drafts suggests that he was working on the poem at Northborough well into the Autumn of 1841, and it may well be that the completion of the poem was interrupted by his enforced removal to Northampton. Whatever the reason for thus breaking off, MS. 6 contains only part of what was to be transcribed from MS. 8, so that a considerable part of the poem remains in MS. 8 alone, while MS. 6 also draws on sources other than MS. 8. The editorial problem is therefore, in part, one of sequence: which comes first?

Since MS. 6 is later than MS. 8, our answer is to follow MS. 6 as far as it goes, and then to follow it with that part of the poem which appears only in the draft of MS. 8. We have made no attempt to break the poem down into a series of cantos, as Mr. Grigson has done (*GS.* pp.179 ff.). Although Clare speaks of writing 'a new Canto' in his letter of July 1841 to Elizabeth Phillips (see *supra*, p.22), he himself never uses the word, to the best of our knowledge, in any of the manuscripts of poems, and it is our opinion that when he speaks of a new canto, he uses the term to signify a continuation of a poem rather than to indicate a clearly defined section of a poem. Mr. Grigson's supposition that Clare 'seems to have planned it as a poem of four cantos' (*GP*, p.16), with a correspondence to the four seasons of the year, is quite ingenious but quite supererogatory, since the references to the seasons, which occur frequently in the poem, are due rather to the stimulus of the season in which he happened to be writing a particular part of the poem than to an over-all preconceived formula. The fact, moreover, that his method was of an *ad hoc* kind rather than schematic is demonstrated by the way in which particular details make their way into the poem. For example, the stanza 'How beautifull this hill of fern swells on . . .' (p.40) is of the same period as his letter to Mary which we quote (*Introduction*, pp.3-4) and the peculiar importance of Fern Hill to Clare at that time is emphasized by another entry in his notebook:

> Fern hill
> At the back of the chapple a beautifull retreat from a mad house
> (Ms 8, p.25)

Similarly, the autumnal stanzas, with their references to Glinton church spire and to the nakedness of the fens, were clearly written in the Autumn at Northborough, as the drafts in the margins of the *Lincoln Rutland & Stamford Mercury* of 3 September 1841 testify.

The unrhymed stanza, 'Honesty and good intentions . . .' and the song which precedes it (p.61) may not have been intended as an integral part of *Child Harold*. In MS. 6, the stanza, 'The blackbird startles from the homestead hedge . . .', is followed by some prose passages, some Biblical paraphrases, and some quotations,[1] together with the couplet:

> Nature says 'Mary' but my pen denies
> To write the truth and so it lives in sighs

The unrhymed stanza and the song are both found among these *miscellanea*, whereas the next stanza of *Child Harold*, 'The lightenings vivid flashes rend the cloud . . .' is preceded by the title, *Child Harold*, which serves to indicate the stanza's place in the sequence. We have, nevertheless, included both the song and the unrhymed stanza, in the interests of completeness; there is no evidence to indicate categorically that they are *not* part of the poem.

We have made no attempt to rearrange the stanzas from MS. 8, but have chosen to print them in the order in which Clare left them. Whereas Mr. Grigson has re-numbered these stanzas, we have preferred to retain Clare's order, even in the case of stanza 27 (p.68) which was clearly intended to follow stanza 26 (p.79) but occurs out of place simply because there was no room for it in the space following stanza 26. Since, however, MS. 8 does not contain stanzas numbered 1 and 2, but contains *two* stanzas numbered 18, any rearrangement would necessarily be based, in part, on inference. One could, of course, argue that the stanza, 'Where are my friends and childern . . .', should be numbered 28, and that the 18 is obviously Clare's error. Similarly, one could argue that the two unnumbered stanzas (p.79) on the theme of Solitude, with their opening apostrophe, were intended as stanzas 1

[1] See *GP*, p.19.

and 2, particularly since the 'green trees' of the second stanza, line 5, are taken up in the first line of the stanza numbered 3. We have decided, however, that since Clare's poetry has in the past been subjected to an excess of editorial zeal, it were better to leave Clare as near as possible as we found him, and to content ourselves with adding suggestions on how he might tentatively be rearranged.

In MS. 8, Clare wrote a two-part *Note for Child Harold*. Since it does not lodge conveniently in a footnote, we give it here:

Note for Child Harold

Easter Sunday—1841 Went In The Morning To Buckhurst Hill Church And Stood In The Church Yard—When A Very Interesting Boy Came Out While Organ Was Playing Dressed In A Slop Frock Like A Ploughboy And Seemingly About Nine Years Of Age He Was Just Like My Son Bill When He Was About The Same Age And As Stout Made—He Had A Serious Interesting Face And Looked As Weary With The Working Days As A Hard Working Man I Was Sorry I Did Not Give Him The Last Halfpenny I Had And Ask Him A Few Questions As To His Age And Name And Parents But Perhaps I May See Him Agen

Easter Monday—At The Easter Hunt I Saw A Stout Tall Young Woman Dressed In A Darkish Flowerd[1] Cotton Gown As A Milkmaid Or Farm Servant And Stood Agen Her For Some Minutes Near A Small Clump Of Furze—I Did Not Speak To Her But I Now Wish I Had And Cannot Forget Her—Then I Saw Another Get Out Of A Gig With A Large Sctoch Shawl On And A Pretty Face

(MS. 8, pp.43-4)

MS. 110

Although *Child Harold* was apparently left unfinished, the combination of reflective stanza and lyrical song was obviously congenial to Clare, for he returned to it in MS. 110. Here the Byronic *persona* has been supplemented and at times displaced by others, Burns and Cowper in particular. Byron persists clearly in the invocation of Italy, Greece and Turkey, and in the portrayal of Haidee whom Clare has transplanted from the second Canto of

[1] Grigson (*GP*, p.9) gives: Fox-red.

c

Byron's *Don Juan*; but Burns is the more pervasive influence in MS. 110, which contains clear evidence to support the view that in his delusions Clare saw himself not only as Byron but also as Burns:

> Anecdotes of Burns Poems the 'On the daisey' and 'The Mouse'
> On turning up a mouse with the plough
> This poem was written on the west wide of Royce Wood while driving Plough for my brother Jem occasioned by turning one up with a Plough   Robt Burns
> On the daisey on burying one under the furrow was written in the same field at Royce wood end which had been part of the green or Cowpasture   Robt Burns
> Tam O'Shanter was written in a part of the same field called Tenters Nook while at work in a garden of his master a Publican of the Bluebell Public house   Robt Burns
> (MS. 110, p.119)

This identification serves to explain the use of the Burns idiom in MS. 110, not always to very happy effect, although one should recognize that Clare sometimes improved on Burns. Compare, for example, Burns's 'O, wert thou in the cauld blast . . .' with Clare's 'O wert thou in the storm . . .' (pp. 165-6).

When Clare made his first visit to London, Octavius Gilchrist, who was accompanying him, pointed out Cowper's house in Huntingdon. Clare recalled this moment when he was writing his autobiography and, characteristically, 'thought of his tame hares'.[1] It is a mark of their affinities that MS. 110 should open with a quotation from *The Task* (Book II, lines 1-5) and that on two other occasions also he should invoke the shade of Cowper. The reference to the *Koran* may, however, seem outlandish, and yet not only did Clare possess a copy,[2] but it is clear that he drew on it for his poetry. There is no evidence to suggest that he was particularly attracted to Chapter XIX (entitled *Mary*) but Clare may certainly have observed the marked affinities between certain sections of the *Koran* and *Job* of which he had been making a metrical paraphrase at the time of writing *Child Harold*.

[1] MS. 63, Peterborough Museum. In *Prose*, p.80, Professor and Mrs. Tibble give this incorrectly as 'his time here'.

[2] *The Holy Koran; commonly called The Alcoran of Mohammed*, London, 1826.

Clare's mental state at this time is probably best demonstrated by a letter to his wife:

My dear Wife
I have wrote some few times to enquire about yourself and the Family and thought about yourself and them a thousand other things that I use to think of the childern—Freddy when I led him by the hand in his childhood I see him now in his little pink frock—seal skin cap—and gold band—with his little face as round as a apple and as red as a rose— and now a stout Man both strangers to each other the father a prisoner under a bad government so bad in fact that its no government at all but prison discipline where everybody is forced to act contrary to their own wishes 'the mother against the daughter in law and the daughter against the mother in law' 'the father against the son and the son against the father'—in fact I am in Prison because I wont leave my family and tell a falshood—this is the English Bastile[1] a government Prison where harmless people are trapped and tortured till they die— English priestcraft and english bondage more severe than the slavery of Egypt and Affrica while the son is tyed up in his manhood from all the best thoughts of his childhood bye lying & falshood—not dareing to show love or remembrance for Home or home affections living in the world as a prison estranged from all his friends still Truth is the best companion for it levels all distinctions in pretentions Truth wether it enters the Ring or the Hall of Justice shows a plain Man that is not be scared at shadows or big words full of fury and meaning nothing when done and said with them truth is truth and no further and the rights of man—age of reason and common sense are sentences full of meaning and the best comment of its truth is themselves—an honest man makes priestcraft an odious lyar and coward and a filthy disgrace to Christianity—that coward I hate and detest—the Revelations has a placard in capitals about 'The Whore of Babylon and the mother of Harlots' does it mean priestcraft I think it must—this rubbish of cant must soon die—like all others—I began a letter and ended a sermon— and the paper too

> I am dear Wife yours ever
> John Clare
> (MS. 110, pp.125–7)

[1] A recurrent image in Clare's mythology: in his letter to his wife, 19 July 1848, he describes the Asylum as 'the purgatorial hell and French Bastile of English liberty' (*KT*, II, p.103).

The bizarre anticlericalism of this letter, which may have had both personal and political causes, was to find voice yet again in 1849:

> In cant and mystery there lurks a wrong
> Poisonous as fangs within the Serpent head
> The subtleset one to Priestcraft does belong
> They humbug till the living turn the dead
> ⟨............⟩ the highest holds her head
> In Pulpit placed with fair and smirking face
> With tongues new oiled and hearts as cold as lead
> The priests descending into hells embrace
> The surplus[1] leaves and shows a harlots face
>
> (Ms. 10, p.91)

Similarly his answer to the moral anarchy with which he had felt himself to be surrounded in Dr. Allen's Asylum had been an outrageous and shockingly uncompromising honesty:

> Ballad—Fragment
>
> O Lord God Almighty How Usefull Art Thou
> To Darn The Knaves Cloak And To Paint The Thieves Brow
> As Good As A Laundress Thy Kindness Has Been
> To Help Starving Sinners And Wash The Unclean
> Thou'rt As Good As A Nurse To the Sickly And Lame
> That Live In Bad Houses And Die In Ill Fame
> For The Worst In The World Have A Passport For Heaven
> While The Best Go To Hell Like A Deed Unforgiven
>
> And Ill Hazard Hell Upon Life's Roughest Waves
> Before Ill Be Cheated By Ruffians and Knaves
> Plain Honesty Still Is The Truth Of My Song
> And Ill Still Stick For Right To Be Out Of The Wrong
> The Honest And True My Example Shall Be
> For While A Mans Honest His Conscience Is Free
>
> (MS. 8, p.49)

The voice of MS. 110 is quieter than this, but equally concerned with stating the truth in the reflective stanzas and finding a clear direct style in the songs. The confusions of the manuscript are

[1] i.e. surplice.

due to its being a draft only, so that we are—as it were—allowed to look over Clare's shoulder as he grappled with his muse. And we have made no attempt to interfere with the sequence: as in other notebooks, he worked at both ends of the book, so we have placed the front of the book at the beginning and then followed this with the verse from the back: we are tempted to add that, had we not indicated in a footnote, where this break occurs, it would not be very easy to find it.

Child Harold

CHILD HAROLD

Many are poets—though they use no pen
To show their labours to the shuffling age
Real poets must be truly honest men
Tied to no mongrel laws on flatterys page
No zeal have they for wrong or party rage
—The life of labour is a rural song
That hurts no cause—nor warfare tries to wage
Toil like the brook in music wears along—
Great little minds claim right to act the wrong[1]

Ballad[2]

Summer morning is risen
And to even it wends
And still Im in prison
Without any friends

I had joys assurance
Though in bondage I lie
—I am still left in durance
Unwilling to sigh

Still the forest is round me
Where the trees bloom in green
As if chains ne'er had bound me
Or cares had ne'er been

Nature's love is eternal
In forest and plain
Her course is diurnal
To blossom again

For homes and friends vanished
I have kindness not wrath
For in days care has banished
My heart possessed both

---

[1] *MS. 6, p.4; MS. 8, p.3.*   [2] *MS. 6, pp.4–5; MS. 8, p.3.*

My hopes are all hopeless
My skys have no sun
Winter fell in youths mayday
And still freezes on

But Love like the seed is
In the heart of a flower
It will blossom with truth
In a prosperous hour

True love is eternal
For God is the giver
And love like the soul will
Endure—and forever

And he who studies natures volume through
And reads it with a pure unselfish mind
Will find Gods power all round in every view
As one bright vision of the almighty mind
His eyes are open though the world is blind
No ill from him creations works deform
The high and lofty one is great and kind
Evil may cause the blight and crushing storm
His is the sunny glory and the calm[1]

Song[2]

The sun has gone down with a veil on her brow
While I in the forest sit museing alone
The maiden has been oer the hills for her cow
While my hearts affections are freezing to stone
Sweet Mary I wish that the day was my own
To live in a cottage with beauty and thee
The past I will not as a mourner bemoan
For abscence leaves Mary still dearer to me

---

[1] *MS. 6, p.5; MS. 8, p.32.*
[2] *MS. 6, pp.5–6; MS. 8, p.14.*

How sweet are the glooms of the midsummer even
Dark night in the bushes seems going to rest
And the bosom of Mary with fancys is heaving
Where my sorrows and feelings for seasons were blest
Nor will I repine though in love we're divided
She in the Lowlands and I in the glen
Of these forest beeches—by nature we're guided
And I shall find rest on her bosom agen

How soft the dew falls on the leaves of the beeches
How fresh the wild flower seems to slumber below
How sweet are the lessons that nature still teaches
For truth is her tidings wherever I go
From school days of boyhood her image was cherished
In manhood sweet Mary was fairer then flowers
Nor yet has her name or her memory perished
Though absence like winter oer happiness lowers

Though cares still will gather like clouds in my sky
Though hopes may grow hopeless and fetters recoil
While the sun of existance sheds light in my eye
I'll be free in a prison and cling to the soil
I'll cling to the spot where my first love was cherished
Where my heart nay my soul unto Mary I gave
And when my last hope and existance is perished
Her memory will shine like a sun on my grave

Mary thou ace of hearts[1] thou muse of song
The pole star of my being and decay
Earths coward foes my shattered bark may wrong
Still thourt the sunrise of my natal day
Born to misfortunes—where no sheltering bay
Keeps off the tempest—wrecked wheree'er I flee
I struggle with my fate—in trouble strong—
Mary thy name loved long still keeps me free
Till my lost[2] life becomes a part of thee[3]

---

[1] [arts] *MS. 6, p.6; MS. 8, p.18, reads* the *for* thou twice *in this line.*
[2] {lorn} *MS. 8, p.18.*   [3] *M.S. 6, p.6; MS. 8, p.18.*

Song[1] a

I've wandered many a weary mile
Love in my heart was burning
To seek a home in Mary[s] smile
But cold is loves returning[2]
The cold ground was a feather bed
Truth never acts contrary
I had no home above my head
My home was love and Mary

I had no home in early youth
When my first love was thwarted
But if her heart still beats with truth
We'll never more be parted
And changing as her love may be
My own shall never vary
Nor night nor day I'm never free
But sigh for abscent Mary

Nor night nor day nor sun nor shade
Week month nor rolling year[3]
Repairs the breach wronged love hath made
There madness—misery here
Lifes lease was lengthened by her smiles
—Are truth and love contrary
No ray of hope my life beguiles[4]
I've lost love home and Mary

Love is the main spring of existance–It
Becomes a soul wherebye I live to love
On all I see that dearest name is writ
Falsehood is here—but truth has life above
Where every star that shines exists in love

---

[1] MS. *8, p.23. See p.39, n.2, below. This song also occurs at MS. 6, p.1.*
[2] [loves sojourning] MS. *6, p.1;* {lifes sojourning} MS. *8, p.23.*
[3] {Nor week nor month nor rolling year} MS. *8, p.23.*
[4] [fate beguiles] MS. *6, p.1;* {fate beguiles} MS. *8, p.23.*

Skys vary in their clouds—the seasons vary
From heat to cold—change cannot constant prove
The south is bright—but smiles can act contrary
My guide star gilds the north—and shines with Mary[1]

Song[2] b

Heres where Mary loved to be
And here are flowers she planted
Here are books she loved to see
And here the kiss she granted

Here on the wall with smileing brow
Her picture used to cheer me
Both walls and rooms are naked now
No Marys nigh to hear me

The church spire still attracts my eye
And leaves me broken hearted
Though grief hath worn their channels dry
I sigh o'er days departed

The churchyard where she used to play
My feet could wander hourly[3]
My school walks there was every day
Where she made winter flowery

But where is angel Mary now
Loves secrets none disclose 'em
Her rosey cheeks and broken vow
Live in my aching bosom

[1] MS. 6, p.6; MS. 8, p.18.
[2] MS. 6, pp.6–7; MS. 7, p.55. Clare's own note on this song and that on p.38 above
is as follows: The above songs were written directly after my return home to
Northborough last Friday evening the rest of the stanzas and songs were written
on Epping Forest Essex. MS. 7 and MS. 6, p.7.
[3] {My [eyes] feet could [daily visit] hourly wander} MS. 7, p.55.

My life hath been one love—no blot it out
My life hath been one chain of contradictions
Madhouses Prisons wh–re shops—never doubt
But that my life hath had some strong convictions
That such was wrong—religion makes restrictions
I would have followed—but life turned a bubble
And[1] clumb the giant stile of maledictions
They took me from my wife and to save trouble
I wed again and made the error double[2]

Yet abscence claims them both and keeps them too
And locks me in a shop in spite of law
Among a low lived set and dirty crew
Here let the Muse oblivions curtain draw
And let man think—for God hath often saw[3]
Things here too dirty for the light of day
For in a madhouse there exists[4] no law—
Now stagnant grows my too refined clay
I envy birds their wings to flye away[5]

How servile is the task to please alone
Though beauty woo and love inspire the song
Mere[6] painted beauty with her heart of stone
Thinks the world worships while she flaunts along
The flower of sunshine butterflye of song
Give me the truth of heart in womans life
The love to cherish one—and do no wrong
To none—o peace of every care and strife
Is true love in an estimable wife[7]

How beautifull this hill of fern swells on
So beautifull the chappel peeps between
The hornbeams—with its simple bell—alone
I wander here hid in a palace green

---

[1] {I} MS. 8, p.18.
[2] MS. 6, p.7; MS. 8, p.18.
[3] {hath often saw} MS.8, p. 18.
[4] 'extends' GP, p.74.
[5] MS. 6, p.7; MS. 8, pp.18–19.
[6] {Here} MS. 8, p.19.
[7] MS. 6, p.8; MS. 8, p.19.

Mary is abscent—but the forest queen
Nature is with me—morning noon and gloaming
I write my poems in these paths[1] unseen
And when among these brakes and beeches roaming
I sigh for truth and home and love and woman[2]

I sigh for one and two—and still I sigh
For many are the whispers I have heard
From beautys lips—loves soul in[3] many an eye
Hath pierced my heart with such intense regard
I Looked for joy and pain was the reward
I think of them I love each girl and boy
Babes of two mothers—on this velvet sward
And nature thinks—in her so sweet employ
While dew's fall on each blossom weeping joy[4]

Here is the chappel yard enclosed with pales
And oak trees nearly top its little bell
Here is the little bridge with guiding rail
That leads me on to many a pleasant dell
The fernowl chitters[5] like a startled knell
To nature—yet tis sweet at evening still—
A pleasant road curves[6] round the gentle swell
Where nature seems to have her own sweet will
Planting her beech and thorn about the sweet fern hill[7]

I have had many loves—and seek no more—
These solitudes my last delights shall be
The leaf hid forest—and the lonely shore
Seem to my mind like beings that are free
Yet would I had some eye to smile on me
Some heart where I could make a happy home in
Sweet Susan that was wont my love to me
And Bessey of the glen—for I've been roaming
With both at morn and noon and dusky gloaming[7]

---

[1] {on these paths} *MS. 8, p.19.*   [2] *MS. 6, p.7; MS. 8, p.19.*
[3] *'on' GP, p.75.*
[4] *MS. 6, pp.7–8; MS. 8, pp.19–20.*
[5] *'chatters' GP, p.75.*   [6] {sweeps} *MS. 8, p.20.*
[7] *MS. 6, p.8; MS. 8, p.20.*

Cares gather round I snap their chains in two
And smile in agony and laugh in tears
Like playing with a deadly serpent—who
Stings to the death—there is no room for fears
Where death would bring me happiness—his sheers
Kills[1] cares that hiss to poison many a vein
The thought to be extinct my fate endears
Pale death the grand phis[i]cian cures all pain
The dead rest well—who lived for joys in vain[2]

Written in a Thunder storm July 15th 1841[3]

The heavens are wrath—the thunders rattling peal
Rolls like a vast volcano in the sky
Yet nothing starts the apathy I feel
Nor chills with fear eternal destiny

My soul is apathy—a ruin vast
Time cannot clear the ruined mass away
My life is hell—the hopeless die is cast
And manhoods prime is premature decay

Roll on ye wrath of thunders—peal on peal
Till worlds are ruins and myself alone
Melt heart and soul cased in obdurate steel
Till I can feel that nature is my throne

I live in love sun of undying light
And fathom my own heart for ways of good
In its pure atmosphere day without night
Smiles on the plains the forest and the flood

Smile on ye elements of earth and sky
Or frown in thunders as ye frown on me
Bid earth and its delusions pass away
But leave the mind as its creator free

---

[1] '*Kill*' *GP, p.76.*
[2] *MS. 6, p.8; MS. 8, p.20.*   [3] *MS. 6, p.8; MS. 8, p.17.*

This twilight seems a veil of gause and mist
Trees seem dark hills between the earth and sky
Winds sob awake and then a gusty hist
Fanns[1] through the wheat like serpents gliding bye
I love to stretch my length 'tween earth and sky
And see the inky foliage oer me wave
Though shades are still my prison where I lie
Long use grows nature which I easy brave
And think how sweet cares rest within the grave[2]

Remind me not of other years or tell
My broken hopes of joys they are to meet
While thy[3] own falshood rings the loudest knell
To one fond heart that aches too cold to beat[4]
Mary how oft with fondness I repeat
That name alone to give my troubles rest
The very sound though bitter seemeth sweet—
In my loves home and thy own faithless breast
Truths[5] bonds are broke and every nerve distrest[6]

Life is to me a dream that never wakes
Night finds me on this lengthening road alone
Love is to me a thought that ever aches
A frost bound thought that freezes life to stone
Mary in truth and nature still[7] my own
That warms the winter of my aching breast
Thy name is joy nor will I life bemoan—
Midnight when sleep takes charge of natures rest
Finds me awake and friendless—not distrest[8]

Tie all my cares up in thy arms O sleep
And give my weary spirits peace and rest
I'm not an outlaw in this midnight deep
If prayers are offered from sweet womans breast

---

[1] {Fanned} *MS. 8, p.23.*   [2] *MS. 6, p.9; MS. 8, p.23.*
[3] *'they' GP, p.76.*
[4] {that [loved thy own too well] aches too cold to beat} *MS. 7, p.55.*
[5] {Faiths} *MS. 7, p.55.*   [6] *MS. 6, p.9; MS. 7, p.55.*
[7] {yet} *MS. 8, p.6.*   [8] *MS.6, p.9; MS. 8, p.6.*

D

One and one only made my being blest
And fancy shapes her form in every dell
On that sweet bosom I've had hours of rest
Though now through years of abscence doomed to dwell
Day seems my night and night seems blackest hell[1]

England my country though my setting sun
Sinks in the ocean gloom and dregs of life
My muse can sing my Marys heart was won
And joy was heaven when I called her wife
The only harbour in my days of strife
Was Mary when the sea roiled[2] mountains high
When joy was lost[3] and every sorrow rife
To her sweet bosom I was wont to flye
To undecieve by truth lifes treacherous agony[4]

Friend of the friendless from a host of snares
From lying varlets and from friendly foes
I sought thy quiet truth to ease my cares
And on the blight of reason found repose
But when the strife of nature ceased her throes
And other hearts would beat for my return
I trusted fate to ease my world of woes
Seeking loves harbour—where I now sojourn
—But hell is heaven could I cease to mourn[5]

For her for one whose very name is yet
My hell or heaven—and will ever be
Falsehood is doubt—but I can ne'er forget
Oaths virtuous falsehood volunteered to me
To make my soul new bonds which God made free
Gods gift is love and do I wrong the giver
To place affections wrong from Gods decree
—No when farewell upon my lips did quiver
And all seemed lost—I loved her more than ever[6]

---

[1] *MS. 6, p.9; MS. 8, p.6.* {nights are blackest hell} *MS. 8, p.6;* {day brings me
night and night seems blackest hell} *MS. 8, p.6, n.*
[2] {roil'd} *MS. 8, p.6.*   [3] {not} *MS. 8, p.6.*
[4] *MS. 6, p.9; MS. 8, p.6.*
[5] *MS. 6, pp.9–10.*   [6] *MS. 6, pp.9–10.*

I loved her in all climes beneath the sun
Her name was like a jewel in my heart
Twas heavens own choice—and so Gods will be done
Love ties that keep unbroken cannot part
Nor can cold abscence sever or desert
That simple beauty blessed with matchless charms
Oceans have rolled between us—not to part
E'en Icelands snows true loves delirium warms
For there Ive dreamed—and Mary filled my arms[1]

Song[2]

O Mary sing thy songs to me
Of love and beautys melody
My sorrows sink beneath distress
My deepest griefs are sorrowless
So used to glooms and cares am I
My fearless troubles seem as joy
O Mary sing thy songs to me
Of love and beautys melody

'To be beloved is all I need
'And them I love are loved indeed'[3]
The soul of woman is my shrine
And Mary made my songs divine
O for that time that happy time
To hear thy sweet Piana's[4] chime
In music so divine and clear
That woke my soul in heaven to hear

But heaven itself without thy face
To me would be no resting place
And though the world was one delight
No joy would live but in thy sight

---

[1] *MS. 6, p.10.*   [2] *MS. 6, p.10; MS. 8, p.28.*
[3] *Cf. Coleridge, 'The Pains of Sleep':*
　　　　　'To be beloved is all I need,
　　　　　And whom I love, I love indeed'.
[4] {Piana} *MS. 8, p.28.*

The soul of woman is my shrine
Then Mary make those songs divine
For music love and melody
Breath all of thee and only thee

Song[1]

Lovely Mary when we parted
I ne'er[2] felt so lonely hearted
As I do now in field and glen
When hope says 'we shall[3] meet agen'
And by yon[4] spire that points to heaven
Where my earliest vows was given
By each meadow field and fen[5]
I'll love thee till we meet agen

True as the needle to the pole
My life I love thee heart and soul
Wa'n't thy love in my heart enrolled[6]
Though love was fire 'twould soon be cold
By thy[7] eyes of heavens own blue
My heart for thine was ever true
By sun and moon by[8] sea and shore
My life I love thee more and more

And by that[9] hope that lingers last
For heaven when lifes hell[10] is past
By time the present—past and gone
I've loved thee—and I love thee on[11]
Thy beauty made youths life divine
Till my soul grew a part of thine
Mary I mourn no pleasures gone—
The past has made us both as one

---

[1] *MS. 6, p.11; MS. 8, p.67.*   [2] {near} *MS. 8, p.67.*
[3] {may} *MS. 8, p.67.*   [4] {By yon} *MS.8, p.67.*
[5] {By these meadow fields and glen} *MS. 8, p.67.*
[6] {If thy love wa'n't with mine enrolled} *MS. 8, p.67.*
[7] {thine} *MS. 8, p.67.*   [8] {and} *MS. 8, p.67.*
[9] {the} *MS. 8, p.67.*   [10] {our life} *MS.8, p. 67.*
[11] {I loved thee and I loved thee on} *MS. 8, p.67.*

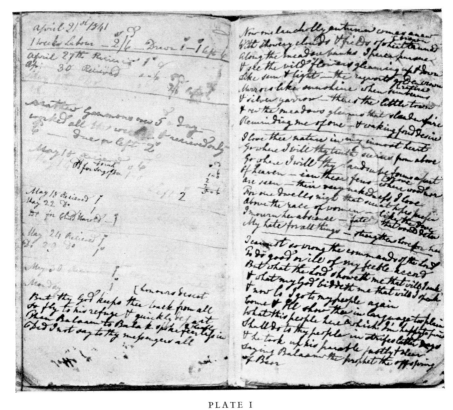

PLATE I

MS. facsimile: *Child Harold* (MS. 8, pages 46–7)

Now melancholly autumn comes anew
With showery clouds and fields of wheat tanned brown
Along the meadow banks I peace pursue
And see the wild flowers gleaming up and down
Like sun and light—the ragworts golden crown
Mirrors like sunshine when sunbeams retire
And silver yarrow—there's the little town
And oer the meadows gleams that slender spire
Reminding me of one—and waking fond desire[1]

I love thee nature in my inmost heart
Go where I will thy truth seems from above
Go where I will thy landscape forms a part
Of heaven—e'en these fens where wood nor grove
Are seen—their very nakedness I love
For one dwells nigh that secret hopes prefer
Above the race of women—like the dove
I mourn her abscence—fate that would deter
My hate for all things—strengthens love for her[1]

Thus saith the great and high and lofty one
Whose name is holy—home eternity
In the high and holy place I dwell alone
And with them also that I wish to see
Of contrite humble spirits—from sin free
Who trembles at my word—and good receive
—Thou high and lofty one—O give to me
Truths low estate and I will glad believe
If such I am not—such I'm feign to live[2]

That form from boyhood loved and still loved on[3]
That voice—that look—that face of one delight
Loves register for years, months, weeks—time past and
    gone[4]
Her looks was ne'er forgot or out of sight

---

[1] *MS. 6, p.11; MS. 8, p.47.*
[2] *MS. 6, p.11; MS. 57: fain.*
[3] [That voice—that look—that face of one delight] *MS. 6, p.11.*
[4] [each day and night] *MS. 6, p.11. GS, p.195, reads 'tis' for* time.

—Mary the muse of every song I write
Thy cherished memory never leaves my own
Though cares chill winter doth my manhood blight
And freeze like Niobe my thoughts to stone—
Our lives are two—our end and aim is one[1]

Ballad[2]

Sweet days while God your blessings send
I call your joys my own
—And if I have an only friend
I am not left alone

She sees the fields the trees the spires
Which I can daily see
And if true love her heart inspires
Life still has joys for me

She sees the wild flower in the dells
That in my rambles shine
The sky that oer her homstead[3] dwells
Looks sunny over[4] mine

The cloud that passes where she dwells
In less then half an hour
Darkens around these orchard dells
Or melts a sudden shower

The wind that leaves the sunny south
And fans the orchard tree
Might steal the kisses from her mouth
And waft her voice to me

O when will autumn bring the news
Now harvest browns the fen
That Mary as my vagrant muse
And I shall meet agen

---

[1] *MS. 6, p.12.*   [2] *MS. 6, p.12; MS. 7, p.55.*
[3] {homestead} *MS. 7.*   [4] {oer} *MS. 7.*

Tis pleasant now days hours begin to pass
To dewy Eve—To walk down narrow close
And feel ones feet among refreshing grass
And hear the insects in their homes discourse
And startled blackbird flye from covert close
Of white thorn hedge with wild fears fluttering wings[1]
And see the spire and hear the clock toll hoarse
And whisper names—and think oer many things
That love hurds up[2] in truths imaginings[3]

Fame blazed upon me like a comets glare
Fame waned and left me like a fallen[4] star
Because I told the evil[5] what they are
And truth and falshood never wished to mar
My Life hath been a wreck—and I've gone far
For peace and truth—and hope—for home and rest
—Like Edens gates—fate throws a constant bar—
Thoughts may o'ertake the sunset in the west
—Man meets no home within a woman's breast[6]

Though they are blazoned in the poets song
As all the comforts which our lifes contain[7]
I read and sought such joys my whole life long
And found the best of poets sung[8] in vain
But still I read and sighed and sued again.[9]
And lost no purpose where I had the will
I almost worshiped when my toils grew vain
Finding no antidote my pains to kill
I sigh a poet and a lover still[10]

---

[1] {Of white thorn hedge and flees on fluttering wings} *MS. 7.*
[2] 'hurls' *GS, p.195, & GP, p.86.*
[3] *MS. 6, p.12; MS. 7.*
[4] 'falling' *GP, p.86.*
[5] {Evil} *MS. 7.*
[6] *MS. 6, p.12; MS. 7.* {But neer met love in a womans breast} *MS. 7.*
[7] {all worlds contain} *MS. 7.*
[8] {of bards had sung} *MS. 7.*
[9] [in vain] *MS. 6, p.13.*
[10] *MS. 6, pp. 12–13; MS. 7.* {I am a poet and a lover still} *MS. 7.*

Song[1]

Dying gales of sweet even
How can you sigh so
Though the sweet day is leaving
And the sun sinketh low
How can you sigh so
For the wild flower is gay
And her dew gems all glow
For the abscence of day

Dying gales of sweet even
Breath music from toil
Dusky eve is loves heaven
And meets beautys smile
Love leans on[2] the stile
Where the rustic brooks flow
Dying gales all the while
How can you sigh so

Dying gales round a prison
To fancy may sigh
But day here hath risen
Over prospects of joy
Here Mary would toy
When the sun it got low
Even gales whisper joy
And never sigh so

Labour lets man his brother
Retire to his rest
The babe meets its mother
And sleeps on her breast—
The sun in the west
Has gone down in the ocean
Dying gales gently sweep
O'er the hearts ruffled motion
And sing it to sleep

---

[1] *MS. 6, p.13; MS. 57.*   [2] {oer} *MS. 57.*

Song[1]

The spring may forget that he reigns in the sky
And winter again hide her flowers in the snow[2]
The summer may thirst when her fountains are dry
But I'll think of Mary wherever I go
The bird may forget that her nest is begun
When the snow settles white on the new budding tree
And nature in tempests forget the bright sun
But I'll ne'er forget her—that was plighted to me

How could I—how should I—that loved her so early
Forget—when I've sung of her beauty in song[3]
How could I forget—what I've worshiped so dearly
From boyhood to manhood—and all my life long—
As leaves to the branches in summer comes duly
And blossoms will bloom on the stalk and the tree
To her beauty I'll cling—and I'll love her as truly
And think of sweet Mary wherever I be

Song[4]

No single hour can stand for nought
No moment hand can move
But calenders a aching thought
Of my first lonely love

Where silence doth the loudest call
My secrets to betray
As moonlight holds the night in thrall
As suns reveal the day

I hide it in the silent shades
Till silence finds a tongue
I make its grave where time invades
Till[5] time becomes a song

---

[1] MS. 6, p.13; MS. 57. [2] {flower} MS. 57.
[3] {[so long] in song} MS. 57.
[4] MS. 6, p.14; MS. 57. [5] {And} MS. 57.

I bid my foolish heart be still
But hopes will not be chid
My heart will beat—and burn—and chill
First love will not be hid

When summer ceases to be green
And winter bare and blea—
Death may forget what I have been
But I must cease to be[1]

When words refuse before the crowd
My Marys name to give
The muse in silence sings aloud
And there my love will[2] live

Now harvest smiles embrowning all the plain[3]
The sun of heaven oer its ripeness shines
'Peace-plenty' has been sung nor sung in vain
As all bring forth the makers grand designs
—Like gold that brightens in some hidden mines
His nature is the wealth that brings increase
To all the world—his sun forever shines
—He hides his face and troubles they increase
He smiles—the sun looks out in wealth and peace[4]

This life is made of lying and grimace
This world is filled with whoring and decieving
Hypocrisy ne'er masks an honest face
Story's are told—but seeing is believing
And I've seen much from which there's no retrieving
I've seen deception take the place of truth
I've seen knaves flourish—and the country grieving
Lies was the current gospel in my youth
And now a man—I'm further off from truth[5]

---

[1] [When I shall cease to be] *MS. 6, p.14*; {When I shall cease to be} *MS. 57.*
[2] [can] *MS. 6, p.14.*
[3] {plains} *MS. 7, p.49.*
[4] *MS. 6, p.14; MS. 7, p.49.*   [5] *MS. 6, p.14.*

Song[1]

They near[2] read the heart
Who would[3] read it in mine
That love[4] can desert
The first truth on his shrine
Though in Lethe I steep it
And sorrows prefer
In my hearts core I keep it
And keep it for her

For her and her only
Through months and through years
I've wandered thus lonely
In sorrow and fears
My sorrows I smother
Though troubles anoy
In this world and no other
I cannot meet joy

No peace nor yet pleasure
Without her will stay
Life looses its treasure
When Mary's away
Though the nightingale[5] often
In sorrow may sing
—Can the blast of the winter
Meet blooms of the spring

Thou first best and dearest
Though dwelling apart
To my heart still the nearest
Forever thou art
And thou wilt be the dearest
Though our joys may be o'er
And to me thou art nearest
Though I meet thee no more

[1] MS. 6, p.15; MS. 7, p.47.
[2] {ne'er} MS. 7, p.47.
[3] {Love} MS. 7, p.47.
[4] {can} MS. 7, p.47.
[5] {Nightingale} MS. 7, p.47.

Song[1]

Did I know where to meet thee
Thou dearest in life
How soon would I greet thee
My true love and wife
How soon would I meet thee
At close of the day
Though cares would still cheat me
If Mary would meet me
I'd kiss her sweet beauty and love them away

And when evening discovers
The sun in the west
I long like true lovers
To lean on thy breast
To meet thee my dearest
—Thy eyes beaming blue
Abscent pains the severest
Feel Mary's the dearest
And if Mary's abscent—how can I be true

How dull the glooms cover
This meadow and fen
Where I as a lover
Seek Mary agen
But silence is teazing
Wherever I stray
There's nothing seems pleasing
Or aching thoughts easing
Though Mary live's near me—she seems far away.

O would these gales murmur
My love in her ear
Or a birds note inform her
While I linger here

---

[1] *MS. 6, pp.15–16; MS. 7, p.47.*

But nature contrary
Turns night into day[1]
No bird—gale—or fairy
Can whisper to Mary
To tell her who seeks[2] her—while Mary's away

Dull must that being live who sees unmoved
The scenes and objects that his childhood knew
The school yard and the maid he early loved
The sunny wall where long the old Elms grew
The grass that e'en till noon retains the dew
Beneath the wallnut shade I see them still
Though not such fancys do I now pursue[3]
Yet still the picture turns my bosom chill
And leaves a void—nor love nor hope may fill[4]

After long abscence how the mind recalls
Pleasing associations of the past
Haunts of his youth—thorn hedges[5] and old walls
And hollow trees that sheltered from the blast
And all that map of boyhood overcast
With glooms and wrongs and sorrows not his own
That oer his brow like the scathed lightening past[6]
That turned[7] his spring to winter and alone
Wrecked name and fame[8] and all—to solitude unknown[9]

So on he lives in glooms and living death
A shade like night forgetting and forgot
Insects that kindle in the springs youth breath
Take hold of life and share a brighter lot

---

[1] *Clare actually wrote in MS. 6, p.16: a* [Is still all the] day *b* Turns night into
The rejected line also occurs in MS. 7, p.47.

[2] {recks} *MS. 7, p.47.*

[3] {not the fancys I was wont pursue} *MS. 7, p.15.*

[4] *MS. 6, p.16; MS. 7, p.15.* {can fill} *MS. 7, p.15.*

[5] {quick hedges} *MS. 7, p.15.*

[6] {passed} *MS.7, p.15.*　　　　[7] {And turned} *MS. 7, p.15.*

[8] {And wrecked his name and fame} *MS. 7, p.15.*

[9] *MS. 6, p.16; MS. 7, p.15.*

Then he the tennant of the hall[1] and Cot
The princely palace too hath been his home
And Gipseys camp when friends would know him not
In midst of wealth a beggar still to roam
Parted from one whose heart was once his home[2]

And yet not parted—still loves hope illumes
And like the rainbow brightest in the storm
It looks for joy beyond the wreck of tombs
And in lifes winter keeps loves embers warm
The oceans roughest tempest meets a calm
Cares thickest cloud shall break in sunny joy
O'er the parched waste showers yet shall fall like balm
And she the soul of life for whom I sigh
Like flowers shall cheer me when the storm[3] is bye[4]

Song[5]

O Mary dear three springs have been
Three summers too have blossomed here
Three blasting winters crept between
Though abscence is the most severe
Another summer blooms in green
But Mary never once was seen

I've sought her in[6] the fields and flowers
I've sought her in the forest groves
In avanues and shaded bowers
And every scene that Mary loves
E'en round her home I seek her here
But Marys abscent every where

Tis autumn and the rustling corn[7]
Goes loaded on the creaking wain
I seek her in the early morn
But cannot meet her face again
Sweet Mary she is abscent still
And much I fear she ever will

---

[1] {Hall} MS. 7, p.15.   [2] MS. 6, p.16; MS. 7, p.15.
[3] [blast] MS. 7, p.15.   [4] MS. 6, p.16; MS. 7, p.15.
[5] MS. 6, p.17; MS. Da8.   [6] {on} MS. Da8.   [7] [grain] MS. Da8.

The autumn morn looks mellow as the fruit
And ripe as harvest—every field and farm
Is full of health and toil—yet never mute
With rustic mirth and peace the day is warm
The village maid with gleans upon her arm
Brown as the hazel nut from field to field
Goes cheerily—the valleys native charm—
I seek for charms that autumn best can yield
In mellowing wood and time ybleaching field[1]

Song[2]

Tis autumn now and natures scenes
The pleachy fields and yellowing trees
Looses their blooming hues and greens[3]
But nature finds no change in me
The fading woods the russet grange
The hues of nature may desert
But nought in me shall find a change
To wrong the angel of my heart
For Mary is my angel still
Through every month and every ill

The leaves they loosen from the branch
And fall upon the gusty wind
But my hearts silent love is staunch
And nought can tear her from my mind
The flowers are gone from dell and bower
Though crowds from summers lap was given
But love is an eternal flower
Like purple amaranths in heaven[4]
To Mary first my heart did bow
And if she's true she keeps it now

---

[1] MS. 6, p.17.
[2] MS. 6, pp.17–18; MS. Da8.
[3] 'Lose all their blooming hues and greens——' GP, p.103.
[4] {Amaranths of heaven} MS. Da8.

Just as the summer keeps the flower
Which spring conscealed[1] in hoods of gold
Or unripe harvest met the shower
And made earths blessings manifold
Just so my Mary lives for me
A silent thought for months and years
The world may live in revellry
Her name my lonely quiet cheers
And cheer it will what e'er may be
While Mary lives to think of me[2]

Sweet comes the misty mornings in September
Among the dewy paths how[3] sweet to stray[4]
Greensward or stubbles as I well remember
I once have done—the mist curls thick and grey[5]
As cottage smoke[6]—like net work on the sprey
Or seeded grass the cobweb draperies run
Beaded with pearls of dew at early day
And oer the[7] pleachy stubbles peeps the sun
The lamp of day when that of night is done[8]

What mellowness these harvest days unfold
In the strong glances of the midday sun
The homesteads very grass seems changed to gold
The light in golden shadows seems to run
And tinges every spray it rests upon
With that rich harvest[9] hue of sunny joy
Nature lifes sweet companion cheers alone—
The hare starts up before the shepherd boy[10]
And partridge coveys wir on russet wings of joy[11]

---

[1] {spring [did to her] consceald} *MS. Da8.*
[2] {lives in bloom for me} *MS. Da8.*   [3] 'now' *GP, p.88.*
[4] {dewey paths tis sweet to stray} *MS. Da8.*
[5] {I have done—and the mist it curleth grey} *MS. Da8.*
[6] {And thick as smoke} *MS. Da8.*   [7] {And on the} *MS. Da8.*
[8] *MS. 6, p.18; MS. Da8.*   [9] [autumn] *MS. 6, p.18;* {autumn} *MS. Da8.*
[10] {up starts the hare before the shepherd boy} *MS. Da8.*
[11] *MS. 6, p.18; MS. Da8.* {And partridge coveys wir above his head with joy}
*MS. Da8. GP, p.89 prints this as an 8-line stanza omitting line 7, presumably because
Grigson relied solely on MS. Da8.*

The meadow flags now rustle bleached and dank
And misted oer with down as fine as dew
The sloe and dewberry[1] shine along the bank
Where weeds[2] in blooms luxuriance lately grew
Red rose the sun and up the morehen flew
From bank to bank the meadow arches stride
Where foamy floods in winter tumbles through
And spread a restless ocean foaming wide
Where now the cowboys sleep nor fear the coming tide[3]

About the medows now I love to sit
On banks bridge walls and rails as when a boy
To see old trees bend oer the flaggy pit
With hugh roots bare that time does not destroy
Where sits the angler at his days employ
And there Ivy leaves the bank to climb
The tree—and now how sweet to weary joy
—Aye nothing seems so happy and sublime
As sabbath bells and their delightfull chime[3]

Sweet solitude thou partner of my life
Thou balm of hope and every pressing care
Thou soothing silence oer the noise of strife
These meadow flats and trees—the autumn air
Mellows my heart to harmony—I bear
Lifes burthen happily—these fenny dells
Seem Eden in this sabbath rest from care
My heart with loves first early memory swells
To hear the music of those village bells[4]

For in that hamlet lives my rising sun
Whose beams hath cheered me all my lorn life long
My heart to nature there was early won
For she was natures self—and still my song
Is her through sun and shade through right and wrong

---

[1] {dewbery} MS. Da8.   [2] {[flowe] weeds} MS. Da8.
[3] MS. 6, p.18; MS. Da8.
[4] MS. 6, p.19.

E

On her my memory forever dwells
The flower[1] of Eden—evergreen of song
Truth in my heart the same love story tells
—I love the music of those village bells[2]

Song[3]

Heres a health unto thee bonny lassie O
Leave the thorns o' care wi' me
And whatever I may be
Here's happiness to thee
Bonny lassie O

Here's joy unto thee bonny lassie O
Though we never meet again
I well can bear the pain
If happiness is thine
Bonny lassie O

Here is true love unto thee bonny lassie O
Though abscence cold is ours
The spring will come wi' flowers
And love will wait for thee
Bonny lassie O

So heres love unto thee bonny lassie O
Aye wherever I may be
Here's a double health to thee
Till life shall cease to love
Bonny lassie O

The blackbird startles from the homestead hedge
Raindrops and leaves fall yellow as he springs
Such images are natures sweetest pledge
To me there's music in his rustling wings

---

[1] *'flowers'* GP, *p.90.*   [2] *MS. 6, p.19.*
[3] *MS. 6, p.19; MS. Da8.*

'Prink prink' he cries and loud the robin sings
The small hawk like a shot drops from the sky
Close to my feet for mice and[1] creeping things
Then swift as thought again he suthers[2] bye
And hides among the clouds from the pursueing eye[3]

Song[4]

Her cheeks are like roses
Her eyes they are blue
And her beauty is mine
If her heart it is true

Her cheeks are like roses—
And though she's away
I shall see her sweet beauty
On some other day

Ere the flowers of the spring
Deck the meadow and plain
If theres truth in her bosom
I shall see her again

I will love her as long
As the brooks they shall flow
For Mary is mine and
Wheresoever I go

Honesty and good intentions are
So mowed and hampered in with evil lies
She hath not room to stir a single foot
Or even strength to break a spiders web

---

[1] {or} *MS. Da8.*

[2] *Glossary, p.311:* 'Suther. To sigh heavily, as the wind among the trees.' *Clare is Baker's only authority for the word.*

[3] *MS. 6, p.19; MS. Da8.* {each} *MS. Da8.*

[4] *MS. 6, p.20. Not necessarily a part of the 'Child Harold' sequence, since a passage of prose intervenes between this song and the previous stanza.*

—So lies keep climbing round loves sacred stem
Blighting fair truth whose leaf is evergreen
Whose roots are the hearts fibres and whose sun
The soul that cheers and smiles it into bloom
Till heaven proclaims that truth can never die[1]

The lightenings vivid flashes—rend the cloud
That rides like castled crags along the sky
And splinters them to fragments—while aloud[2]
The thunders heavens artillery vollies bye
Trees crash, earth trembles—beast[s] prepare to flye
Almighty what a crash—yet man is free
And walks unhurt while danger seems so nigh—
Heavens archway now the rainbow seems to be
That spans the eternal round of earth and sky and sea[3]

A shock, a moment, in the wrath of God
Is long as hell's eternity to all
His thunderbolts leave life but as the clod
Cold and inna[ni]mate—their temples fall
Beneath his frown to ashes—the eternal pall
Of wrath sleeps oer the ruins where they fell
And nought of memory may their creeds recall
The sin of Sodom was a moments yell
Fires death bed theirs their first grave the last hell[4]

The towering willow with its pliant boughs
Sweeps its grey foliage to the autumn wind
The level grounds where oft a group of cows
Huddled together close—or propped behind
An hedge or hovel ruminate and find
The peace—as walks and health and I pursue[5]
For natures every place is still resigned
To happiness—new life's in every view
And here I comfort seek and early joys renew[6]

[1] MS. 6, p.22. This unrhymed stanza, which is probably part of the 'Child Harold' sequence, does not appear in GP nor in GS.
[2] {while [the] aloud} MS. 6, p.36.   [3] MS. 6, p.36.
[4] MS. 6, p.36. {Fires [was their] deathbed theirs [and] their first grave the [was] last hell} MS. 6, p.36.
[5] [health and I was wont to find] MS. 6, p.36.   [6] MS. 6, p.36.

The lake that held a mirror to the sun
Now curves with wrinkles in the stillest place
The autumn wind sounds hollow as a gun
And water stands in every swampy place
Yet in these fens peace harmony and grace
The attributes of nature are alied
The barge with naked mast in sheltered place
Beside the brig close to the bank is tied
While small waves plashes by its bulky side[1]

Song[2]

The floods come oer the meadow leas
The dykes are full and brimming
Field furrows reach the horses knees
Where wild ducks oft are swimming
The skyes are black the fields are bare
The trees their coats[3] are loosing
The leaves are dancing in the air
The sun its warmth refusing[4]

Brown are the flags and fadeing sedge
And tanned the meadow plains[5]
Bright yellow is the osier hedge
Beside the brimming drains[6]
The crows sit on the willow tree
The lake is full below[7]
But still the dullest thing I see
Is self that wanders slow[8]

---

[1] *MS. 6, p.36.*
[2] *MS. 6, p.37; MS. 49, p.R5.*
[3] [leaves] *MS. 6, p.37.*
[4] {The trees their leaves are looseing
  The leaves are flitting on the air
  And trees their coats are loosing} *MS. 49, p.R5.*
[5] {And russet turns the meadow plains} *MS. 49, p.R5.*
[6] {That sweas beside the brimming drains} *MS. 49, p.R5.*
[7] {The muddy lake lyes full below} *MS. 49, p.R5.*
[8] {Is self lorn wandering to and fro} *MS. 49, p.R5.*

The dullest scenes are not so dull
As thoughts I cannot tell[1]
The brimming dykes are not so full
As my hearts silent swell[2]
I leave my[3] troubles to the winds
With none to share a part[4]
The only joy my[5] feeling finds
Hides in an aching heart[6]

Abscence in love is worse then any fate
Summer is winters desert and the spring
Is like a ruined city desolate
Joy dies and hope retires on feeble wing
Nature sinks heedless—birds unheeded sing
Tis solitude in citys—crowds[7] all move
Like living death—though all to life still cling
The strongest bitterest thing that life can prove
Is womans undisguise of hate and love[8]

Song[9]

I think of thee at early day
And wonder where my love can be
And when the evening shadows grey
O how I think of thee

Along the meadow banks I rove
And down the flaggy fen
And hope my first and early love
To meet thee once agen

---

[1] {As thoughts that in his bosom dwell} *MS. 49, p.R5.*
[2] {As is his bosoms silent swell} *MS. 49, p.R5.*
[3] {He leaves his} *MS. 49, p.R5.*
[4] {With none to hear or share a part} *MS.49, p.R5.*
[5] {his} *MS. 49, p.R5.*
[6] {Is silence in an aching heart} *MS. 49, p.R5.*
[7] {citys crowds} *MS. 49, p.R5.*
[8] *MS. 6, p.37; MS. 49, p.R.5.*
[9] *MS. 6, p.45; MS. 49, p.4.*

I think of thee at dewy[1] morn
And at the sunny noon
And walks with thee—now left forlorn
Beneath the silent moon

I think of thee I think of all
How blest we both have been—
The sun looks pale upon the wall
And autumn shuts the scene

I can't expect to meet thee now
The winter floods begin
The wind sighs throu the[2] naked bough
Sad as my heart within

I think of thee the seasons through
In spring when flowers I see
In winters lorn and naked view
I think of only thee

While life breaths on this earthly ball
What e'er my lot may be
Wether in freedom or in thrall
Mary I think of thee

Tis winter and the fields are bare and waste[3]
The air one mass of 'vapour clouds and storms'
The suns broad beams are buried and oercast
And chilly glooms the midday light deforms
Yet comfort now the social bosom warms
Friendship of nature which I hourly prove
Even in this winter scene of frost and storms
Bare fields the frozen lake and leafless grove[4]
Are natures grand religion and true love[5]

---

[1] [dewey] *MS. 49, p.4.*   [2] {through the} *MS. 49, p.4.*
[3] {[waste and] bare and waste} *MS. Dc64.*
[4] {[The naked] Bare} *MS. Dc64.*   [5] *MS. 6, p.45; MS. Dc64.*

Song[1]

Thourt dearest to my bosom
As thou wilt ever be
While the meadows wear[2] a blossom
Or a leaf is on the tree
I can forget thee never[3]
While the meadow grass is green
While the flood rolls down the river
Thou art still my bonny queen

While the winter swells the fountain
While the spring awakes the bee
While the chamois loves the mountain
Thou'lt be ever dear to me
Dear as summer to the sun[4]
As spring is to the bee
Thy love was soon as won[5]
And so twill ever be

Thou'rt loves eternal summer
The dearest maid I prove
With bosom white as ivory[6]
And warm as virgin love
No falsehood gets between us
Theres nought the tie can sever[7]
As cupid dwells with venus
Thou'rt my own love forever

---

[1] *MS. 6, p.45; MS. 49, p.R10.*
[2] {bear} *MS. 49, p.R10.*
[3] {Or the leaves come on the tree
    And I will leave thee never} *MS.49, p.R10.*
[4] {Dear as to summer is the sun} *MS. 49, p.R10.*
[5] {Thy love appeared as soon as won} *MS. 49, p.R10.*
[6] {With breasts as white as ivory} *MS.49, p.R10.*
[7] {No cares love's ties can sever} *MS. 49, p.R10.*

Song[1]

In this cold world without a home
Disconsolate I go
The summer looks as cold to me
As winters frost and snow
Though winters scenes are dull and drear
A colder lot I prove
No home had I through all the year
But Marys honest love

But Love inconstant as the wind
Soon shifts another way
No other home my heart can find
Life wasting day by day[2]
I sigh and sit and sit and sigh
for better days to come
For Mary was my hope and joy
Her truth and heart my home

Her truth and heart was once my home
And May was[3] all the year
But now through seasons as I roam
Tis winter everywhere
Hopeless I go through care and toil
No friend I e'er possest
To reccompence for Marys smile
And the love within her breast

My love was ne'er so blest as when
It mingled with her own
Told often to be told agen
And every feeling known
But now loves hopes are all bereft
A lonely man I roam
And abscent Mary long hath left
My heart without a home

---

[1] MS. 6, p.57; MS. Dc64.
[2] {Love wasting life away} MS. Dc64.   [3] {lived} MS. Dc64.

27[1]

The Paigles Bloom In Shower's In Grassy Close
How Sweet To Be Among Their Blossoms Led
And Hear Sweet Nature To Herself Discourse
While Pale The Moon Is Bering Over Head
And Hear The Grazeing Cattle Softly Tread
Cropping The Hedgerows Newly Leafing Thorn
Sounds Soft As Visions Murmured Oer In Bed
At Dusky Eve or Sober Silent Morn
For Such Delights Twere Happy Man Was Born[2]

3

Green bushes and green trees where fancy feeds
On the retireing solitudes of May
Where the sweet foliage like a volume reads
And weeds are gifts too choice to throw away
How sweet the evening now succeeds the day
The vevelt[3] hillock forms a happy seat
The white thorn bushes bend with snowey may
Dwarf furze in golden blooms[4] and violets sweet
Make this wild scene a pleasure grounds retreat[5]

18

Where are my *friends*[6] and childern where are they
The childern of two mothers born in joy
One roof has held them—all have been at play
Beneath the pleasures of a mothers eye
—And are my late hope's blighted—need I sigh
Hath care commenced his long perpetual reign
The spring and summer hath with me gone bye
Hope views the bud a flower and not in vain
Long is the night that brings no morn again[7]

---

[1] MS. 6 ceases as a primary source and is replaced by MS. 8. The stanza numbering
is from MS. 8. For comments upon this and upon the stanza sequence, see editorial note
above, p. 26.

[2] MS. 8, p.33.   [3] velvet.   [4] [blossoms] MS. 8, p.50.
[5] MS. 8, p.50.   [6] Clare's italics.   [7] MS. 8, p.51.

4

Now Come The Balm And Breezes Of The Spring
Not With The Pleasure's Of My Early Day's
When Nature Seemed One Endless Song To Sing
A[1] Joyous Melody And Happy Praise
Ah Would They Come Agen—But Life Betrays
Quicksands and Gulphs And Storms That Howl And Sting
All Quiet Into Madness And Delays
Care Hides The Sunshine With Its Raven Wing
And Hell Glooms Sadness Oer The Songs Of Spring[2]

5

Like Satans Warcry First In Paradise
When Love Lay Sleeping On The Flowery Slope
Like Virtue Wakeing In The Arms Of Vice
Or Deaths Sea Bursting In The Midst Of Hope
Sorrows Will Stay—And Pleasures Will Elope
In The Uncertain Cartnty[3] Of Care
Joys Bounds Are Narrow But A Wider Scope
Is Left For Trouble Which Our Life Must Bear
Of Which All Human Life Is More Or Less The Heir[4]

6

My Mind Is Dark And Fathomless And Wears
The Hues Of Hopeless Agony And Hell
No Plummet Ever Sounds The Souls Affairs
There Death Eternal Never Sounds The Knell
There Love Imprisoned Sighs The Long Farewell
And Still May Sigh In Thoughts No Heart Hath Penned
Alone In Loneliness Where Sorrows Dwell
And Hopeless Hope;[5] Hopes On And Meets No End
Wastes Without Springs And Homes Without A Friend[6]

---

[1] 'Of' GP, p.78. [2] MS. 8, p.52.
[3] Certainty. [4] MS. 8, p.52.
[5] Clare's semi-colon is here clearly unwanted and interrupts the sense of the line.
[6] MS. 8, p.52.

Song[1]

Say What Is Love—To Live In Vain
To Live And Die And Live Again

Say What Is Love—Is It To Be
In Prison Still And Still Be Free

Or Seem As Free—Alone And Prove
The Hopeless Hopes Of Real Love

Doe's Real Love On Earth Exist
Tis Like A Sun beam On The Mist

That Fades And No Where Will Remain
And Nowhere Is Oertook Again

Say What Is Love—A Blooming Name
A Rose Leaf On The Page Of Fame

That Blooms Then Fades—To Cheat No More
And Is What Nothing Was Before

Say What Is Love—What E'er It be
It Center's Mary Still With Thee

7

What is the Orphan Child Without A Friend
That Knows No Fathers Care Or Mothers Love
No Leading Hand His Infant Steps Defend
And None To Notice But His God Above
No Joy's Are Seen His Little Heart To Move
Care[2] Turns All Joys to Dross And Nought To Gold[3]
And He In Fancys Time May Still Disprove
Growing To Cares And Sorrow's Menifold
Bird[4] Of The Waste A Lamb Without A Fold[5]

---

[1] MS. 8, p.53.   [2] [Chills] MS. 8, p.54.

[3] This is followed in MS. 8 by the deleted line: [In Strangers Faces He May Friends Behold].

[4] 'Bud' GP, p.79.   [5] MS. 8, p.54.

8

No Mothers Love or Fathers Care Have They
Left ToThe Storms Of Fate Like Creatures Wild
They Live Like Blossoms In The Winters Day
E'en Nature Frowns Upon The Orphan Child
On Whose Young Face A Mother Never Smiled
Foolhardy Care Increasing With His Years
From Friends And Joys Of Every Kind Exiled
Even Old In Care The Infant Babe Appears
And Many A Mother Meets Its Face In Tears[1]

9

The Dog Can Find A Friend And Seeks His Side
The Ass Can Know Its Owner And Is Fed
But None Are Known To Be The Orphans Guide
Toil Breaks His Sleep And Sorrow Makes His Bed
No Mothers Hand Holds Out The Sugared Bread
To Fill His Little Hand—He Hears No Song
To Please His Pouting Humours—Love Is Dead
With Him And Will Be All His Whole Life Long
Lone Child Of Sorrow And Perpetual Wrong[1]

10

But Providence That Grand Eternal Calm[2]
Is With Him Like The Sunshine In The Sky
Nature Our Kindest Mother Void Of[3] Harm
Watches The Orphan's Lonely Infancy
Strengthening The Man When Childhoods Cares[4] Are Bye
She Nurses Still Young Unreproached Distress
And Hears The Lonely Infants Every Sigh
Who Finds At Length To Make Its Sorrows Less
Mid Earths Cold Curses There Is One To Bless[5]

---

[1] *MS. 8, p.54.*
[2] [Good] *MS. 8, p.55.*   [3] [Means No] *MS. 8, p.55.*
[4] 'care' *GP, p.80.*
[5] *MS. 8, p.55.*

11

Sweet Rural Maids Made Beautifull By Health
Brought Up Where Natures Calm Encircles All
Where Simple Love Remains As Sterling Wealth
Where Simple Habits Early Joys Recall
Of Youthfull Feelings Which No Wiles Enthrall
The Happy Milk Maid In Her Mean Array
Fresh As The New Blown Rose Outblooms Them All
E'en Queens Might Sigh To Be As Blest As They
While Milkmaids Laugh And Sing Their Cares Away[1]

12

How Doth Those Scenes Which Rural Mirth Endears
Revise Old Feelings That My Youth Hath Known
And Paint The Faded Bloom Of Earlier Years
And Soften Feelings Petrefied To Stone
Joy[2] Fled And Care Proclaimed Itself My Own
Farewells I Took Of Joys In Earliest Years
And Found The Greatest Bliss To Be Alone
My Manhood Was Eclipsed But Not In Fears
—Hell Came[3] in Curses And[4] She Laugh'd At Tears[5]

13

But Memory Left Sweet Traces Of Her Smiles
Which I Remember Still And Still Endure
The Shadows Of First ⟨L . . . ⟩s[6] My Heart Beguiles
Time Brought Both[7] Pain and Pleasure But No Cure
Sweet Bessey Maid Of Health And Fancys Pure
How Did I Woo Thee Once—Still Unforgot
But Promises In Love Are Never Sure
And Where We Met How Dear Is Every Spot
And Though We Parted Still I Murmur Not[8]

---

[1] MS. 8, p.55.   [2] 'Joys' GP, p.80.
[3] [lives] MS. 8, p.55.
[4] [But], MS. 8, p.55.   [5] MS. 8, p.55.
[6] GS, p.188, 'Love', but the word is clearly in the plural.
[7] 'Birth' GP, p.80.
[8] MS. 8, p.56.

14

For Loves[1] However Dear Must Meet With Clouds
And Ties Made Tight Get[2] Loose And May Be Parted
Springs First Young Flowers The Winter Often Shrouds
And Loves First Hopes Are Very Often Thwarted
E'en Mine Beat High And Then Fell Broken Hearted
And Sorrow Mourned In Verse to Reconscile
My Feelings To My Fate Though Lone And Parteded[3]
Loves Enemies Are Like The Scorpion Vile
That Oer Its Ruined Hopes Will Hiss And Smile[4]

Ballad[5]

The Blackbird Has Built In The Pasture Agen
And The Thorn Oer The Pond Shows A Delicate Green
Where I Strolled With Patty Adown In The Glen
And Spent Summer Evenings And Sundays Unseen
How Sweet The Hill Brow
And The Low Of The Cow
And The Sunshine That Gilded The Bushes So Green
When Evening Brought Dews Natures Thirst To Allay
And Clouds Seemed To Nestle Round Hamlets And Farms
While In[6] The Green Bushes We Spent The Sweet Day
And Patty Sweet Patty Was Still in My Arms

The Love Bloom That Redded Upon Her Sweet Lips
The Love Light That Glistened Within Her Sweet Eye
The Singing Bees There That The Wild Honey Sips
From Wild Blossoms Seemed Not So Happy As I
How Sweet Her Smile Seemed
While The Summer Sun Gleamed
And The Laugh Of The Spring Shadowed Joys From On High
While The Birds Sung About[7] Us And Cattle Grazed Round
And Beauty Was Blooming On Hamlets and Farms
How Sweet Steamed The Inscence Of Dew From The Ground
While Patty Sweet Patty Sat Locked In My Arms

---

[1] 'love' GP, p.80.   [2] [May] MS. 8, p.56; 'yet' GP, p.80.
[3] Thus in MS. 8, p.56; 'love departed' GP. p.81.   [4] MS. 8, p.56.
[5] MS. 8, p.57.   [6] [Through] MS. 8, p.57.   [7] [Around] MS. 8, p.58.

15

Yet Love Lives On In Every Kind Of Weather
In Heat And Cold In Sunshine And In Gloom[1]
Winter May Blight And Stormy Clouds May Gather
Nature Invigorates And Love Will Bloom
It Fears No Sorrow In A Life To Come
But Lives Within Itself From Year To Year
As Doth The Wild Flower In Its Own Perfume
As In The Lapland Snows Springs Blooms Appear
So True Love Blooms And Blossoms Every Where[2]

Ballad[3]

The Rose Of The World Was Dear Mary To Me
In The Days Of My Boyhood And Youth
I Told Her In Songs Where My Heart Wished To Be
And My Songs Where[4] The Language Of Truth

I Told Her In Looks When I Gazed In Her Eyes
That Mary Was Dearest To Me
I Told Her In Words And The Language Of Sighs
Where My Whole Hearts Affections Would Be

I Told her in love that all nature was true[5]
I convinced her that nature was kind
But love in his trials had labour to do
⟨   ⟩[6] Mary would be in the mind

Mary met me in spring where the speedwell knots grew
And the king cups were shining like flame
I chose her all colours red yellow and blue
But my love was one hue and the same

Spring summer and winter and all the year through
In the sunshine the shower and the blast
I told the same tale and she knows it all true
And Marys my blossom at last

---

[1] 'glooms' GP, p.81.   [2] MS. 8, p.58.   [3] MS. 8, pp.58–9.
[4] Were.   [5] Change of hand, and capitals abandoned.   [6] Clare has left a hiatus.

16

⟨ . . . . ⟩¹ is of heaven still the first akin
⟨ . . . s⟩² born in paradise and left its home
For desert lands stray hearts to nurse and win
Though pains like plagues pursue them where they roam
Its joys are ever green and blooms at home
The sailor rocking on the giddy mast
The soldier when the cannons cease to boom
And every heart its doubts or dangers past
Beats on its way for love and home at last³

17

Nature thou truth of heaven if heaven be true
Falsehood may tell her ever changeing lie
But natures truth looks green in every view
And love in every Landscape glads the eye
How beautiful these slopeing thickets lie
Woods on the hills and plains all smooth and even
Through which we see the ribboned evening skie
Though Winter here in floods and snows was driven
Spring came like God and turned it all to heaven³

18

There Is A Tale For Every Day⁴ To Hear
For Every Heart To Feel And Tongue To Tell
The daughters Anzious⁵ Dread The Lovers Fear
Pains That In Cots And Palaces May Dwell
Not Short And Passing Like The Friends Farewell
Where Tears May Fall And Leave A Smile Beneath
Eternal Grief Rings In The Passing Bell
Tis Not The Sobs of Momentary Breath
Ties Part Forever In The Tale Of Death⁶

---

¹ GS, p.189, surmises 'Love'.   ² GS, p.189, surmises "Twas'.
³ MS. 8, p.59.
⁴ 'everyone' GP, p.81.
⁵ anxious.   ⁶ MS. 8, p.61.

F

19

The Dew falls on the weed[1] and on the flower
The rose and thistle bathe their heads in dew
The lowliest heart may have its prospering hour
The sadest bosom meet its wishes true
E'een[2] I may joy[3] love happiness renew
Though not the sweets of my first early days
When one sweet face was all the loves I knew
And my soul trembled on her eyes to gaze
Whose very censure seemed intended praise[4]

20

A soul within the heart that loves the more
Giving to pains and fears eternal life
Burning the flesh till it[5] consumes the core
So Love is still the eternal calm[6] of strife[7]
Thou soul within a soul thou life of life
Thou Essence of my hopes and fears and joys
M—y[8] my dear first love and early wife
And still the flower my inmost soul enjoys
Thy love's the bloom no canker worm destroys[9]

21

Flow on my verse though barren thou mayest be
Of thought—Yet sing and let thy fancys roll
In Early days thou sweept a mighty sea
All calm in troublous deeps and spurned controul
Thou fire and iceberg to an aching soul
And still an angel in my gloomy way
Far better opiate then the draining bowl
Still sing my muse to drive cares fiends away
Nor heed what loitering listener hears the lay[10]

---

[1] [rose] *MS. 8, p.61.*   [2] *E'en.*
[3] *GP, p. 82, omits joy.*   [4] *MS. 8, p.61.*
[5] [and then] *MS. 8, p.61.*   [6] [storm] [death] *MS. 8, p.61.*
[7] [life] *MS. 8, p.61.*   [8] *'Mary' GP, p.82.*
[9] *MS. 8, p.61.*   [10] *MS. 8, p.62.*

My themes be artless cots and happy plains
Though far from man my wayward fancies flee
Of fields and woods rehearse in willing strains
And I mayhap may feed on joys with thee
These cowslip fields this sward my pillow be
So I may sleep the sun into the west
My cot this awthorn hedge this spreading tree
—Mary and Martha once my daily guests
And still as mine both wedded loved and blest[1]

23

I rest my wearied life in these sweet fields
Reflecting every smile in natures face
And much of joy this grass—These hedges yields
Not found in cities where crowds daily trace
Heart[2] pleasures there hath no abideing place
The star gemmed early morn the silent even
⟨ . . . l⟩ pleasures that our broken hopes deface
To love too well leaves nought to be forgiven
The Gates of Eden is the bounds[3] of heaven[4]

24

The apathy that fickle love wears through
The doubts and certaintys are still akin
Its every joy has sorrow in the view
Its holy truth like Eve's beguileing sin[5]
Seems to be losses even while we win
Tormenting joys and cheating into wrong
And still we love—and fall into the Gin
My sun of love was short—and clouded long
And now its shadow fills a feeble song[6]

---

[1] *MS. 8, p.62.*   [2] *'Scant' GP, p.83.*
[3] *[life] MS. 8, p.62.*   [4] *MS. 8, p.62.*
[5] *MS. 8, p.62, deletes after this line: [Seems to torment and cheats us into wrong].*
[6] *First five lines of this stanza appear in MS. 8, p.62. The stanza is completed on p.64 after Clare's heading:* 24 Continued; *GP omits the last four lines.*

Song[1]

I saw her in my springs young choice
Ere loves hopes looked upon the crowd
Ere loves first secrets found a voice
Or dared to speak the name aloud

I saw her in my boyish hours
A Girl as fair as heaven above
When all the world seemed strewn with flowers
And every pulse and look was love

I saw her when her heart was young
I saw her when my heart was true
When truth was all the themes I sung
And Love the only muse I knew

Ere infancy had left her brow
I seemed to love her from her birth
And thought her then as I do now
The dearest angel upon earth

25

O she was more then fair—divinely fair
Can language paint the soul in those blue eyes
Can fancy read the feelings painted there
—Those hills of snow that on her bosom lies
Or beauty speak for all those sweet replies
That through loves visions like the sun is breaking
Waking new hopes and fears and stifled sighs
From first love's dreame's my love is scarcely waking
The wounds might[2] heal but still the heart is aching[3]

---

[1] MS. 8, pp.64–5. Clare gives no title.
[2] [may] MS. 8, p.65.   [3] MS. 8, p.65.

26

Her looks was like the spring her very voice
Was springs own music more then song to me
Choice of my boyhood nay my souls first choice
From her sweet thralldom I am never free
Yet here my prison is a spring to me
Past[1] memories bloom like flowers where e'er I rove
My very bondage though in snares—is free
I love to stretch me in this shadey Grove
And muse upon the memories[2] of love[3]

Hail Solitude still[4] Peace and Lonely good
Thou spirit of all joys to be alone
My best of friends these glades and this green wood
Where nature is herself and loves her own
The hearts hid anguish here I make it known
And tell my troubles to the gentle wind
Friends cold neglects have froze my heart to stone
And wrecked the voyage of a quiet mind
With wives and friends[5] and every hope disjoined[6]

Wrecked of all hopes save one to be alone
Where Solitude becomes my wedded mate
Sweet Forest with rich beauties overgrown
Where solitude is queen and riegns in state
Hid in green trees I hear the clapping gate
And voices calling to the rambling cows
I Laugh at Love and all its idle fate
The present hour is all my lot alows
An age of sorrow springs from lovers vows[7]

---

[1] 'But' GP, p.84. [2] [memory] MS. 8, p.65.
[3] MS. 8, p.65. [4] [thou] MS. 8, p.65.
[5] [hopes] MS. 8, p.66. [6] MS. 8, pp.65–6.
[7] MS. 8, p.66.

Sweet is the song of Birds for that restores
The soul to harmony the mind to love
Tis natures song of freedom out of doors
Forests beneath free winds and clouds above
The Thrush and Nightingale and timid dove
Breathe music round me where the gipseys dwell—
Pierced hearts left burning in the doubts of love[1]
Are desolate where crowds and citys dwell—
The splendid palace seems the gates of hell[2]

---

[1] [hell]ˌMS. *8, p.66.*   [2] MS. *8, p.66.*

Don Juan

DON JUAN[1]

'Poets are born'—and so are whores—the trade is
Grown universal—in these canting days[2]
Women of[3] fashion must of course be ladies
And whoreing is the business—that still pays
Playhouses Ballrooms[4]—there the masquerade is
—To do what was of old—and now adays
Their maids—nay wives[5] so innocent and blooming
Cuckold their spouses to seem honest women[6]

Milton sung Eden and the fall of man[7]
Not woman for the name imples a wh—e
And they would make a ruin of his plan[8]
Falling so often they can fall no lower
Tell me a worse delusion if you can
For innoscence—and I will sing no more[9]
Wherever mischief is tis womans brewing
Created from manself—to be mans ruin

The flower in bud hides from the fading sun
And keeps the hue of beauty on its cheek
But when full blown[10] they into riot run
The hue turns pale and lost each ruddy streak
So 't is with woman who pretends to shun
Immodest actions which they inly seek
Night hides the wh—e—and cupboards tart and pasty[11]
Flora was p–x–d—and womans quite as nasty

---

[1] *Our text is taken from Northampton MS. 6. Variants from other Northampton MSS., principally MS. 8, are given in the footnotes.*
[2] in religious days *MS. 8, p.60.*   [3] in *MS. 8, p.60.*
[4] churches *MS. 8, p.60.*   [5] Where maids and wives *MS. 8, p.60.*
[6] *MS. 6, p.38.*   [7] *The following four stanzas appear on p.43 of MS. 6.*
[8] For they *MS. 7.*
[9] Then woman—and I'll teaze the muse no more *MS. 7.*
[10] *The word* blown *is repeated and struck through the second time.*
[11] cupboards the apple pasty *MS. 7;* 'Night hides the wh–c– cupboard's tart and pasty' *GP, p.65.*

Marriage is nothing but a driveling hoax
To please old codgers when they're turned of forty
I wed and left my wife like other folks
But not untill I found her false and faulty
O woman fair—the man must pay thy jokes
Such makes a husband very often naughty[1]
Who falls in love will seek his own undoing
The road to marriage is—'the road to ruin'[2]

Love worse then debt or drink or any fate
It is the damnest smart[3] of matrimony
A hell incarnate is a woman-mate
The knot is tied—and then we loose[4] the honey
A wife is just the protetype to hate
Commons for stock and warrens for the coney
Are not more tresspassed over in rights plan
Then this incumberance on the rights of man

There's much said about love and more of women
I wish they were as modest as they seem
Some borrow husbands till their cheeks are blooming
Not like the red rose blush—but yellow cream
Lord what a while those good days are in coming[5]
Routs Masques and Balls—I wish they were a dream
—I wish for poor men luck—an honest praxis
Cheap food and cloathing—no corn laws or taxes

---

[1] [malty].
[2] *Another version of this stanza is found on p.27 of MS. 7. The first four lines are identical and then:*

> O woman fair how can you be so naughty
> I cursed the marriage tye—false love and wooing
> —a wh—e—g woman always looks so haughty—
> Who falls in love will seek his own undoing
> The way to marriage is 'the road to ruin'.

[3] [part].
[4] *'love'* GP, *p.65. lose.*
[5] comeing MS. *8, p.31.*

I wish—but there is little got bye wishing
I wish that bread and great coats ne'er had risen
I wish that there was some such word as 'pishun'
For ryhme sake for my verses must be dizen
With dresses fine—as hooks with baits for fishing
I wish all honest men were out of prison
I wish M.P's. would spin less yarn—nor doubt
But burn false bills and cross bad taxes out

I wish young married dames were not so frisky[1]
Nor hide the ring to make believe they're single[2]
I wish small beer was half as good as whiskey
And married dames with buggers would not mingle
There's some too cunning far and some too frisky
And here I want a ryhme—so write down 'jingle'
And there's such putting in—in whores crim con[3]
Some mouths would eat forever and eat on

Childern are fond of sucking sugar candy
And maids of sausages—larger the better
Shopmen are fond of good sigars and brandy
And I of blunt—and[4] if you change the letter
To C or K it would be quite as handy
And throw the next away—but I'm your debtor
For modesty—yet wishing nought between us
I'd hawl close to[5] a she as vulcan did to venus

I really cant tell what this poem will be
About—nor yet what trade I am to follow
I thought to buy old wigs—but that will kill me
With cold starvation—as they're beaten hollow
Long speeches in a famine will not fill me
And madhouse traps still take me by the collar
So old wig bargains now must be forgotten
The oil that dressed them fine has made them rotten

---

[1] friskey MS. 8, p.31. [2] [wed]. [3]Cf. Byron's 'Don Juan', Canto XV, stanza 84.
[4] blunt or MS. 8, p.31. 'Blunt' was current slang for money: it occurs in 'The Fancy: A Selection from the Poetical Remains of the late Peter Corcoran', London, 1820, which Clare possessed.
[5] too MS. 8, p.32.

I wish old wigs were[1] done with ere they're mouldy
I wish—but heres the papers large and lusty
With speeches that full fifty times they've[2] told ye
—Noble Lord John[3] to sweet Miss Fanny Fusty
Is wed—a lie good reader I ne'er sold ye
—Prince Albert goes to Germany[4] and must he
Leave the queens snuff box where all fools are strumming
From addled eggs no chickens can be coming

Whigs strum state fiddle strings untill they snap
With cuckoo cuckold cuckoo year by year
The razor plays it on the barbers strap
—The sissars grinder thinks it rather quere
That labour wont afford him 'one wee[5] drap'
Of ale or gin or half and half or beer
—I wish prince Albert and the noble dastards
Who wed the wives—would get the noble bastards

I wish prince Albert on his german journey
I wish the Whigs[6] were out of office and
Pickled in law books of some good atorney
For ways and speeches few can understand[7]
They'll bless ye when in power—in prison scorn ye
And make a man rent his own house and land—
I wish prince Alberts queen was undefiled
—and every man could get his *wife* with child

I wish the devil luck with all my heart[8]
As I would any other honest body
His bad name passes bye me like a f—t
Stinking of brimstone—then like a whisky toddy

---

[1] was MS. *8, p.32.*   [2] Ive MS. *8, p.32.*
[3] *The marriage of Lord John Russell to Lady Fanny Elliott, second daughter of the Earl and Countess of Minto, was announced as about to take place on 26 July 1841 in the Northampton Mercury, 12 June 1841 and 17 July 1841.*
[4] *Albert's first absence from England was in fact in March 1844. Until that date he had not been separated from the Queen since their marriage.*
[5] we MS. *8, p.7.*   [6] wigs MS. *8, p.7.*
[7] For speeches which men never understand MS. *8, p.7.*
[8] *GP, p.67, omits the whole of this stanza without explanation.*

We swallow sin which seems to warm the heart
—There's no imputing[1] any sin to God—he
Fills hell with work—and is'n't it a hard case
To leave old whigs[2] and give to hell the carcass

Me-b——ne may throw his wig to little Vicky
And so resign his humbug and his power
And she with the young princess mount the dickey[3]
On ass milk diet for her german tour
Asses like ministers are rather tricky
I and the country proves it every hour
W–ll—gt–n and M–lb——n[4] in their station
Coblers to queens—are phisic to the nation[5]

These batch of toadstools on this rotten tree
Shall be the cabinet of any queen
Though not such coblers as her servants be
They're of Gods making[6]—that is plainly seen
Nor red nor green nor orange—they are free
To thrive and flourish as the Whigs have been
But come tomorrow—like the Whigs forgotten
You'll find them withered stinking dead and rotten

Death is an awfull thing it is by God
I've said so often and I think so now
Tis rather droll to see an old wig nod
Then doze and die the devil dont know how
Odd things are wearisome and this is odd—
Tis better work then kicking up a row
I'm weary of old Whigs[7] and old whigs heirs[8]
And long been sick of teazing God with prayers

---

[1] imputeing *MS. 8, p.7.*   [2] wigs *MS. 8, p.7.*
[3] And with the princess mount the donkey Dickey *MS. 8, p.7.*
[4] Wellington and Melbourn *MS. 8, p.8.*
[5] *GP, pp.67–8, runs this stanza and the next together.*
[6] makeing *MS. 8, p.8.*
[7] wigs *MS. 8, p.8.*   [8] 'hairs' *GP, p.68.*

I've never seen the cow turn to a bull[1]
I've never seen the horse[2] become an ass
I've never seen an old brawn cloathed in whool[3]
But I have seen full many a bonny lass
And wish I had one now beneath the cool
Of these high elms—Muse tell me where I was
O—talking of turning[4] I've seen Whig and Tory
Turn imps of hell[5] and all for Englands glory

I love good fellowship and wit and punning
I love 'true love'[6] and God my taste defend
I hate most damnably[7] all sorts of cunning—
I love the Moor and Marsh and Ponders end[8]—
I do not like the song of 'cease your funning'
I love a modest wife and trusty friend
—Bricklayers want lime as I want ryhme for fillups
—So here's a health to sweet Eliza Phillips[9]

Song

Eliza now the summer tells
Of sports where love and beauty dwells
Come and spend a day with me
Underneath the forest tree
Where the restless water flushes
Over mosses mounds and rushes
And where love and freedom dwells
With orchis flowers and foxglove bells
Come dear Eliza set me free
And oer the forest roam with me

Here I see the morning sun
Among the beachtree's shadows run
That into gold the short sward turns
Where each bright yellow blossom burns

---

[1] Bull MS. 8, p.8.   [2] a horse MS. 8, p.8.   [3] wool MS. 8, p.8.
[4] Imps of Hell MS. 8, p.8.   [5] 'twining' GP, p.68.
[6] MS. 8, p.9 has no quotation marks here.   [7] damably MS. 8, p.9.
[8] Three miles to the West of High Beech, one mile from Enfield.
[9] See above, p.7.

With hues that would his beams out shine
Yet nought can match those smiles of thine
I try to find them all the day
But none are nigh when thou'rt away
Though flowers bloom now on every hill
Eliza is the fairest still

The sun wakes up the pleasant morn
And finds me lonely and forlorn
Then wears away to sunny noon
The flowers in bloom the birds in tune
While dull and dowie all the year
No smiles to see no voice to hear
I in this forest prison lie
With none to heed my silent sigh
And underneath this beachen tree
With none to sigh for Love but thee

Now this new poem is entirely new
As wedding gowns or money from the mint
For all I know it is entirely true
For I would scorn to put a lie in print
—I scorn to lie for princes—so would you
And ere I shoot I try¹ my pistol flint
—The cattle salesman—knows the way in trying
And feels his bullocks ere he thinks of buying

Lord bless me now the day is in the gloaming
And every evil thought is out of sight
How I should like to purchase some sweet woman
Or else creep in with my two wives to night
Surely that wedding day is on the coming²
Abscence like phisic poisons all delight—
Mary and Martha both an evil omen
Though both my own—they still belong to no man

---

¹ trie *MS. 8, p.9.*   ² comeing *MS. 8, p.9.*

But to our text again—and pray[1] where is it
Begin as parsons do at the beginning
Take the first line friend and you cannot miss it
'Poets are born' and so are whores for sinning
—Here's the court circular—o Lord is this it
Court cards like lists of —— not the naked meaning
Here's Albert going to germany they tell us
And the young queen down in the dumps and jealous

Now have you seen a tramper on race courses
Seeking an honest penny as his trade is
Crying a list of all the running horses
And showing handbills of the sporting ladies
—In bills of fare you'll find a many courses
Yet all are innoscent as any maid is
Put these two dishes into one and dress it
And if there is a meaning—you may guess it

Don Juan was Ambassador from russia
But had no hand in any sort of tax
His orders hung like blossoms of the fushia
And made the ladies hearts to melt like wax
He knew Napoleon and the king of prusia
And blowed a cloud oer spirits wine or max
But all his profits turned out losses rather
To save[2] one orphan which he forced to father

Theres Doctor Bottle[3] imp who deals in urine[4]
A keeper of state prisons for the queen
As great a man as is the Doge of Turin
And save in London is but seldom seen
Yclep'd old A–ll–n[5]—mad brained ladies curing
Some p–x–d like Flora and but seldom clean
The new road oer the forest is the right one
To see red hell and further on the white one

---

[1] prey *MS. 8, p.9.*   [2] He saved *MS. 8, p.10.*
[3] bottle *MS. 8, p.10.*   [4] '*wine*' *GP, p.70.*
[5] Allen *MS. 8, p.10.*

Earth hells or b–gg–r sh–ps or what you please
Where men close prisoners are and women ravished
I've often seen such dirty sights as these
I've often seen good money spent and lavished
To keep bad houses up for doctors fees
And I have known a b–gg–rs tally travers'd[1]
Till all his good intents began to falter
—When death brought in his bill and left the halter

O glorious constitution what a picking
Ye've had from your tax harvest and your tythe
Old hens which cluck about that fair young chicken
—Cocks without spurs that yet can crow so blythe
Truth is shut up in prison while ye're licking
The gold from off the gingerbread—be lythe
In winding that patched broken old state clock up
Playhouses open—but mad houses lock up[2]

Give toil more pay where rank starvation lurches
And pay your debts and put your books to rights
Leave whores[3] and playhouses and fill your churches
Old clovenfoot your dirty victory fights
Like theft he still on natures manor poaches
And holds his feasting on anothers rights
To show plain truth you act in bawdy farces
Men show their tools—and maids expose their arses[4]

Now this day is the eleventh of July
And being sunday I will seek no flaw
In man or woman—but prepare to die
In two days more I may that ticket draw
And so may thousands more as well as I
To day is here—the next who ever saw
And In a madhouse I can find no mirth pay
—Next tuesday used to be Lord Byrons birthday

---

[1] buggers . . . traversed *MS. 8, p.10.*
[2] Playhouses open your gaols and madshops lock up *MS. 8, p.11.*
[3] *'whore' GP, p.71.*   [4] ar–es *MS. 8, p.11.*

G

Lord Byron poh—the man wot rites the werses
And is just what he is and nothing more
Who with his pen lies like the mist disperses
And makes all nothing as it was before
Who wed two wives and oft the truth rehearses
And might have had some twenty thousand more
Who has been dead so fools their lies are giving
And still in Allens madhouse caged and living

If I do wickedness to day being sunday
Can I by hearing prayers or singing psalms
Clear off all debts twixt god and man on monday
And lie like an old hull that dotage calms
And is there such a word as Abergundy[1]
I've read that poem called the 'Isle of Palms'[2]
—But singing sense pray tell me if I can
Live an old rogue and die an honest man

I wish I had a quire of foolscap paper
Hot pressed—and crowpens—how I could endite
A silver candlestick and green wax taper
Lord bless me what fine poems I would[3] write
The very tailors they would read and caper
And mantua makers would be all delight
Though laurel wreaths my brows did ne'er environ
I think myself as great a bard as Byron

I have two wives and I should like to see them
Both by my side before another hour
If both are honest I should like to be them
For both are fair and bonny as a flower
And one o Lord—now do bring in the tea mem
Were bards pens steamers[4] each of ten horse power
I could not bring her beautys fair to weather
So I've towed both in harbour blest together[5]

---

[1] abergundy *MS. 8, p.12.*
[2] *i.e. 'The Isle of Palms'*, by '*Christopher North*' (*John Wilson*), *London, 1812.*
[3] could *MS. 8, p.12.*
[4] '*streamers*' *GP, p.72.*   [5] So now both's towed *MS. 8, p.12.*

Now i'n't this canto worth a single pound
From anybodys pocket who will buy
As thieves are worth a halter I'll be bound
Now honest reader take the book and try
And if as I have said it is not found
I'll write a better canto bye and bye
So reader now the money till unlock it
And buy the book and help to fill my pocket[1]

---

[1] *This stanza is followed (MS. 8, p.13) by the letter to Eliza Phillips; see above, p. 22.*

MS. 110

'O for a Lodge in some vast wildernesss[1]
Some boundless contiguity [of] shade
Where rumour of oppression and deciet
Of unsuccessful or successful war
Might never reach me more' Cowper[2]

And in the maple bush there hides the style
And then the gate the awthorn stands before
Till close upon it you cannot see't the while
Tis like to Ivy creeping oer a door
All green as spring nor gap is seen before
And still the path leads on—till neath your hand
The gate waits to be opened and then claps—the sower
Scatters the seeds of spring beneath his hand
And then the footpath tracks the elting land

Song

The Fruit is fair to luik upo'
And the flower is fair to see
But my ain flower wi' her sweet clais on
Is the sweetest gem for me
The flower's o' garden's and o' fields
Right bonny flowers may be
The fruit o' orchards flowers o' braes
Are na' sae sweet to me
She beets them a' in sunday claes
There's na sich like on banks and braes

Her gown is red and white and blue
The tartan rainbow coloured shade
Her face is roses blushing true
And lilys grow beneath the plaid

---

[1] MS. 110. See editorial note, p.28.
[2] These are the first five lines of Book II of 'The Task'.

Her waist a single arm may span
Her ancle gimp her leg sae bra'
A proper angel for a man
Her foot the smallest o' the sma'
There's na sick like in Sunday claes
On scotlands banks and scotlands braes

I've travelled scotland three times oer
And the flower upo' the heather know
I never saw the like before
By hill or flood or birkenshaw
There's fruits and flower's in many a glen
But o' the like they've nane to show
She beats them oer and oer agen
The maid upo' the heather know
She beats them a' when i' her sunday clais
Theres nae sic like on banks or brae's

Land of perpetual summer Italy
Land of the golden City of the sun
Cradle of Europes Empire but for thee
The rest were darkness and perpetual dun
Celestial clime and garden of the sun
Country of Virgil Hessiod—once the free
Latium and Greece both kingdoms of the sun
Their infant cradles rocked by Liberty
And still the sunniest Land is Italy

Greece[1] Land of Homer and the muses fire
How nations read and kindle at thy name
The freemans sword the poets native lyre
Have filled thy history with a classic fame
And is not Greece that Land of Isles the same
The sun shines oer its freedom and wars cease
The despots chains near[2] made it stoop
Its hills and classic sky's repose in peace
And freedom owns it as the soil of greece

---

[1] *Followed by deletion of the word* the.　　　[2] *ne'er.*

Song

I sit upo' a simmer bank
To view the flower sae bloomin'
I think my sweetheart may cum bye
And she's a luvley woman
Her Sunday gown's gat yellow flowers
Her sunday gown's gat green
And she's gat twa three sunday gowns
The sweetest e'er war seen

Her cheeks are like the buddin' rose
Her face the rose fu' blown
Her lukes are what a' natur' knows
I think my heart my ain
I wish she'd cum amang the flowers
And be a flower her sell
I'd press her in these hartsum[1] hours
And luv' her beauty well

Her bonnet is a hat o' strae
Which village maids adorn
Not ane o' mayday seemed sae bra'
She had it new at morn
The ribbons they war green and blue
And naethin luked sae sweet
Ane colour spring the tuther true
Her smiles I luvd to greet

I wish that she wud wanner bye
Amang the flowers and bee's
She'd in this arbour see me lie
The place war sure to please
I see her now i' gown o' green
I' fancies happy ee —
Strae hat the sweetest e'er was seen
I wish she'd wanner bye

---

[1] *heartsome.*

Infants are but cradles for the grave
And death the nurse as soon as life begins
Time keeps accounts books for him and they save
Expences for his funeral out of sins
The stone is not put down—but when death wins
Churchyards are chronicles were[1] all sleep well
The gravestones there as afterlives live in
Go search the Scriptures they will plainly tell
That God made heaven—Man himself the hell

There is a chasm in the heart of man
That nothing fathoms like a gulph at sea
A depth of darkness lines may never span
A shade unsunned in dark eternity
Thoughts without shadows—that eye can see
Or thought imagine tis unknown to fame
Like day at midnight such its youth to me
At ten years old it boyhoods care came
Now manhoods forty past tis just the same

Song

She's like the daisey on the hill
That upward turns his eye
As if he thought the small white clouds
Where[2] daiseys in the sky

She is the wood Anemonie
Sae droopin and sae true
In sic' like shades she luvs to be
Bloomin' in draps o' dew

She is the goud spink on the thorn
Sae lovley in her sang
She is the gouden light o' morn
As beautifull and young

The richest chord of Poesy
The sweetest note they sing
She is the poets pleasant dreams
And every pleasant thing

---

[1] *where.*   [2] *Were.*

The all thats beautifull and sweet
The all thats good and fair
Is my true lover when we meet
Where summers wild flowers are

Temple of Minerva

The ruin of a ruin—man of mirth
Pause oer the past and meditate decay
The very stones are perishing to earth
Foundations though alls left will waste away
Time's chissel on whats left still writes 'Decay'
Which every season wrecks and wears away[1]

A shadow it was present—but tis past
Time sickened and lifes nature met decay
Convulsive winds seemed sobbing out their last
When ruins piecemeal Temple past away
The very stores like clay dissolving lye
And solitude half fearing learns to sigh[2]

See'st thou the steps of yesterday
The night before the last
See'st thou when darkness went away
And daylight winnowed past
The present is—and shadows are
What was so very bright and fair

Spring meadow flowers was suns and joy
Of present happiness
But when the summer filled the sky
All was another dress
They changed to seed among the hay
And dyed when summer went away[3]

---

[1] *Then follows:* [Times chissel on its wreck has wrote decay
          Which every season wrecks and wears away].
[2] *Then follows:* [And virtues self half fearing learned to sigh].
[3] *Here follows a verse paraphrase of Revelations Chap. 6.*

Now evening rosey streaks—a ribbond sky
Spreads in the golden light[1] of the far west
And mighty rocks are pillowed dark and high[2]
The image and the prototype of rest
The heavens prophecy where peace is blest[3]
A stillness soft as fall of silent dews
Is felt around—the very dusk looks blest
As is the maiden while her heart pursues
Her evening walk oer fields in silent dews

Ave Maria tis the hour of love
When sighs and pains and tears on beautys breast
Are whispered into blessings from above
Ave Maria tis the hour of rest
For man and woaman and the weary beast
And parents love the minature delights
That blesses all with sleep and quiet rest[4]
Ave Maria tis the hour of night
Like to an Indian Maiden dressed in white[5]

The winter time is over love
White thorns begin to bud
And brown and green of freshness love
Enlivens all the wood

Theres white clouds got agen the sun
One daisey open on the green
The primrose shows its sulphur bud
Just where the hazel stulps are seen

And ere the april time is out
Along the ridings gravel walk
The bedlams primrose blooms about
Wi' twenty blossoms on a stalk

How happy seems the drop of dew
That nestles in the daiseys eye
How blest the cloud seems in the blue
That near the sun appears to lie

---

[1] [streaks].   [2] [on the sky].   [3] [of peace and rest].
[4] [with slumber Ave Maria].
[5] *This stanza clearly derives from Byron's 'Don Juan', Canto III, Stanza 103.*

How happy does thy shadows seem
That stretches oer the morning grass
They seems to walk as in a dream
I know their shadows as they pass

The primrose over withered leaves
Now beautifully shines
  ★ ★ ★   ★
   ★ ★ ★

Song[1]

I wish I was were[2] I would be
Alone with beauty and the free
I wish I was where I have been
A lover[3] on the village green
Where old pits swell'd and mosses grew
Along with one who loved so true

Hath time made no change and then love is the same
Through calm and through danger dishonour and fame
What e'er I encounter what e'er I pursue
Human love may be frail—but mans honour is true

Canst thou feel what I breathed on thy bosom that eve
If thy love was a womans thoult ne'er disbelieve
But walk in thy fancys through meadow and glen
Aye walk and be happy and think it agen
There's the hills in thy fancy the Park in thy eye
And in midnight so guiltless that beautiful sky
And the stars looked upon us so lovely and warm[4]
And thy own native star shed its beauty so calm
That said in bright colours love never should part
When I lay on thy bosom the man of thy heart

---

[1] *Cf. GP, p.140 and TP2, p.523.*   [2] *where.*
[3] *Grigson gives 'shower'—a misreading. The 'l' of 'lover' is written over two other letters to give the effect of 'sh'.*
[4] [calm].

The prude may rail on love and falsehood declaim
Mock love is their liscence and falshood their fame
In abscence they scandalize wrong and decieve
And laugh at their fondness when women believe
But man never wronged them and Eden I see
Where man ever loved and a woman is free
Then leave me still free with thy love to be blest
On the bosom of woman thy wishes are blest
Oer the hills and the hollows on that happy Eve
True love was the welcome that cannot decieve

1

There is[1] a day a dredfull day
Still following the past
When sun and moon shall pass away
And mingle with the blast
There is a vision in my eye
A vacuum oer my mind
Sometimes as on the sea I lye
Mid roaring waves and mind[2]

3

The very shore if shore I see
All shrivels like a scroll
The heavens rend away from me
And thunders sulphurs roll[3]

2

When valleys rise to[4] mountain waves
And mountains sink to seas
When towns and cities temples graves
All vanish like a breeze

---

[1] [I wis].   [2] [*sic*] *wind*.
[3] And thunders [seem to] sulphurs [shadows] roll.
   These four lines are clearly an abortive attempt to make a third stanza. Clare later wrote the stanza below beginning: Pays in destructions. *See below, p.109.*
   [4] [seem to] rise [in].

The skys that was are past and oer
That chronicle of months weeks days
Years reckonings there are kept no more
Oblivion's ruins pay's

3

Pays in destructions—shades and hell
Sin goes in darkness down
And there in sulphurs shadows dwell
Worth wins and wears the crown
Strange shapes and void afflict the soul
And shadow to the eye
A world on fire while smoke seas roll
And lightenings rend the sky

4

The morn shall be be as blood the sun
Black as a thunder cloud
The stars shall turn to blue and dun
And heaven by[1] darkness bowed
Shall make suns dark[2] and give no day
When stars like skys[3] shall be
When heaven and earth shall pass away
Wilt thou Remember me

Spring

The sweet spring now is coming
In beautifull sunshine
Thorns buds and wild flowers blooming
Daisey and Celadine
Somthing so sweet there is about the spring
Silence is music ere the birds will sing

---

[1] [in].   [2] [When] suns [turn] dark.   [3] [all dark].

And theres the hedgerow pootys
Blackbirds from mossy cells
Pick them where the last year's shoot is
Hedge bottoms and wood dells
Stript,[1] spotted, yellow, red, to spring so true
For which the schoolboy looks with pleasures new

On gates the yellow hammer
As bright as Celadine
Sits—green linnets learn to stammer
And Robins sing divine
On brown land furrows stalks the crow
And magpies on the moor below

In small hedged closes lambkins stand
Its cud the heifer chews
Like snow clumps upon fallow land
They shine among the Ewes
Or sheets of water by moonlight
The Lambkins shine so very white

The lane the narrow lane
With daisy beds beneath
You scarce can see the light again
Untill you reach the heath
Thorn hedges grow and meet above
For half a mile a green alcove

The nettles by garden walls
Stand angrily and dun
Summer on them like prison falls
And all their blossoms shun
The abby's haunted heaps of stone
Is by their treachery overgrown

Theres verdure in the stony street
Decieving earnest[2] eyes
The bare rock has its blossom's sweet
The micriscope espies[3]
Flowers leaves and foliage everywhere
That cloaths the animated year

---

[1] *Striped.*   [2] [the most] earnest.   [3] [Decieving earnest eyes].

Fields meadows woods and pastures
Theres spring in every place
From winters wild disasters
All wear her happy face
Beast[s] on their feet and birds upon the wing
The very clouds upon the sky look spring

Sunshine presses by the hedge
And there's the pileworts sure to come
The primrose by the rustling sedge
And largest cowslips first in bloom
All show that spring is every where
The flowery herald of the year

The present is the funeral of the past[1]
And man the living sepulchre of life
Still in the past he lives—O would it last
In its own dreams of beauty where the strife
Of passion died—yet trouble ever rife
Dwells on its sweetest tones and[2] harsh all[3] sound
That chord that used to sound the name of wife[4]
On life's jarred [music] now emits no sound
And sweetheart melodys youth[5] lost are nowhere to be found

Beautifull poetry I bow to thee
Here in the midst of winter and of dearth
I trace the sunny climes of Italy
And all the gorgeous Edens upon earth
Far from the land that chilled my early birth
To Stambouls plains and rich perenial hours
Rich[6] Turkeys climes and all[7] the wealth of earth
O poesy thy unexausted powers
Gives me these summers of eternal flowers

---

[1] Cf. TP2, p.464 and GP, p.142, which prints this as a ten-line stanza.
[2] [till].   [3] [things].
[4] [That melody called sweetheart is not found
    And wife on lifes jarred music has no sound].
[5] Clare leaves the word youth above are. Presumably a variant not rejected. Tibble and Grigson, probably with justification, here omit are.
[6] [To].
[7] Clare leaves as a variant, unrejected, To Stambouls plain and rich.

Sweet Italy and Turkey full as sweet
When shall I meet agen in heavens own eye
Those angels and those houris that would greet
My wanderings in romes hills and Stambouls sky
Where Eden in mans reach would bloom and lie
With womans smiles about him on loves wing
Fluttered around me in the sweetest sky
Joy realized the love my memories sing
Beautys fond smiles and loves eternal spring

A Favourite Place

Beautiful gravel walks overgrown
With moss and grass little places where
the poet sat to write

Song Last Day[1]

There is a day a dreadfull day
Still following the past
When sun and moon are past away
And mingle with the blast
There is a vision in my eye
A vacuum oer my mind
Sometimes as on the sea I lye
Mid roaring waves and wind

When valleys rise to mountain waves
And mountains sink to seas
When towns and cities temples graves
All vanish like a breeze
The skyes that was are past and oer
That almanack of days[2]
Year chronicles are kept no more
Oblivions ruin pays

---

[1] See above p.104.
[2] At this point the stanza is interrupted by the interpolation of the stanza beginning:
The red bagged bee on never weary wing.

Pays in destruction shades and hell
Sin goes in darkness down
And therein sulphurs shadows dwell
Worth wins and wears the crown
The very shore if shore I see
All shrivelled to a scroll
The Heaven's rend away from me
And thunders sulphurs roll[1]

Black as the deadly thunder cloud
The stars shall turn to dun
And heaven by that darkness bowed
Shall make days light be done
When stars and skys shall all decay
And earth no more shall be
When heaven itself shall pass away
Then thou'lt remember me

The red bagged bee on never weary wing[2]
Pipe's his small trumpet round the early flowers
And the white nettles by the hedge in spring
Hears his low music all the sunny hours
Till clouds come on and leaves the falling showers
Herald of spring and music of wild blooms[3]
It seems the minstrel of springs early flowers
On banks where the red nettle flowers it comes
And there all the long sunny morning hums

---

[1] *GP, p.141, prints the last four lines as a separate fragment. In the first of the four lines Grigson reads 'of' for 'if' and in the second 'shrivels like' for 'shrivelled to'.*

[2] *This stanza is published by TP2, p.403 as stanza 6 of a sequence of which the other stanzas appear in the Clare MSS., thus:*

> *1 and 2: MS. 9, p.13;*
> *3: MS. 110, Flyleaf verso;*
> *4: MS. 110, p.72; 5: MS. 110, p.87;*
> *6: MS. 110, p.30; 7: MS. 110, p.34.*

Mrs. Tibble informed the editors that the authority for this arrangement was a transcript made by Mr. Blunden.

[3] *[flowers].*

When reason and religion goes a benting
Christianity grows lean as specters—and
Pines off to somthing else—none seem repenting
But each get notions none else understand
Wives from their husbands pare off unrelenting
And like pined pigeons mope about the land
Couple's awake go silently and dreaming
And love and faith and madness are but seeming[1]

Summer is on the earth and in the sky
The days all sunny and the fields all green
The woods spread oer her hills a canophy[2]
Of beautys harmony in every scene
Like to a map the fields and valleys lie
Winds dash in wildest motions the woods green
And every wave of leaves and every billow
Lies in the sun like Beauty on a pillow[3]

There is a freshness in the leafy sprays
That dashes oer the forest from the wind
The wild sublimity of windy days
Like the rich thinkings of a master mind
Or dashes on the canvass none can find
In works inferior—when the woods all blaze
With a wild sunset and the winds unbind
Their foliage to the heavens wild amaze
Field meadow wood rolling oer stormy days

The roaring of the woods is like a sea
All thunder and comotion to the shore
The old oaks toss their branches to be free
And urge the fury of the storm the more
Louder then thunder is the sobbing roar
Of leafy billows to their shore the sky[4]
Round which the bloodshot clouds like fields of gore
In angry silence did at anchor lie
As if the battles roar was not yet[5] bye

---

[1] *Clare indicates by a double line that this stanza is separated from the one that follows*
[2] *Canopy.*
[3] *A defective stanza. It should have nine lines.*
[4] to their shore the [shore the] sky.   [5] [hardly].

Anon the wind has ceased the woods are still
The winds are sobbed to sleep and all is rest[1]
The clouds like solid rocks too jagged for hills
Like[2] quietly ashore upon the west
The cottage ceases rocking—each tired guest
Sleeps sounder for the heavy storm's uproar
—How calm the sunset blazes in the west
As if the waking storms would burst no more
And this still even seems more calmer than before

Bluebells how beautifull and bright they look[3]
Bowed oer green moss and pearled in morning dew
Shedding a shower of pearls as soon as shook
In every wood hedgegap they're shineing through
Smelling of spring and beautifully blue
—Childhood and Spring how beautifully dwells
Their memories in the woods we now walk through
O balmy days of spring in white thorn dells
How beautifull are woods and their bluebells

Song

Tis spring my love tis spring
And the birds begin to sing
If twas winter left alone with you
Your happy form and face
Would make a sunny place
And prove a finer flower then ever grew

Tis spring my love tis spring
On the hazels catkins hing[4]
And the snow drop wi' blebs o' dew
Is not more white within
Then your bosoms hidden skin
The sweetest bonny flower that ever grew

---

[1] [calm].　　　[2] *Lie.*
[3] *See above, p.109, n. 2.*　　　[4] [sing].

The suns arose from bed
All strewn with roses red
But the brightest crimson place
Is nought so fresh and fair
Or so lovely to compare
As thy blushing bonny face

I love springs early flowers
And their bloom in her first hours
They never half so bright or lovely seem
They are like the happy grace
Of young womans blushing face
And the green happiness of loves young dream

The sinking sun sheds through the window glass
A roseiate light upon the painted walls
Green looks the trees cornfields and meadow grass
As golden on the road the low sun falls
Loud at their play the citys childern calls
And happy minds seek green spots in the fields
Ere yet the heavy dew of evening falls
While the lone partridge to their ramble calls[1]

Song

My bonny Mary Ann
My winsome Mary Ann
The sweetest thing in natures plan
Is my ain true love Mary Ann
Sae bonny is her witching size
Sae pretty is her rosey face
Sae red her lips sae bright her eyes
She's mans delight in ony place

O the bonny Mary Ann
Slender waste and proper size
O the luvly Mary Ann
Cherry cheeks and sparkling eyes

---

[1] *Defective nine-line stanza.*

Nay never turn those smiles away
Thy frowns will turn me crazy
Thou kingcup of the sunny may
Thou bonny April daisy

My bonny Mary Ann
My charming Mary Ann
The sweetest thing in natures plan
Is my ain true love Mary Ann
The thing that I shud like the best
In natures sweetest plan
Is luv' in Islands of the blest
Wi' bonny Mary Ann

A cozey place with Mary Ann
Ne'er haunted by the foot o' man
But blest with natures choicest plan
Me and my bonny Mary Ann
Her cherry cheeks and proper size
Her luiks that turn frae idle man
I'll worship nature in her eyes
And ever luv' my Mary Ann

My bonny dearest Mary Ann
Soft neck and breasted like a swan
Thy cherry cheeks aye beat the wan
My rosey bonny Mary Ann
I pu' a flower and think o' thee
I cant contrary natures plan
The sweetest flower maist dear to me
Is my ain bonny Mary Ann

Song

The Larks in the sky love
The flowers on the lea
The white thorn's in bloom love
To please thee and me

Neath its shade we can rest love
And sit on the hill
And as we met last love
Enjoy the spring still

The spring is for lovers
The spring is for joy
Oer the moor where the plovers
Wir hover and cry
We'll seek the white thorn love
And sit on the hill
On some sunny morn love
And be lover's still

Where the partridge is craiking
From morning to e'en
In the wheatlands awaking
That sprouts young and green
Where the brook dribbles past love
Down the willowy glen
And as we met last love
Be lovers agen

The larks in the grass love
Abuilding her nest
And the brook runs like glass love
Neath the carrion crows nest
There the wild woodbines twine love
And till the days gone
Sun sets and stars shine love
I'll call thee my own

Song

Theres pleasure on the pasture lea
And peace within the cottage
But theres na peace at a' for me
While love is in its dotage

I never have a thought o'gude[1]
But worser thoughts will soil[2] it
When heaven is man's happiest mood
The deil is[3] sure to spoil it

Mans sweetest choice is womans yet[4]
Scenes where her kiss was granted
The[5] choicest place[6] where first they met
Mid flowers by nature planted

And there they dwell in fancys flights
In valley field and glen
In pleasant dreams and heart delights
Till neist they meet agen

Song

The bird cherrys white in the dews o' the morning
The wildings are blushing along the hedgeside
The gold blossomed furze the wild heaths are adorning
And the brook in the hollow runs light by my side
But where is the charmer the voice of[7] the maiden
Whose presence once charmed me the whole summers day
The bushes wi' gold and wi' silver oerlaiden
Looks cold i' the morning when Phebe's away

The sun rises bright oer the oaks in the spinney
Bringing gold unto gold on the winbushes there
Blossoming bright as a new minted guinea
And moist wi' the mist of the morns dewy air
The flower is bowed down and I let the tired Bee be
All wet wi' night dew and unable to flye
Such a kindness in me would be pleasure to Phebe
A poor trampled insect[8] would cause her to sigh

---

[1] [happy thought].   [2] [spoil].   [3] [devils].
[4] [still].   [5] [Are].   [6] [spots].
[7] *Clare repeats this word in error.*   [8] [beetle].

The white thorn is[1] coming wi' bunches of blossoms
The broad sheets of daiseys spread out on the lea
The bunches of cowslips spread out their gold bosoms
While the oak balls appear on the old spinney tree
Come forward my Phebe wi dews of the morning
By the old crooked brook let thy early walk be
Where the brambles arched stalks—glossy leaves are adorning
And bits o' woo'[2] hang on the bark o' the tree

Come forward my Phebe by times in the morning
Come forward my Phebe in blebs o' the dew
They bead the young cowslip like pearls i' the dawning
And we'll mark the young shower where the green linnet flew
I'll court thee and woo thee from morning to e'ening
Where the primrose looks bright in the ivy's dark green
And the oak oer the brook in its white bark is leaning
There let me and Phebe wi morning be seen

Tall grows the nettle by the hedgeway side[3]
And bye the old barn end they shade the wall
In sunshine nodding to the angry tide
Of winds that winnows bye—these one and all
Makes up the harmony of Spring—and all
That passes feel a sudden love for flowers
They look so green—and when the soft showers fall
They grow so fast—Dock Burdocks Henbane—all
Who loves not wild flowers bye the old stone wall

Verses on Onley[4]

A charm is thrown oer Olney plains
By Cowper's rural muse
While sunshine gilds the river Ouse
In mornings meadow dews

---

[1] [is] [was].   [2] wool.
[3] See above, p.109, n. 2.   [4] Olney.

Sally Frisby

Song

Sally Frisbys fair and bonny
Frae[1] the bosom to the feet
Rose and lily there's not ony
Half sae fair and half sae sweet
As hedge woodbine's streaks o' red
Bonny Sally's far more dear
Her heelthy hue o' white and red
Is like the rose upo' the brere[2]

Bonny Sally blooming Sally
Fairest flower of a' the town
I' the woodbine lane to dally
And walk wi' Sally up and down
The woodbine to the summer dear
Is nothing half sae sweet[3]
The hue of roses on the brere
Turns pale thy face to meet

There is a colour on thy cheek
A brightness in thy eye
Twere vain in any flower to seek
Or any painted sky
There is a rose upon thy cheek
Not found on any tree
There is a ruby on thy lip
Not found in either sea

Dew drops that upon heath bells lye
Their colour shining through
Is just the hue o' thy bright eye
And half as luvly too
We'll wander down the pebbly brook
Where clearest waters dally
And hide us i' the 'clover nook'
Myself and beautious Sally

---

[1] [Bonny].   [2] briar.   [3] [Red hues o' rose].

Song

How sweet the happy evening hails
The fields as sinks the sun
While leans the maid agen the rails
Where clear the waters run
A bonny maid with eyes as sweet
As beams[1] o' e'ening sun
A bonny maid and dressed as neat
As sweethearts when they're won

The hedges by the e'ening sun
Was gilt in every place
But the sweetest look that e'er was won
Was in her bonny face
In gown o' pink and hat o' straw
How sweet the maid did seem
Her face as round as ony ba'[2]
Her bosom fair as cream

How white her hands how very white
Like angels hands they be
The sweetest thing that e'enings light
Has ever brought to me
She stood agen the fountains[3] head
And leaned agen the rails
The setting sun was going to bed
And gilding all the vales

I passed the maid a flower o' grace
That did my fancys strike
The rose it blossomed in her face
No garden owns the like
Her gown o' pink her hat o' straw
Have won my fancy clean
She is the fairest o' them a'
The maid I met at e'en

---

[1] [sun].   [2] *ball*.   [3] [rails].

Oundle Phebe

My bonny blooming Oundle Lassie
More beautiful than Hebe
Let's wander in the meads sae grassy
My bonny blaiming[1] Oundle Phebe
The beautifull and true my love
The beautifull and true
Are in that rosey face my love
And those bright eyes o' blue

They're brighter then a bleb o' dew
On the rose leaves underside
That trembles as the wind blows through
Brighter then onything beside
I never saw a fairer face
E'er since the days of Hebe
The sweetest flower o' ony place
Is beautys pastoral Phebe

O my bonny rosey Phebe
Beautifull as greece's Hebe
Bright eyed pastoral blooming Phebe
O my blooming bonny Phebe
Had I the world the land and sea
I'd gi' it wi' myself to Phebe
My queen and goddess she shud be
The bright and beauteous Phebe

I snatch the bell flower frae the dew[2]
Frae woods the valleys lilly
Thy bosom had the selfsame hue
When I stood shally shilly
Beside thee by the bright green thorn
Agazing upo' Phebe
The sweetest rosebud o' the morn
Art thou my lovely Phebe

---

[1] *blooming.*   [2] [thorn].

I look upo' the heat o'day
I look upo' the dawning
The morning red the e'ening grey
The blooming and adorning
The gouden plumage o' the dove
Is not sae bright as Phebe
The pink o' a' the warld's luv
Is fascinating Phebe

To Sorrow[1]

'Sorrow is my joy'
Beautiful Sorrow in thy silence thou
Art more then beautiful—not[2] charms of youth
A rosey[3] skin or lily painted brow
Can match thy looks thou beautiful in truth
Rebeccas faith warm with the love of Ruth
Leave heavens sunshine on thy thoughtfull brow
Thou beautifull of sorrow and of truth
Hiding no secret sin no broken vow
While in thy raven hair white snow drops glow

Song

O beautiful Sorrow
Joys shadow divine
Where day canna borrow
Nae sunbeams to shine
I think that the shadow
'Maist[4] beats the sunbeam
Thy face it looks gladder
In sorrowfull dreams

---

[1] *Cf. TP2, p.464.*   [2] [the].
[3] [lily].   [4] *Almost.*

I think the pale shadow[1]
Of[2] beauty more dear
Then the beautifull blushes
Of roseys when near
Thou beautifull sorrow
How warmer and fair
Then the bunch of cold snowdrops
In thy raven hair

Thou'rt a beautifull sorrow
Of fancys and dreams
Where the gloomy tomorrow
The darkest day seems
Where the snowdrops may wither
That nae sunlight can borrow
Where the sunshine come hither
My beautifull Sorrow

With thy hair like the raven
A' glossy[3] and black
Thy bosom o' snowdrops
And bonny broad back
My luv is in shadows
Where no one can borrow
Real joy makes me sadder
My pleasure is sorrow

Song

There is a feeling nought can calm
A passion nought can quell
The mention of a sweetheart's name
That fond thoughts dare not tell
To know thee thus my dearest maid
And then to part in twain
The thunder making earth affraid
Will smile upon the main

---

[1] [shade of].   [2] [Thy].   [3] [Thy breas'].

The just may fall by thunder shocks
That never knew a crime
And earthquakes rend the lonely rocks
That upward used to climb
But love fond love that wedlock ties
Each other as their own
Then choked to tears and stifled sighs
And petrified to stone

For thee dear maid I touch the strings
And keep my heart awake
Tis simple truth the ballad sings
That love will not forsake
And stubborn are the hands that strike
The chords to melody
That loved the many all[1] alike
With a double love for thee

Thy pedigree and titles high
As[2] shadows pass away
And that fine face and brighter eye
Must also meet decay
But love that warmed us at the first
Can live and love[3] alone
Nor ever die bye fate accursed
Though petrified to stone

The thunder mutters louder and more loud
With quicker motion hay folks ply the rake
Ready to burst slow sails the pitch black cloud
And all the gang a bigger haycock make
To sit beneath—the woodlands winds awake
The drops so large wet all thro' in an hour
A tiney flood runs down the leaning rake
In the sweet hay yet dry the hay folks cower
And some beneath the waggon shun the shower

---

[1] [great and small].   [2] [I pass].
[3] [never thrive].

Song

O aince I loved the lily
As the first and fairest flower
And aince I luved the rose
On simmers hedge row tower
And I luv'd the white thorn bower
Clad softly green at spring
But sweeter then the flower
Is my luv' Mary King

I luved her in her childhood
In sorrow and in joy[1]
Red as blossoms i' the wild wood
And brown as any boy
As the linnet luv's its young
I' the green leaves o' the spring
So I've often said and sung
Of my true luv' Mary King

Sae I've often said and sung
When her links o'[2] flaxen hair
Oer her fair shoulders hung[3]
And her little breast was bare
I luved her more and more[4]
Till she got a fair young thing
Fond and tender as before
Was the bonny Mary King

And now she's ripe and blooming
I' the prime o' rosey may
And her bosoms luv' untombing
Bursts lace and pins away
'All sueing to be prest'
White as snowdrops o' the spring
Love warms the lily breast
O sweet bonny Mary King

---

[1] [I luved her all the year].   [2] [little].
[3] [Was hanging oer her shoulders].   [4] [Twas pleasure to behold her].

I

My bonny Mary King
Ripe and rosey Mary King
Sweetest flower o' a' the spring
Is my ain true luv' Mary King
Sae I luv' her night and day[1]
A ripe and bonny thing
Till lifes sands waste away
Young handsome Mary King

O Woman lovely woman how beguiling
Is thy sweet voice of music and thy smiles
Thy cheeks all roses and thy lips all smiling
And where's the treachery that thy heart beguiles
For thy sweet self man labours sweats and toils
Mines the whole earth and raviges the deep
For thee the summer in its glory smiles
Yet 'Man was made to mourn and women weep'[2]
And briars and thorns as harvests both must reap

Song

Sweet Susan Chaplin was a maid
That I loved late and early
When down the wheatfield path we strayed
Or 'mong the shocks o' barley
O Susan Chaplin was the maid
That I loved late and early

My Kildare's bonny Susan
With her glossy raven hair
Wi'out her theres nae chusing
Or joy or pleasure mair
Sae I loved my bonny Susan
With the glossy raven hair

Thy eyes the mirrors brightness
Or brooks that show the sky
Thy neck the lilys whiteness

---

[1] [more and more].
[2] *At the beginning of this line is inserted the name* Ann Preston.

Thy lips like rubys lye
A kissing ane anither
She's the diamond in my eye

Her cheeks are like the rosey flower
Then aiblins[1] like the lily
Shes gloomy in a lonely hour
Then tricksome as a filly
Of Kildare she's the rosy bower
And ⟨. . . . .⟩[2] the snow white Lily

Sweet Susan is the girl for me
My bright and bonny Susan
She's slender as a poplar tree
My bonny black eyed Susan
There's but ain only chusing
While I'm making love to thee

Poets and Poesy are aspirations
Of minds superior to the common lot
The light and life and ornament of nations
That leave no writing they could wish to blot
Time mossed in centurys finds them unforgot
Green with the leaves of laurel and the bay
The poets dwelling is a sacred spot
Where pilgrims Love when ages pass away
The low mossed cot—the steeple crack'd and grey

Song

The winter stays till e'en the spring it canna cum
And every cannie bud is nipt up before the bloom
The winter winna gae and it stays a day oer lang
Sae the flowers they canna bloom and the birdies get nae sang

---

[1] *The word appears to be thus. Burns's 'Address to the Unco Guid and the Rigidly Righteous' contains the line:*
        Ye're aiblins nae temptation . . .
Aiblins = perhaps.

[2] *The word appears to be* sgive *or* sgine.

The young and cannie maiden canna gang by her ain gate
But brazen ruffian winter mun teaze her suin and late
Her gown to shun the dirt of leaves her ancle bare
For her gown it is the best and her ony sabbath ware[1]

Then brazen ruffian winter begins his bawdry sang
And calls her foul and filthy names and does her mickle wrang
But I lov to see her ancle and I lov to see her gown
Held up by her lily hand when rains are dripping doon

And if I see her bonny cauf it set me in a bleeze[2]
The pillars o' king Salomon are nat sae sweet as these
But winter blites wi' chilblains where love would leave a kiss
And woman lovely woman is ever used amiss

The winter stays till e'en and the spring it canna get
There's near[3] a way for maids to gaing and neer a blossom yet
There's ne'er a wa' for womans gate luik which a wa we will
Yet still I lov a' womankind and winna do her ill

I winna wrang a woman for the best bluid in my veins
I winna wrang a woman till the last of life remains
Though the spring it canna cum and the winter winna gang
I maun luv' aye worship woman in every tale and sang

Look through the naked bramble and black thorn
And see the arum show its vivid green
Glossy and rich and some ink spotted like the morn
Ing[4] sky with clouds—in sweetest neuks Ive been
And seen the arum sprout its happy green
Full of spring visions and green thoughts
Dead leaves a' litter where its leaves are seen
Broader and brighter green from day to day
Beneath the hedges in their leafless spray

---

[1] *wear.*   [2] *blaze.*   [3] *ne'er.*
[4] *At this point it seems that Clare intended the* ing *of* morning *to be carried over from the previous line.*

Here is the scenes[1] the rural poet made
So famous in his songs—the very scenes
He painted in his words that warm and shade
In winters wild waste and springs young vivid greens
Alcove and shrubbery—and the tree that leans
With its overweight of Ivy—Yardley oak
The peasants nest and fields of blossomed beans
The bridge and avenue of thick set oak
The wilde[r]ness—here Cowpers spirit spoke

The Awthorn

I love the awthorn well
The first green thing
In woods and hedges—black thorn dell
Dashed with its green first spring
When sallows shine in golden shene
These white thorn places in the black how green

How beautifully green
Though March has but begun
To tend primeroses planted in the suns
The roots that further in
Are not begun to bud or may be just begun

I love the white thorn bough
Hung over the mole hill
Where the spring feeding cow
Rubs off the dew drop chill
When on the cowslip pips and glossy thorn
The dews hang shining pearls at early morn

Song

Theres a little odd house by the side of the Lane
Where the daisys smiles sweet in the spring
Where the morning sun glitters like gold on the pane
And the hedgesparrow trembles his wing
Where chaffinch green linnet and Sparrows have tones
That make the green Lane and the cottage their own

---

[1] [awll].

The sparrows they chirp and make nests i' the eaves
The chaffinch sings 'pink' in the hedge o' white thorn
That fences the garden and there the bird weaves
A nest of grey lichen soon as light i' the morn
And there bonny Susan will sit at the door
And see the green linnet at work at its nest
Where the robin flyes in for a crumb on[1] the floor
And seems as if longing to sit on her breast

Song

Come dwell with me
Neath the greenwood tree
And nature will teach thee plain
That peace and health is liberty
We nowhere else shall gain
Come dwell with me
Neath the greenwood tree
Where life is not spent in vain

Come where the wilding blows
Like the hedge dog rose
With its pale and pinky stain
Where the hugh oak rocks
While the tempest blows
Come dwell with me
Neath the hugh oak tree
Where nature no ill bestows

Full green is the spring
And thrushes they sing
In the hazle and maple tree
Come to the green wood
And twill set[2] thy heart free[3]
In such a still place to be
With all thats beautiful and good

---

[1] [at].   [2] [do].   [3] [good].

I love the little pond to mark at spring[1]
When frogs and toads are croaking round its brink
When blackbirds yellow bills gin first to sing
And green woodpecker rotten trees to clink
I love to see the cattle muse and drink
And water crinkle to the rude march wind
While two ash dotterels[2] flourish on its brink
Bearing key bunches children run to find
And water buttercups they're forced to leave behind

Spring[3]

Pale sun beams gleam
That nurtur a few flowers
Pile wort and daisey and a sprig o' green
On white thorn bushes
In the leaf strewn hedge

These harbingers
Tell spring is coming fast
And these the schoolboy marks
And wastes an hour from school
Agen the old pasture hedge

Cropping the daisey
And the pile wort flowers
Pleased with the Spring and all he looks upon
He opes his spelling book
And hides her blossoms there

Shadows fall dark
Like black in the pale Sun
And lye the[4] bleak day long
Like blackstock under hedges
And bare wind rocked trees

---

[1] Cf. *TP2, p.402. Tibble* reads 'meet'. See *p.109, n. 2 above.*

[2] *Clare has sketched in pencil above this verse the pond with the two ash dotterels. In the first volume of Knight's transcripts at Northampton, pp.284–5, there occurs a poem entitled 'Recolections of Home', where Clare writes of:*

    That sweet little homestead with pollard ash and pond
    Leads back a hundred miles wherever I may roam . . .

[3] *Cf. TP2, p.404.*   [4] [all].

Tis dull but pleasant
In the hedge bottom lined
With brown seer[1] leaves the last
Year littered there and left
Mopes the hedge sparrow

With trembling wings and cheeps
Its welcome to pale sunbeams
Creeping through and further on
Made of green moss
The nest and green blue eggs are seen

All token spring and everyday
Green and more green hedges and close
And every where appears
Still tis but March
But still that March is Spring

The wind blows happily on everything
The very weeds that shake beside the fold
Bowing they dance—do anything but sing
And all the scene is lovely to behold
Blue mists of morning evenings of gold
How beautiful the wind will play with spring
Flowers beam with every colour light beholds
Showers oer the Landscape flye on wet pearl wings
And winds stir up unnumbered pleasant things

I love the luscious green before the bloom
The leaves and grass and even beds of moss
When leaves gin bud and spring prepares to come
The Ivys evergreen the brown green gorse
Plots of green weeds that barest roads engross
In fact I love the youth of each green thing
The grass the trees the bushes and the moss
That pleases little birds and makes them sing
I love the green before the blooms of spring

---

[1] *sere.*

Sorrow is felt not seen—the grief of verse[1]
Is writ by those who share not in our pain
The pawl embrodered and the sable hearse
Are symbols not of sorrow but of gain
What of the scutcheoned hearse and pawl remain
When all is past—there sorrow is no more
Sorrows heart aches—and burning scars will stain
As morning dews—as april showers is o'er
Some tears fall on their graves [again][2]

Katharine Airlie

O a' the flowers o' scottish land
Oer hill and valley blooming
There's nane that has the warld's command
And looks sae sweet as woman
She is the pink of each paterre[3]
Though three times doubled fairley
And war they sweeter then they are
They'd not match Cathrine Airlie

Ive often trod the scatterd dells
And clomb her mountains high
Where bush and tree upon the fells
Touched the cieling of the sky
And maids I've a'maist seen them a'
And talked baith late and early
But fews sae fair and nane sae bra'
As bonny Catharine Airlie

O bonny is the gowan blue
Beneath the Lammie's claie's
And never bluimed a flower mair true
On vales or mountain braes
To catch the dew and tell the spring
With showers that sprinkle's early
But nae flower fanned by birdies wing
Can match with Katharine Airly

---

[1] *Pages 131–77 of MS. 110 are used in reverse. This section thus begins on p.131.*
[2] Cf. *TP2, p.468.*   [3] *parterre.*

Mair fair¹ then lilies o' the vale
Mair sweet then roses are
That bluims in bonny Teviotdale
There's ne'er a rose sae fair
As is her sweet and bonny face
The lik is² seen but rarely
There's near³ a rose in ony place
Like bonny Katharine Airlie

Sae lang as scotland hills are green
And vallies pour their floods
Sae lang as nature's soveriegn queen
Oer mountains plains and woods
Sae lang the lily o' the land
The flower o' late and early
The dearest flower in loves command
Is my sweet Katharine Airlie

False time what is it but a rogues account
Of books wrong kept—times keystone is the sun
True natures wronged—and what is the amount
But deaths diseases—that their circuit run
Through error and through deeds that fate has done
Religion is the health—the suns bright ray
By which the goal of Love and Freedoms won
The oceans tide will flow its natural way
And none its speed and none its course will stay

The North Star

There is a Star⁴ I know it well
Sun of the northern sky
That cheers the hermits lonely cell
Like heavens unerring eye
Twas there a thousand thousand years
And still in the same place appears

---

¹ [flowr].   ² [has].   ³ ne'er.   ⁴ [lamp].

The other stars they flye about
Like lights lit in a cell
Lit up awhile and then put out
There's none knows where they dwell
But where God lit thou'rt shining still
A Lamp of heaven's eternal will

The compass to the problem true
As sun is to the day
The even star that gems the dew
Take's day's last light away
Yet shines in heaven no stationed space[1]
But wanes and others take her place

But there thou wert when Noahs ark
Its shoreless voyage went
Just where thourt stealing from the dark
Like tapers from a tent
And there thou wert at Waterloo
In the same place as now I view

When Moses stood on Sions hight
Thy light was faithfull then
And thy beams shed unerring light
On sons of lesser men
The same as on that glorious night
When Israel slew th' Amelakites

Thou lone and solitary star
A lamp oer oceans pathless brine[2]
Beacon to those who travel far
Upon this hemisphere is thine
Such light[3] is by religion given
To light our blinded way to heaven

---

[1] [place].
[2] [shine].   [3] [&] Such [the] light.

All nature has a feeling wood brooks fields[1]
Are life eternal—and in silence they
Speak happiness—beyond the reach of books
There's nothing mortal in them—their decay
Is the green life of change to pass away
And come again in blooms revifified[2]
Its birth was heaven eternal is its stay
And with the sun and moon shall still abide
Beneath their night and day and heaven wide

Twilight

Twilight meek nurse of dews
And mother of refreshing births to flowers
Sweet now a walk to chuse
And roam in thy cool hours
To be an hour away unseen of men
In the green lane or whitethorn studded glen

Sweet twilight swarth[3] or pale meek nurse of dews
Mother of sweet sleep to many flowers
The birth of dewwebbed[4] breezes that imbues
Our hearts to meditation in sweet hours
Sweet twilight nurse of sleep
In watchet stole and web of sober[5] grey

Old times forgetfull memories of the past
Are cold and drear as snow upon our graves
In books less then a shadows doom will last
But Fragments there each stranded volume saves
Like some rich gems washed up from ocean waves
But now no summer dwells upon the spot
Nor flower to blossom—the eternal blast
Oblivion leaves the earth in which they rot
Darkness in which the very lights forgot

---

[1] Cf. TP2, p.475. [2] Originally revivified, but amended.
[3] [nurse]. [4] [cobbwe]. [5] [mantle].

Where are the citys Sodom and Gommorrah
The marble pallaces upon the plain
Citys to day and a dead sea tomorrow
And what they was they ne'er will be again
That earth is lost and all its city slain
By the oerwhelming waves entombed and gone
Search for its ruins now is void and vain
And but one witness saw that ruin done
The ever burning bright eternal Sun[1]

Song

Twas just when early springs begin
To open daiseys eyes agin
And shaw the gouden light wi'in
Upon a sunny mornin'

Twas just when buds will swell to shoot
And buddin' primrose at the root
Begins to show its sulphur[2] suit
All on the dewy morning

And violets peep afore the dawn
Upon woodbanks beneath the thorn
Ere yet a single leaf is born
To shield the chilly morning

I saw a maid i mornin's grey
Upon her misty milkin' way
When dead grass tufts and naked spray
Bent wi' the weet[3] o mornin'

As ony flower her face was fair
And had the rose i' june been there
There'd bin nout[4] in it to compare
Wi' her I met that mornin

---

[1] *Two lines crossed out before this line:*
        Star and still that witness is the lasting sun
        That eye all seeing bright eternal sun.
[2] [sunday].   [3] *wet.*   [4] *nought or nowt.*

There may be many flowers a bloomin'
And monie mair wi' simmer comin'
The sweetest that I cau'd a woman
Upon that dewy mornin'

And may the smiles o' heaven keep it
And may the dews o' april steep it
And nought on earth ha' cause to weep it
The flower o' aprils mornin

'Blessed be thy bloom thou lovely gem
Unscathed by ruffian hand
And from thee many a happy stem
Arise to deck our land'   Burns[1]

And what is Love the sweetest of all pains
Yet teazing more then madness to the mind
It wants no setoffs garniture or gains
Better acceptance in the heart to find
On lily breasts and rosey mouths love binds
Its image which no power on earth can free
Though called inconstant as the shifting winds
Tis Truth on earth as heaven itself can be
I've felt it ever since I loved Haidee[2]

---

[1] *The last stanza of Burns's 'On the Birth of A Posthumous Child', which reads:*
    Blest be thy bloom, thou lovely gem,
    Unscath'd by ruffian hand!
    And from thee many a parent stem
    Arise to deck our land.

[2] *The reconstruction of some of the stanzas which follow this is difficult. Clare evidently changed his mind several times. The stanza beginning 'Haidee the lovliest of all thats loved' has its first four lines immediately following this, but is then interrupted to make way for a complete stanza, 'Those turband roses vide Turkish girls'. Then come five lines of a first draft of the stanza ' "The Lord of Daybreak" soars on high'. Next come two blank lines and then five lines beginning 'When once thy smile is seen what else may seem'. Now comes the final version of the complete stanza ' "The Lord of Daybreak" soareth now on high' incorporating a revised version of 'Where once thy smile is seen— what else may seem'. Finally, after a space of twelve pages, Clare completes the stanza beginning 'Haidee the lovliest of all thats loved', and indicates the connection by use of asterisks. In order to make this procedure clearer to the reader, we have brought the two parts of this stanza together, but have left the remainder in the original order, simply enclosing the rejected drafts in square brackets.*

Haidee the lovliest of all that loved
The venus of young life the poets dreams
A vision of the mind by all approved
A beauty of the heart that all esteems[1]
Where all is beautifull—theres no part seems[2]
Diviner—all is best—none better—Haidees real
—Angels are good mens hopes[3] and poets dreams
Haidee is flesh and blood—with eyes that steal
Man from himself—love's soul beneath Gods seal

Those turband roses vide[4] Turkish girls
How shaped and young and beautifull they are
All garnitured in rubies gold and pearls[5]
The lilies whiteness even is not fair
Beside their lovliness—but droop despair
And sicken in their sunshine—there love dwells
The houris's of Eden—long dark hair
And wreathing tresses loves bewitching spells
And 'large black eyes like pearls hid in their shells'[6]

['The Lord of the daybreak'[7] soars on high
And turns the grecian sea to mirrourd gold[8]
Like Edens round the grecian Islands lie
Where seasons green and beautifull unfold[9]
Thy smiles are charms that turned all to gold][10]

[When once thy smile is seen what else may seem
So beautifull—for nought more loved could be
Then thou in boyhoods fancy or loves dream
And still as then thy prescence I behold[11]
I never think of Greece without Haidee]

---

[1]*Here comes the first break, with Clare's note: (quote from Koran). As will be seen below this note refers to the last line of the next stanza. See below, n. 6.*

[2] *These five lines are inserted after 'Mary Green' on p.102 of MS. 110. See below pp.142-3.*

[3] *Clare seems to prefer this to* fancies *but has not deleted* fancies.

[4] *A piece of Clare naïveté.*   [5] [shells].

[6] *Clare has an asterisk here and the note:* Koran. *See above, n. 1.*

[7] *This is a quotation from the Koran, chapter 113.*

[8] *The words* to mirrored gold *are deleted before* the grecian sea.

[9] [With the green shadows of eternity].

[10] *Then follow two blank lines.*   [11] [thou art a sweet young dream to me].

'The Lord of Daybreak' soareth now on high
And turns to mirrored gold each wood and stream
Like Edens round the grecian Islands lie
As beautifull as a midsummer dream—
Where once thy[1] smile is seen—what else may seem
So beautifull—for nought more loved can be
Then thou in boyhoods fancy or loves dream
And still thou art a sweet young dream to me
I never think of greece without Haidee

The heaven of earths visions[2]—boyhoods dreams—
But too much love turns dirty—here we halt
And face about from heaven and extremes
Ale cant be good if they forget the malt
And earth has lost its savour without salt
Love—hate are nearer kindred then life seems
To own too—if her fault I cannot tell
That sweet that turns to sour and never creams
Makes strange reallities the heaviest dreams

Love tickled is by any bents or straws
A lady likeing whisper in the dark
A rebel doubtfullness unknown to laws
That looks all eyes and greedy as a shark
Swallows the mall the promenade[3] and park
But such is sham love fond of different faces
Not that which hears the ballads of the lark
True loves the inward self in secret places
Whats felt by two in love a third but guesses

Nelly Giles

O Nelly Giles o Nelly Giles
I canna rest i' sleep
I wander over gates and stiles
And over rivers deep

---

[1] [ones].

[2] *Although this appears to be a separate movement from the Haidee section, these words echo the last lines of the stanza above on p.137 and the next words follow on from the stanza just completed.*

[3] *Clare has written* the maul the promede.

Your face it is sae sweet to see
Sae rich the rosey smiles
Ye've often made a fool o' me
My charming Nelly Giles

The summer is a luscious flower
And sae is Nelly Giles
The clover bottles makes the hour
Sae sweet frae stile to stile
Down paths that gae accross the fields
Bean flowers smell sweet and smile
But nae aen thing sic pleasures yields
As a walking[1] Nelly Giles

The water like the bright sun smiles
In white thorns linnets sing
And yonder wanders Nelly Giles
A lily by the spring
The clover bottles luscious smiles
The cowslip by the way
But ten times over Nelly Giles
Is handsomer then they

Sweet Nelly Giles sweet Nelly Giles
Is sweeter then the rose
That on the white thorn hedges smiles
In summer times repose
The sma' white lily by the well
The bell flower by the stile
Looks nothing in their class so well
As charming Nelly Giles

There is an eye there is a look
That wins by choicest smile
You cannot find it i' the brook
But ony Nelly Giles
O Nelly Giles thou pink o' May
And summertime o' smiles
I think about thee every day
Thou charming Nelly Giles

---

[1] [courting].

K

Song

My bonny Ann Sharp[1]
It was rapture to meet thee
My bonny Ann Sharp
It was pleasure to greet thee
With the leaves on the bushes
The meadows all hay
When we sat on green rushes
And courted all day

When the wild flower close bye us
Was wooed by the bee
Nought in life gave such joy as
A armfull of thee
My bonny Ann Sharp
Thou art first o' the many
There is nane i' the whole warld
Can equal my Nannie

Its a beautifull place
I still visit my sen
Where wild flowers may blossom
That blossomed there then
My bonnie Ann Sharp
And the grass luiked sae green
That I thought o' thy beauty
Both morning and e'en

My bonny Ann Sharp
And rich[2] beautys ain Nannie
Thy frowns and ill temper
Would bother me scranny
But bonnie Ann Sharp
Will luik kindly on me
And bonnie Ann Sharp
Is the dearest to me

---

[1] *Just above this poem Clare writes* Ann Sharp Flying Horse.
[2] [my].

Of my manhood the queen
Dearest light o' my e'e
And this sweet simmer scene
But reminds me o' thee
O my beautifull Ann
Neath the meadows green tree
Where the clear water ran
I'll thy worshiper be

Song   White Thorn Tree

The may bush smells sae very sweet
The crimson threeds sae fine
The chaffinch builds her nest sae neat
And shepherds sit to dine
Aye dear o' me I love to see
The sweetly scented white thorn tree

The leaves are green and very green
Though bunches o' the may
Whiten till scarcely one is seen
For a whole summers day
Aye dear o' me I love to see
Hedges[1] all white[2] and love the awthorn tree

It spreads above the little pond
And hides the thrushes nest
The hedge is whiter still beyond
With moonlight on its breast
Aye dear o' me I luv' to see
The little pond and awthorn tree

I luv' the thorn the white awthorn
The bonniest thing in may
That bonnily scents the gales o' morn
And sweetens a' the day
Aye dear o' me I love to see
Grass shadows o' the white thorn tree

---

[1] [The].   [2] [in].

It fa's sae black on the wild thyme hills
In the morning and sae lang
And the blackbird hides that merry trills
In its leaves the sweetest song
Aye dear o' me I luv' to see
The blackbird haunted white thorn tree

O the bonny scented awthorn
Bright leaf and snowy flowers
That stands alone tween lands o' corn
Glittered wi' morning dews and showers
Aye dear o' me I luv' to see
The bonny spreading white thorn tree

Mary Green

O Loves bonny Mary Green
Was there ever such a hue[1]
On the rosey pearled in dew
As on thy cheek is seen
On choice carnation leaves
Was there e'er so rich a streak
When thy white bosom heaves
As thy lips that music[2] speak

Shall I twine the weeping willow
Round the bloom of Mary Green
Oer her bosoms snowy pillows
And her face so like a queen
Shall the cypress glooms be wreathing
Like a lump o' coffined clay
Round that form o' beauty breathing
All the witcherys o' May

O my lovely Mary Green
The richest flower o' May
On thy bonny face is seen
Which love winna take away

---

[1] *Clare indicates by numbers that these two lines are to be reversed, but fails to amend* O *to* As.
[2] [essay to].

Thy dress sae neat thy face sae sweet
As bonny as a queen
Thou'rt loves own sweetheart a' compleat
My bonny Mary Green

Song

Mary Ann Abbot[1]
Ive a secret or two
But love dare not blab it
To any but you

Its a[2] secret as simple
As secrets all are
In Mary Anns dimples
And beautifull hair

Dark curls of her youth
And love light o' her eye
In that beautifull truth
Why is Mary so shy

Nature ripened those charms love
Pride never made vain
Why not come to my arms love
And kiss me again

Lay bare[3] those twin roses
That hide in thy hair
Thy eyes light discloses
The sweetness hid there

For thy dark curls lye on them
Like night in the air
Like a nightmare upon them
As nothing were there

Come my sweet Mary Ann
Let me kiss and adore thee
Theres none in this world
That was ever before thee[4]

---

[1] *Cf. GP, p.142.*   [2] [My love].   [3] [Let me].
[4] *Grigson reads 'That ever was before thee'.*

O for one real imaginary blessing
Ideal real blessing blasted through
With sin and yet how rich is the carressing
Of love as mothers kisses sweet as Hermon dew
A bright grey eye or black it knocks mine through
And leaves them dim as stars fall'n from above
Electric shocks they come from God knows who
Milk maids have eyes the pictures of the doves
That thrill through bones and marrow is it Love[1]

It is the very essence of all pleasure
It is earths diamond and the oceans gem
It is of life and soul the dearest treasure
Woman through life is mans own diadem
To love God truly may we worship them
Of life in love how various is the scene
Of infant cherubs Loves the parent stem
I wooed a gipsey wench on sunday e'ens
And worshiped beggar girls and courted queens[2]

---

[1] *This is a conjectural reconstruction of the stanza which actually appears on p.99 of MS. 110 as follows:*

O for one real imaginary blessing
Ideal real blessing blasted through
~~With sin and poxes and the God knows who~~
~~For Love~~
With sin and yet how rich is the carressing
~~Of love as milk in womans breast and true~~
~~Hermon dew~~
As mothers kisses sweet as Hermon dew
A bright grey eye or black it knocks mine through
And leaves them dim as stars fall'n from above
Electric shocks they come from God knows who
Milk maids have eyes the pictures of the doves
That thrill through bones and marrow is it Love

[2] *Then follow three rejected lines of which the first must surely be one of the most grotesque in English verse:*

Sweet milk maid o' may mornings queen Victoria
With bonny bosom white as is the May
With all thy green and cowslip fields before thee

Clare returns to this theme again a little later. See below p.145.

Love is the fire that burns the heart to cinders
Love is the thought that makes the poets sigh
Sweet as Queens portraits stuck in London windows
For loyal subjects in their love to buy
Love is of every heart the painted toy
The idol of man[s] worship—faces fair
Where my enchanted magic from a boy
The pouting lip the colour of the hair
Left me in raptures next of kin to care

I loved and wooed them in the field like gems
Of two[1] much value for the clown who sung
The azure bluebells in their sapphire stems
Among green bushes low their mute[2] bells hung
These seemed love's modest maidens dew[3] bestrung
With blebs o'[4] mornings glittering pearls
I loved them in the vallys where I sung
With their green drapery and crispy curls
I loved them as a crowd of blooming girls

With bonny bosom white as is the May[5]
Sweet milkmaid o' may mornings—queen Victoria
The wild brere[6] blushes wi' the break o' day
Sweet as the cowslip fields that spread before thee
Sweet are the dusky clouds that sprinkle oer thee
Filling the cowslip pips wi pearls untold[7]
Thy crown and scepter fade from natures glory
Like toys for tyrants or like garments old
Be nature's Queen and keep her[8] crown of gold

The wild hedge rose it is a bonny flower
As ever met the sunshine and the sky[9]
Its gold threads beeded with the summer showers
That patter on the glossy leaves and lye

---

[1] *too.*   [2] [bells].   [3] [pearl].   [4] [dewdrops].
[5] *See above, p.144, n. 2.*   [6] *briar.*   [7] [o' gold].
[8] [thy].   [9] [fields].

Like pearls that glitter neath the maidens eye
Who stands admiring by the burning flowers
That from her own looks takes a deeper dye
Like feathers on the hedges at morns hours
They look to fancies happier then ours

I could not walk the fields like common men
And have no fancys nourish—nor could I
Pass the wild rose bush oer the foxes den
And not admire its grandeur silently
Natures own majesty who could pass bye
Things left all beauty like those simple scenes
The wild rose blushing neath a summer sky
The summer morning and the rosey e'en
With all the woodland multitudes of green

Song

We never know the sweets o' joy
Untill it goes away
The sweetest flower no notice wakes[1]
Untill it meets decay

The bright sun shines our heads above
Like rich unnoticed dreams
And when the day is lost in clouds
We value the sunbeams

The spring is nothing when it comes
That seemed so bright before
The merry bee neglected hums
Flowers weeds and nothing more

The present joy we cannot see
The sweetest comes to morrow
But when its past no longer free
Past joys are present sorrow

---

[1] makes *is left as an unrejected alternative.*

Song

I long to think of thee in lonely midnight
When thy spirit comes warm as an[1] angel of light
Thy face is before me in rosey and flame
Which my kiss canna reach and I know not thy name
My heart aches to think on't—tis long sin' we met
If love is the truth love how can I forget
My arms would have clasped thee to pull thy face down
But when I embraced thee the Vision was flown

And was it true luv' and cud[2] I forget
Thy name when I feel how enraptured we met
And can love forget thee sae much and keep true
Thy vision brought daylight before the cock crew
I saw thee above me in roseate hue
Thy cheeks they were red and thy bosom swelled too
My arm couldna reach those pearl shoulders sae white
Nor my lips cud[2] na kiss wi' thy lips to unite

And can it be love to have loved and forget
To see thee in visions nor know thy name yet
Thy face is my own that was worshiped in love
And thou comest before me a light from above
Tis thyself but I canna yet think o' thy name
Though my cells light at midnight before the day came
Thy face is still beauty thy breast roseys hue
But thy name I cant think of and yet love is true

God looks on nature with a glorious eye
And blesses all creation with the sun
Its drapery of green and brown earth ocean lie
In morning as Creation just begun
That safforn[3] east fortells the riseing sun
And who can look upon that majesty
Of light brightness and splendour nor feel won
With love of him whose bright all seeing eye
Feeds the days light with Immortallity

---

[1] *Clare writes* an *twice here.*   [2] *could.*   [3] *saffron.*

March Violet

Where last years leaves and weeds decay[1]
March violets are in blow
I'd rake the rubbish all away
And give them room to grow

Near neighbour to the Arum proud[2]
Where dew drops fall and sleep
As purple as a fallen cloud
March violets bloom and creep

Scenting the gales of early morn
They smell before they're seen
Peeping beneath the old white thorn
That shows its tender green

The lamb will nible by their bloom
And eat them day by day
Till briars forbid his steps to come
And then he skips[3] away

Mid nettle stalks that wither there
And on the greensward lie
All bleaching in the thin march air
The scattered violets lie

I know the place it is a place
In spring where nettles come[4]
There milk white violets show thier face
And blue ones earlier bloom

---

[1] *Underneath* decay *is the word* scene.
[2] *Over* Arum proud *is written* beds of green.
[3] turns *is left as an unrejected alternative.*
[4] [bloom].

Song—Molly Magee

My thoughts are of thee Love though thou thinkest not of me
Yet dearly I love thee sweet Molly Magee
To day i' the morning twas nine o' the clock
Thy arm went behind thee to button thy frock
And in pulling it back wi' sich sweetness and ease
My heart broke in two love as short as you please
So now Im a cripple as well you may see
And all through the beauty of Molly Magee

Tother day she stooped natty to tye up her shoe
It wanted five minutes of a quarter to two
And lauk sich a foot and a ancle war there
I lost both my eyes as I turned me to stare
They left me as blind as an owl before day[1]
And stone heaps and blunders are all in the way
I maun be a blindman and believe I cant see
And its all for the beauty of Molly Magee

She tyed up her shoe string she buttoned her frock
And my heart was shut up like the bolt i' the lock
Like the bolt i' the lock like the chit i' the pea
Sich power had the beauty o' Molly Magee
Her back was so white and her leg was so round
The sight o't war worth half the coin in a pound
But bother the sight it has stolen my e'e
I'm blind wi' the beauty o' Molly Magee

I tumble oer stone heaps and miss the high way
And am lost i' the dark i the middle o day
If ain opes his mouth I'm as deaf as a tree
They a' seem as taulkin o' Molly Magee
If they mutter agen her and I knew it not
My heart leaves my breast like a bird that is shot
I shall ne'er mak' an ould man I plain enough see
I'm kilt through the beauty of Molly Magee

---

[1] [in the dark].

Wreck of the Emelie

The Land it is a dangerous strand
So is the briny Sea
When man has lost his self command
How wretched he must be
Our Ship it was the 'Emmelie'
To Cardiff she was bound
But foundered in a dangerous sea
With dangers all around

The sky was all a ink black rock
The wild fire seaming through
The Emelie recieved the shock
All in that boisterous Seas
Like seething pots the billows boiled
And frothed that briny sea[1]
The sailors on the masts were coiled
When wrecked the Emelie

The night came on in black and brown
And where that chauldron boiled red hot
The foundering Emelie went down
As sudden as a shot
Some clung to spars to hencoops some
Twas but a minutes space
Loud oer them boiling billows boom
And left no resting place

Above them gloomed the angry sky
And through the pitch black rock[2]
Of clouds the splintered lightnings flye
None could resist the shock
Down and in a moment gone
Nine men plunged in the wave
And all the seamen lost but one
There met a watery grave

---

[1] [The sky like rocks on fire].   [2] [cloud].

One still survived that fatal wreck
By billows washed ashore
Though all had hopes that stood on deck
That now can feel no more[1]
He through the boiling[2] waves did beat
All in that boiling sea
And on the beach upon his feet
Viewed the shipwrecked Emelie

The healthfull mind that muses and inhales
The green eyed dews of morning finds his way
To paradise Gods choice self planted vales
The dewy breath of flowers the gales that play
Around them like sleep wakeing half the day
Morning luxuriant in green juicey strife
.   .   .   .
.   .   .   .[3]
Health to faint love and happiness to life

O the first days of summer—mornings blush
Is rife with healthy freshness hung with dew
To dip your hand into a wet rose bush
And crop the fairest flower that ever grew
Pearled with the silver shine of morning dew
How beautifull it looks how sweet it smells
The breath of virgin morning coming new
That from the sweets of flowers her story tells
And voice of song birds in the ecchoing dells

And heres the double pink Hepathica
Another early herald of the spring
That comes before the Daffodils to say
That Winds of march are coming with the spring
And all her pleasant flowers—Birds on the wing
Are chirping in the boxtree bye the roots
Hepathicas are early flowers of Spring
They come before the rich laburnum shoots
And frost and snow the early blossom suits

---

[1] *Followed by* [The coops and spars he spurned aside].
[2] [howling].   [3] *Two lines omitted from this stanza.*

Song[1]

O Edinburough Katys a beautifull girl
Her eyes bright as sunshine her teeth white as pearl
Her waist little mair then the span of baith han's
Yet her bosom and shoulders are broader then man's
This edinborough Katys a beautiful girl
Her eyes bright as sunshine her teeth white as pearl
As soft as a cushion a armfull to span
With a bosom and shoulders as broad as a man

O Edinburough Katy she bluims like a lily[2]
The pride o' a' Scotland the pride o' her Willy
Is Edinbro' Katy as weel as the town
And she waulks on the mountain while the sun gangs down
O Endinbro Katy's a beautifull girl
Her eye[3] is rich auburn her teeth white as pearl
O Edinburough Katy's as red as a rose
As down the fair streets of the city she goes

O Edinburgh Katy[s] suns twa three and twenty
The stranger[4] he luiks on her beauty sae dainty
And scarcely believes her as yet in her teens
And she scarcely can think what the strangers luik means
For Katy cant bear to be speird at bye ony
Her shoulders sae broad and her bosom sae bonny
This Edinburough Katy's the lily sae dear
And the flower o' the city at the Spring o' the year

[1] *This may in fact be the second stanza since Clare inserts the word* Song *before the next stanza.*
[2] *Clare inserts the word* Song *before this stanza.*
[3] *Is this a mistake for* hair?   [4] [And yet to a].

Shorter Poems

Mr Blluds[1]
Song

I'll come to thee at even tide
When the west is streaked wi grey
I'll wish the night thy charms to hide
And daylight all away

I'll come to thee at set o' sun
Where white thorns i' the May
I'll come to thee when work is done
And love thee till the day

When Daisey stars are all turned green
And all is meadow grass
I'll wander down the bank at e'en
And court the bonny Lass

The green banks and the rustleing sedge
I'll wander down at e'en
All slopeing to the waters edge
And in the water green

And theres the luscious meadow sweet
Beside the meadow drain
My lassie there I once did meet
Who I wish to meet again

The water lilies where[2] in flower
The yellow and the white
I met her there at even's hour
And stood for half the night

We stood and loved in that green place
When sundays sun got low
Its beams reflected in her face
The fairest thing below

---

[1] *This cryptic title probably means Ballads for Mary, or Ballads of Mary. He then writes a song to Ann Foot, one of the many women for whom and about whom he wrote poems. The poem is found in MS. 9, p.4, et. seq., interspersed with a letter in code to Mary Ludgate of the White Hart Inn, Northampton.*

[2] *were.*

L

My sweet Ann Foot[1] my bonny **Ann**
The Meadow banks are green
Meet me at even when you can
Be mine as you have been

Song[2]

The meadows fill with cow slips
The grass excessive green
Down oer the splashy slough dips
Where the Wagtail birds are seen
I walked there i' the morning
When awoke the early Bee
I went at evens dawning
For the Rose of Broomilea

Sweet Rose of Broomilea
How it scents the evening gale
Where sings the early Bee
While the other flowers turn pale
The silver daiseys there
Like easter white they be
But nothing upon earths more fair
Then the Rose of Broomilea

How lily white her budding breast
Her eyes soft shade o' blue
The lovely Iris o' the west
Owns not a brighter hue
The emerald meadows oft I pass
When daylight shuts his e'e
And dewpearls hang each blade o'grass
For the Rose o' Broomilea

Like a white lamp the evening star
Shines oer the glimmering stream
When I return from courting her
Oer whom I fondly dream

---

[1] *Ann Foot appears twice in the lists of women's names in MS. 10, pp.101 and 107, in the first case with the place-name, Glinton.*
[2] *MS. 9, pp.1ff. Cf. GP, p.191.*

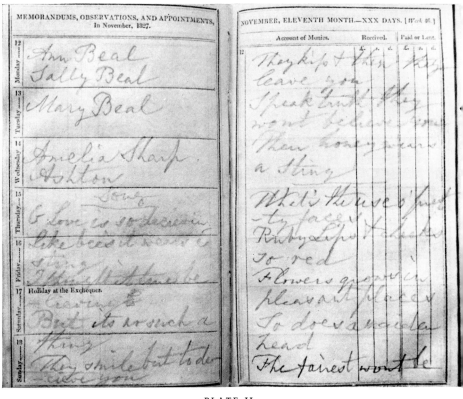

PLATE II

MS. facsimile : MS. 10 (pages 96–7)

Shine on thou mild bright evening light
Shine on oer lake and tree
While I am blest beneath thy sight
Wi' the Rose o' Broomilea

[No Title]

Spring comes and it is may—white as are sheets[1]
Each orchard shines beside its little town
Childern at every bush a poesy meets
Bluebells and primroses—wandering up and down
To hunt birds nests and flowers and a stones throw from town
And hear the blackbird in the coppice sing
Green spots appear like doubling a book down
To find the place agen and strange birds sing
We have no name for in the burst of spring

The sparrow[2] comes and chelps about the Slates[3]
And pops in to her hole beneath the Eaves[4]
While the cock piegon amourously awaits
The Hen on barn ridge crows and then leaves
With crop all ruffled—where the sower heaves
The hopper at his side his beans to sow
There he with timid courage harmless thieves
And whirls around the teams and then drops low—
While plops the sudden gun and great the overthrow

Song[5]

O Love is so decieving
Like bees it wears a sting
I thought it true believing
But its no such a thing
They smile but to decieve you
They kiss and then they leave you
Speak truth they wont believe you
Their honey wears a sting

---

[1] MS. 9, p.13. Cf. TP2, p.401.
[3] MS. 9, p.16. Cf. TP2, p.402.
[5] MS. 10, pp.102–4.

[2] The [little] sparrow.
[4] the [Wall] Eaves.

What's the use o' pretty faces
Ruby lips and cheeks so red
Flowers grow in pleasant places
So does a maidenhead
The fairest wont believe you
The foulest all decieve you
The many laugh and grieve you
Untill your coffin dead

Song[1]

O once I loved a pretty girl
Which caused my heart to ache
With ruby lips and teeth o' pearl
And eyes none could forsake
O she was fair and more then fair
A wild flower of the vale
None in the village could compare
With my sweet Susan Gale[2]

Sweet is the bloom o' the wild brere
That scents the morning dew
And sweet the woodbine flowers appear
That hedges bring to view
Primroses in the old green lane
That scent the evening pale
But there's one flower as sweet again[3]
My own Sweet Susan Gale

O Susan Gale O Susan Gale
How beautifull thou art
Thy face turns many faces pale.
And chills through many an heart
The fairest flower in wood and hill
The first in every vale
Is one would turn a saints heart chill
My bonny Susan Gale

---

[1] MS. 10, pp.108–11.

[2] *Susan Gale seems to have been a real person: her sister, Mary Gale, also appears in a poem in the Knight Transcripts.*

[3] [But nothing can compair to].

Song[1]

Theres beauty in the summer flower
And in the awthorn blossom
Tis sweet to lie at evens hour
Upon a sweet hearts bosom
Tis sweet to lean upon her arm
And loves emotions feel
While walking round the wood and field
With handsome Mary Neal[2]

Young Mary Neal was handsome
And Mary Neal was fair
She was worth a Ladys ransom
With her dark and flowing hair
How fair the flower how soft the wind
Through bushes used to steal
Like woodbine round the thorn entwined
I walked with Mary Neal

How sweet the thorn its tender green
Shot oer the wood side way
Sweet dimples i the brook were seen
I' thorn sweet showers o' may
When down the green we used to hie
And through the wood ride steal
When I kissed her cheek and praised her eye
Of my own Mary Neal

How beautifull the moon arose
And oer the Barley shone
When I clasped her where the hedge briar grows
Young Mary all my own
At broken vows my heart would die
The thought on't makes me reel
For her I live and love and sigh
My lovely Mary Neal

---

[1] *MS. 10, pp.112–16.*   [2] *Cf. 'Mary Neele' (TP2, p.159).*

Song[1]

My old Lover left me I knew not for why
He left me wi' kisses I parted in tears
After painting my cheeks i' the rosey blooms dye
And swearing my eyes were the gems o' the spheres
My Lover has left me I knew not for why
Two years and three months he has wandered afar
The things that were hisn I've put them all bye
And from the fire corner removed the Armchair
I once had a sweet heart I knew not for why
But I think I could love all the days o' my life
But he left me one morning like a bird i th sky[2]
The singing Lark dropt like a stone passing bye[3]
And the cloud racks o' heaven seemed boiling in strife
My sweet heart he left me I knew not for why
He's left me alone for two desolate years
The Swallows on holliday wings chitter bye
And my Eyes looking silent keeping filling wi' tears
I cant be myself let me do as I will
I think till I'm blind and feel willing to die
But my true love has left me and there remains still
He kissed me and left me nor do I know why

[No Title]

Lord hear my prayer when trouble glooms[4]
Let sorrow find a way
And when the day of trouble comes
Turn not thy face away
My bones like hearth stones burn away
My life[5] like vapoury smoke decays

---

[1] MS. 10, pp.97–101, interspersed with lists of women's names. Cf. GP, p.190.
[2] [and wandered away].
[3] [from the sky] Clare should perhaps have cancelled all of this line.
[4] MS. DC. 64. Cf. GP, p.102.
[5] [smoke].

My heart is smitten like the grass
That withered lies and dead
And I so lost to what I was
Forget to eat my bread
My voice is groaning all the day
My bones prick through this skin of clay

The wildernesses pelican
The deserts lonely owl
I am their like a desert man
In ways as lone and foul
As sparrows on the cottage top
I wait till I with faintness drop[1]

I bear[2] my enemies reproach[3]
All silently I mourn
They on my private peace encroach
Against me they are sworn
Ashes as bread my trouble shares
And mix my food with weeping cares

Yet not for them is sorrows toil
I fear no mortals frown
But thou hast held me up awhile
And thou hast cast me down
My days like shadows waste from view
I mourn like withered grass in dew

But thou Lord shalt endure forever
All generations through
Thou shalt to Zion be the giver
Of joy and mercey too
Her very stones are in their trust
Thy servants reverence her dust

Heathens shall hear and fear thy name
All kings of earth thy glory know
When thou shalt build up Zions fame
And live in glory there below
He'll not despise their prayers though mute
But still regard the destitute

---

[1] 'fainting' GP.   [2] 'hear' GP.   [3] [My enemies reproach I bear].

[No Title]

Tis martinmass from rig to rig[1]
Ploughed fields and meadow lands are blea
In hedge and field each restless twig
Is dancing on the naked tree
Flags in the dykes are bleached and brown
Docks by its sides are dry and dead
All but the ivy bows[2] are brown
Upon each leaning dotterels head

Crimsoned with awes the awthorns bend[3]
Oer meadow dykes and rising floods
The wild geese seek the reedy fen[4]
And dark the storm comes oer the woods
The crowds of lapwings load the air
With buzes of a thousand wings
There flocks of sturnels too repair
When morning oer the valley springs

---

[1] MS. DC. 64. Cf. GP, p.104. The first four lines of the second stanza are also found in MS. 49.

[2] boughs.

[3] Crimson with awes the white thorn bends MS. 49.

[4] The wild geese seeks the reedy fens MS. 49.

Poems from the Knight Transcripts

KNIGHT TRANSCRIPTS

Poetry by John Clare
written by him while an
Inmate of the Northampton
General Lunatic Asylum

Copied from the Manuscripts as presented to me by Clare—and favoured with others by some Ladies and Gentlemen, that Clare had presented them to—the whole of them faithfully transcribed to the best of my knowledge from the pencil originals many of which were so obliterated that without refering to the Author I could not decipher. Some pieces will be found unfinished, for Clare will seldom turn his attention to pieces he has been interrupted in while writing—and in no instance has he ever rewritten a single line—whenever I have wished him to correct a single line he has ever shown the greatest disinclination to take in hand what to him seems a great task.

Song[1]

O wert thou in the storm
    How I would shield thee:
To keep thee dry and warm,
    A camp I would build thee.

Though the clouds pour'd again,
    Not a drop should harm thee,
The music of wind, and rain,
    Rather should charm thee.

O wert thou in the storm,
    A shed I would build thee;
To keep thee dry and warm,—
    How I would shield thee.

---

[1] *KT1, p.15; GP, p.127; TP2, pp.460–1. This poem clearly derives from Burns's Address to a Lady, 'O, wert thou in the cauld blast', but improves greatly upon it.*

165

The rain should not wet thee,
　　Nor thunder clap harm thee.
By this side I would sit me,—
　　To comfort, and warm thee.

I would sit by thy side love,
　　While the dread storm was over;—
And the wings of an angel,
　　My charmer would cover.

July 25th 1844

Evening[1]

'Tis evening the black snail has got on his track,
And gone to its nest is the wren;—
And the packman snail too, with his home on his back;
Clings on[2] the bowed bents like a wen.

The shepherd has made a rude mark with his foot,
Where his shaddow reached when he first came;
And it just touched the tree where his secret love cut
Two letters that stand for love's name

The evening comes in with the wishes of love;—
And the shepherd he looks on the flowers;—
And thinks who would praise the soft song of the dove,
And meet joy in these dewfalling hours

For nature is love, and the wishers[3] of love[4]
When nothing can hear or intrude;
It hides from the eagle, and joins with the dove
In beautiful green solitude.

---

[1] *KT1, p.31; CL, p.218, TP2, p.417.*
[2] *'to' CL, p.218; 'to' TP2, p.417.*
[3] *Is this Knight's misreading of 'mistress' or 'wishes'?*
[4] *'and finds haunts for true love' TP2, p.417.*

Sonnet[1]

The flag top quivers in the breeze
That sighs among the willow trees:
In gentle waves the river heaves,
That sways like boats the lily leaves:
The bent grass trembles, as with cold;
And crow flowers nod their cups of gold,
Till every dew-drop in them found,
Is gently shook upon the ground.
Each wild weed, by the river side,
In different motions dignified,
Bows to the wind, quakes to the breeze,
And charms sweet summers harmonies.
The very nettle quakes away,
To glad the summers happy day

Morning[2]

The morning comes—the drops of dew
Hang on the grass and bushes too
The sheep more eager bite the grass
Whose moisture gleams like drops of glass
The hiefer licks in grass and dew
That makes[3] her drink and fodder too
The little bird his morn song gives
His breast wet with the dripping leaves
Then stops abruptly just to fly
And catch the wakened butterfly
That goes to sleep behind the flowers
Or backs of leaves from dews and showers
The yellow hammer haply blest
Sits by the dyke upon her nest
The long grass hides her from the day
The water keeps the boys away
The morning sun is round and red
As crimson curtains round a bed

---

[1] *KT1, p.60; TP2, p.438.*
[2] *KT1, p.74; TP2, p.416.*   [3] *'make' TP2, p.416.*

The dew drops hang on barley horns
As beads the necklace thread adorns
The dew drops hang wheat ears upon
Like golden drops against the sun
Hedge-sparrows in the bush cry 'tweet'
O'er nests larks winnow in the wheat
'Till the sun turns gold and gets more high
And paths are clean, and grass gets dry
And longest shadows pass away   ·
And brightness is the blaze of day

The Invitation[1]

Let us go in the fields love and see the green tree
Let's go in the meadows and hear the wild bee
There's plenty of pleasure for you love and me
    In the mirths and the music of nature
We can stand in the path love and hear the birds sing
And see the woodpigeons snap loud on the wing
While you stand beside me a beautiful thing
    Health and beauty in every feature

We can stand by the brig-foot and see the bright things
On the sun shining water, that merrily springs
Like sparkles of fire in their mazes and rings
    While the insects are glancing and twitters
You see naught in shape but hear a deep song
That lasts through the sunshine the whole summer long
That pierces the ear as the heat gathers strong
    And the lake like a burning fire glitters

We can stand in the fields love and gaze o'er the corn
See the lark from her wing shake the dews of the morn
Through the dew bearded woodbine the gale is just born
    And there we can wander my dearie
We can walk by the wood where the rabbits pop in
Where the bushes are few, and the hedge gapped and thin
There's a wild-rosy bower and a place to rest in
    So we can walk in and rest when we're weary

---

[1] *KT1, pp.87–8.*

The skylark my love from the barley is singing
The hare from her seat of wet clover is springing
The crow to its nest on the tall elm swinging
   Bears a mouthful of worms for its young
We'll down the green meadow, and up the lone glen
And down the woodside far away from all men
And there we'll talk over our love tales again
   Where last year the nightingale sung

Stanzas[1]

The spring is come forth, but no spring is for me,
Like the spring of my boyhood, on woodland and lea,
When flowers brought me heaven, and knew me again
In the joy of their blooming o'er mountain and plain
My thoughts are confined, and imprisoned—O when
Will freedom find me my own vallies again?

The winds breaths[2] so sweet, and the day is so calm;
In the woods and the thicket the flowers look so warm
And the grass is so green, so delicious and sweet,
O when shall my manhood my youth's vallies meet,
The scenes where my children are laughing at Play,
The scenes where my memory is fading away[3]

The primrose looks happy in every field
In strange woods the violets their odours will yield
And flowers in the sunshine all brightly arrayed
Will bloom just as fresh and as sweet in the shade:[4]
But the wild flowers that bring me most joy and content
Are the blossoms that blow[5] where my childhood was spent

---

[1] *KT1, pp.110–11. Knight's pagination goes astray: the next page (i.e. page 112) is numbered 111, and contains 'I am'.*

[2] *'breathes' CL, pp.237–8, TP2, p.476.*

[3] *'The scenes that from memory are fading away?', CL; Tibble follows Cherry in most differences.*

[4] *Alternative reading in Knight: 'as warm as a shade'.*

[5] *'glow' TP2, p.475.*

Then I played like a flower in the shade and the sun
And slept as in Eden when daylight was done
There I lived with my parents, and felt my heart free,
And love—that was yet joy or sorrow to be,
Joy and sorrow it has[1] been, like sunshine and showers
And their sun is still bright o'er my happiest hours[2]

The trees they are naked,[3] the bushes are bare
And the fields they are brown,[4] as if winter lay[5] there
But the violets are there by the dykes and the dell,
Where I played 'hen and chickens'—and heard the church bell
Which called me to prayer-book and sermons in vain
O when shall I see my own vallies again?

The churches look bright as sun at noon day,
There meadows[6] look green e're the winter's away
There the pooty still lies for the school boy to find
And a thought often brings these sweet places to mind
Where the trees waved like thunder[7] no music[8] so well
Then[9] nought sounded harsh but the school-calling bell

There are spots where I played, there are spots where I loved,
There are scenes where the tales of my choice were approved
As green as at first—and their memory will be
The dearest of life's recollections to me!—
The objects seem[10] there in the care of my heart
Are as fair as at first—and will never depart

Though no names are mentioned to sanction my themes
Their heart's[11] beat with mine and make real my dreams:
Their memories with mine their diurnal course run,
True as night to the stars, and as day to the sun.
And as they are now so their memories will be
Long as[12] sense, truth, and reason, remaineth[13] with me.

---

[1] [they have]. [2] Omitted in CL and TP1 and 2.
[3] 'The trees are all naked' CL, p.238. [4] 'as brown' CL, p.238.
[5] 'was' CL, p.238. [6] 'the meadows' CL, p.238.
[7] 'and wind moaned' CL, p.238.
[8] 'sorrows'. [9] [And]. 'There' CL, p.238. [10] seen? 'seen' CL, p.238.
[11] Knight's mistaken punctuation. This should be 'hearts'.
[12] 'While' CL, p.238. [13] 'remain here' CL, p.238.

Some days before the Spring[1]

There's a gladness of heart in the first days of Spring
There's a pleasure in memory to hear the birds sing
The Pink or Hedgesparrow will sing at day break
Though a leaf on the hedges is hardly awake
As for flowers on the grass there's not one to be seen
And the grass in the fields scarce enough to be green
The ruts full of water all muddy and thick
Which the boy tries to stop with a bit of a stick

The bits of brown haystacks all cut to the core
In the grassy close corners show winter is o'er
With the oaks frowning o'er them all mossy and grey
They will stand in the shelter 'till they cut the new hay
The field-fare is there a seeking hedge fruits
And the crow on the grass, is boreing for roots
With the jackdaw that nauntles among the molehills
In their grey powdered wigs, and bright yellow bills

The stones in the brooks, are all covered with green
All trailing and spreading as mosses are seen
In the woods at the spring and the close of the year
When violets and primroses like sisters appear
How level the meadow, how saffron the sun
How fine is the web that the spider has spun
Round the twigs of the hedge and the bents of the vales
In the soft mornings sunshine and sweet evening gales

Then come let us walk and enjoy the brisk air
And fancy the change when sweet spring it is there
Wild flowers in the grass, and nests in the tree
A hedge for the bird and a flower for the bee
So away let us walk while the sun's in the sky
And the paths o'er the greensward and rushes are dry
And Mary will see what there is to be seen
The hedges swelled buds, and the meadows more green

---

[1] *KT1, pp.139–40.*

M

To a Lark singing in Winter[1]

Wing-winnowing lark with speckled breast
Has just shot up from nightly rest
To sing two minuets[2] up the west
    Then drop again
Heres some small straws about her nest
    All hid from men.

Thou farmers minstrel ever cheery
Though winters all about so dreary
I dare say thou sat warm and erie
    Between the furrows
And now thy song that flows unweary
    Scorns earthly sorrows

The little mouse comes out and nibbles
The small weed in the ground of stubbles
Where thou lark sat and slept from troubles
    Amid the storm
The stubbles ic'el[3] began to dribble
    In sunshine warm

Sweet minstrel of the farm and plough
When ploughmans fingers gin to glow
How beautiful and sweet art thou
    Above his head
The stubble field is in a glow
    All else seems dead

All dead without the stubble ground
Without a sight without a sound
But music sunshines all around
    Beneath thy song
Winter seems softened at thy sound
    Nor nips to wrong

---

[1] *KT1, p.155.*
[2] *Clare sometimes spells 'minutes' in this way and may have intended that word.*
[3] *Clare commonly spelt 'icicle', 'icicel' or 'iceicle'. This is presumably his contraction of that word.*

On all the stubble-blades of grass
The melted drops turn beads of glass
Rime feathers upon all we pass
   Everywhere hings
And brown and green all hues that was
   Feathered like wings

It is a morn of ragged rime
The coldest blast of winter time
Is warmth to this Siberian clime
   Dead winter sere
And yet that clod brown bird sublime
   Sings loud and clear

The red round sun looks like a cheat
He only shines blood freezing heat
And yet this merry birds night seat
   Seems warm's a sty
The stubble woods around it meet
   And keep it dry

Each stubble stalk a giant tree
Scarce higher than   [1] knee
Seem woods to stop the winds so blea
   From this snug home
Boundless this stubble wood must be

How safe must be this birds sweet bed
In stubble fields with storms o'er head
Or skies like bluest curtains spread
   Lying so lone
With bit of thurrow o'er her head
   Mayhap a stone

The god of nature guides her well
To choose best dwellings for her sell[2]
And in the spring her nest well[3] tell
   Her choice at least
For God loves little larks as well
   As man or beast

---

[1] *Hiatus in KT1.*   [2] *herself.*   [3] *we'll.*

Thou little bird thou bonny charm
Of every field and every farm
In every season cold and warm
    Thou sing'st thy song
I wish thy russet self no harm
    Nor any wrong

Free from the snares thy nature shuns
And nets and baits and pointed guns
Dangers thy timid nature shuns
    May thou go free
Sweet bird as summer onward runs
    I'll list' to thee

I'd writ one verse, and half another
When thou dropt down and joined a brother
And o'er the stubble swopt together
    To play 'till dark
Then in thy night nest shun cold weather
    As snug's a Lark

Old russet fern I wish thee well
Till next years spring comes by itsel
Then build thy nest and hide it well
    'Tween rig or thurrow
No doubt may be this is the dell
    —Spring comes the morrow

Then blossomed beans will bloom above thee
And bumble bee buz in and love thee
And nothing from thy nest shall moove thee
    When may shines warm
And thy first minstrel[sy][1] above thee
    Sing o'er the farm

---

[1] *KT1 has 'minstrel' only.*

The Round Oak[1]

The Apple top't oak in the old narrow lane
And the hedge row of bramble and thorn
Will ne'er throw their green on my visions again
As they did on that sweet dewy morn
When I went for spring pooteys and birds nest to look
Down the border of bushes ayont the fair spring
I gathered the palm grass close to the brook
And heard the sweet birds in thorn bushes sing

I gathered flat gravel stones up in the shallows
To make ducks and drakes when I got to a pond
The reed sparrows nest it was close to the sallows
And the wrens in a thorn bush a little beyond
And there did the stickleback shoot through the pebbles
As the bow shoots the arrow quick darting unseen
Till it came to the shallows where the water scarce drebbles
Then back dart again to the spring head of green

The nest of the magpie in the low bush of white thorn
And the carrion crows nest on the tree o'er the spring
I saw it in march on many a cold morn
When the arum it bloomed like a beautiful thing
And the apple top't oak aye as round as a table
That grew just above on the bank by the spring
Where every saturday noon I was able
To spend half a day and hear the birds sing

But now there's no holidays left to my choice
That can bring time to sit in thy pleasures again
Thy limpid brook flows and thy waters rejoice
And I long for that tree—but my wishes are vain
All thats left to me now I find in my dreams
For fate in my fortune's left nothing the same
Sweet Apple top't oak that grew by the stream
I loved thy shade once now I love but thy name

June 19/46

---

[1] KT1, p.161.

Twilight[1]

Sweet twilight, nurse of dews
And mother of sweet hours
With thee a walk I choose
Among the hawthorn bowers
That overhang the molehill greenly gray
Made as it were to intercept the way

Beetles are thy trumpeters
And to thy silence play
Where the soft still rustle stirs
O'er[2] dead winds of the day
Mid marshy sedge dull aspens and pasture rushes
O'er green cornfields and hedge row bushes

Thy hours have one light place
Streaky and dunly grey
As if the night was giving place
And bringing back the day
The sun seems coming so the eye believes
But darkness deepens round and undeceives

O'er brooks the weeping ash
Hangs cool and grimly dark
I hear the water splash
And then half fearing mark
In ivy'd ash a robber near the stream
Till from a nearer view I find it but a dream

Sweet twilight nurse of night
Thy path the milk maid treads
With nimble step so light
Scarce bends the cowslips heads
But hastening on ere by thy light forsook
She leaves her cows all resting by the brook

---

[1] *KT1, p.170; TP2, pp.417–18.*　　　　[2] *'of' TP2, p.418.*

Sweet twilight thy cool dews
Are beautifully spread
Where the nightingale its[1] song renews
Close by the old[2] cow shed
In that low hazel oft' I've heard her sing
While sombre evening came on downy wing

The playful rabit too
Its white scut glancing
Amid the silver dew
I've seen them oft advancing
In troops from spiney's[3] where they love to dwell
Dancing on molehills in the open dell[4]

Spring leaves seem old in green
And the dull thorn is lost in the
Dun twilight—but the hazel still is seen
In sleeping beauty by the old oak tree
Giving the woods a beauty and a power
While earth seems Eden in such an hour[4]

Sweet twilight in thy dews
And silence I rejoice
Thy odd stars bid me muse
And give to silence voice
Now twilight ceases on the verge of even'
And darkness like a pawl[5] spreads over heaven

---

[1] 'her' TP2, p.418.　　　[2] 'odd' TP2, p.418.
[3] spinneys.　　　[4] Omitted by Tibble.
[5] pall.

To Jane[1]

The lark's in the sky love
The flowers are[2] on the lea
The white thorn's in bloom love
To please both[3] thee and me
Neath its shade we can rest love
And sit on the hill
And as last we met love
Enjoy the spring still

The spring is for lovers
The spring is for joy
O'er the moor where the plovers
Whir over[4] and cry
We will seek the white thorn[5] love
And sit on the hill
In the sweet sunny morn love
We'll be lovers still

When the partridge is craking
From morning to e'en
In the wheatlands awaking
The sprouts young and green
Where the brook dribbles past love
Down the willowy glen
And as we met last love
Be lovers again

The lark's in the grass love
Building[6] her nest
And the brook's running fast love
'Neath the carrion crows nest
There the wild woodbines twine love
And till the days gone
Suns set and stars shine love
I'll call thee mine own

---

[1] *KT1, pp.185–6; CL, pp.246–7.*   [2] *Cherry omits 'are'.*
[3] *Cherry omits 'both'.*   [4] *'startled' CL, p.246.*
[5] *'hawthorn' CL, p.246.*   [6] *'A-building' CL, p.247.*

Larks and Spring[1]

The sunny end of March is nigh
And not a cloud is in the sky
Along the footpath o'er the farm
The school boy basket[2] on his arm
But not a nest is there to look
He takes a stone to cross the brook
Made wider by the rainy night
And hums the music of delight
To see the rabits seek their burrow
Or ground lark from the fallow'd furrow[3]
Start up and shiver while he sings
Then drop as though he'd lost his wings
As stunt and heavy as a stone
In the brown furrow still and lone
And still I love the ground-larks flight
Starting up the ploughmans height
And more and more unseal his eye
When rose leaves pave the eastern sky
To see the skylark as he springs
Shake mornings moisture from his wings
And rise and sing in music proud
Small as a bee beneath a cloud
'Till mixing with the vapours dun
He's lost in valleys of the sun
And singing on in springs delight
Some moments ere he comes in sight
It drops, and drops from breezy morn
To seek its mate amid the corn
A happy song the skylark brings
And spring's in every note he sings
With coppled crown, and speckled breast
The pilewort blooms above his nest
In rain it seeks the sheltering furrow
But sings when sunshine comes tomorrow
In every field they mount and sing
The songs of Nature and of Spring

---

[1] *KT1, p.195.*   [2] *Knight has in pencil above: 'satchel'.*
[3] *'furrow' is written over 'thurrow'. Possibly Knight's emendation.*

Sonnet[1]

Wood Anemonie

The wood anemonie through dead oak leaves
And in the thickest wood now blooms anew
And where the green briar, and the bramble weaves
Thick clumps o' green, anemonies thicker grew
And weeping flowers, in thousands pearled in dew
People the woods and brakes hid hollows there
White, yellow and purple hued the wide wood through
What pretty, drooping weeping flowers they are
The clipt frilled leaves the slender stalk they bear
On which the drooping flower hangs weeping dew
How beautiful through april time and may
The woods look, filled with wild anemonie
And every little spinney now looks gay
With flowers mid brush wood and the hugh oak tree[2]

No title[3]

How hot the sun rushes
Like fire in the bushes
The wild flowers look sick at the foot of the tree
Birds nests are left lonely
The pewit sings only
And all seems disheartened, and lonely like me

Baked earth and burnt furrows
Where the rabbit he borrows[4]
And yet it looks pleasant beneath the green tree
The crows nest look darkly
O'er fallows dried starkly
And the sheep all look restless as nature and me

---

[1] *KT1, p.214; TP2, p.439.*
[2] *'trees' TP2.*   [3] *KT1, p.234.*   [4] *burrows.*

Yet I love a meadow dwelling
Where nature is telling
A tale to the clear stream—its dearest to me
To sit in green shadows
While the herd turns to gadders
And runs from the hums of the fly and the bee

This spot is the fairest
The sweetest and rarest
This sweet sombre shade of the bright green tree
Where the morehens flag nest
On the waters calm breast
Lies near to this sweet spot thats been mother to me

Mary a Ballad[1]

The skylark mounts up with the morn
The vallies are green with the spring
The linnets sit in the whitethorn
To build mossy dwellings and sing
I see the thorn bush getting green
I see the woods dance in the spring
But Mary can never be seen
Though the all cheering spring doth begin

I see the grey bark of the oak
Look bright thro' the underwood now
To the plough-plodding horses they joke[2]
But Mary is not with her cow
The birds almost whistle her name
Say where can my Mary be gone
The spring brightly smiles—and 'tis shame
That she should be absent alone

---

[1] *KT1, pp.235–7; CL, pp.197–9; TP2, pp.499–501.*
[2] '*yoke*' *CL; Tibble follows Cherry: CL, p.197 and TP2, p.499.* '*yoke*' *requires the omission of the hyphen between* '*plough*' *and* '*plodding*'.

The cowslips are out on the grass
Increasing like crowds at a fair
The river runs smoothly as glass
And the barges float heavily there
The milkmaid she sings to her cow
But Mary is not to be seen
Can Nature such absence allow
At milking on pasture and green

When Sabbath it[1] comes to the green
The maidens are there in their best
But Mary is not to be seen
Though I walk till the sun's in the west
I fancy still each wood and plain
Where I and my Mary have strayed
When I was a country[2] swain
And she was the happiest maid

But woods they are all lovely[3] now
And the wild flowers blow all unseen
The birds sing alone on the bough
Where Mary and I once have been
But for months she now keeps away
And I am a lonely[4] hind
Trees tell me so from day to day[5]
When waving in the wind[6]

Birds tell me so upon the bough[7]
That I'm thread bare and old[8]
The very sun looks on me now
A being dead and cold[9]

---

[1] 'Sabbath-day' CL, p.198.   [2] 'young country' CL, p.198.
[3] 'lonely' CL, p.198.   [4] 'sad lonely' CL, p.198.
[5] 'day after day' CL, p.198.
[6] 'As slowly they wave in the wind' CL, p.198.
[7] 'while swaying the bough' CL, p.198.
[8] 'That I am all threadbare and old' CL, p.198.
[9] 'As one dead, forgotten, and cold' CL, p.198.

Once I'd a place where I could rest
And love and quiet be[1]
That quiet[2] place was Mary's breast
And still a hope to me—[3]

The spring comes brighter by day[4]
And brighter flowers appear
And though she long has kept away
Her name is ever dear
Then leave me still the meadow-flowers
Where daffies blaze and shine
Give but the springs young hawthorn bower
For then sweet Mary's mine

To Miss B[5]

Odd rot it what a shame it is
    That love should puzzles grow
That we the one we seek should miss
    And change from top to toe
The Gilafers a Gilafer
And nature owns the plan
And strange a thing it is to me
A man cant be a man

I traced the woods and mountains brow
    And felt as feels a man
Love pleased me then that puzzles now
    E'en do the best I can
Nature her same green mantle spread
And boundless is her span
The same bright sun is o'er my head
But I can't be a man

---

[1] 'for then I was free' CL, p.198.
[2] Cherry omits 'quiet', CL, p.198.
[3] 'And hope was still left unto me' CL, p.198.
[4] 'day by day' CL, p.199.
[5] KT1, pp.237–8. Presumably the 'Miss B' is the Miss Blunsome referred to in the poem on p.245 below. But see also a reference MS. 10, p.51 to 'Miss Blunson'.

The turf is green and fair the sky
And nature still divine
And summot[1] lovely fills my eye
Just like this love of mine
And though I love—it may not be
For do the best I can
Mong such disordered company
I cannot be a man

Through[2] married ties—affections lies
And all the ties of love
I struggled to be just and wise
But just I cannot prove
The Bible says that God is love
I like so wise a plan
But was it ordered from above
That love was [not] wi' man

This contradiction puzzles me
And it may puzzle all
Was Adam thus foredoomed to be
Our misery by his fall
Eves fall has been a fall to me
And do the best I can
Woman I neither love nor see
And cannot be a man

Song[3]

How silent comes this gentle wind
And fans the grass and corn
It leaves a thousand thoughts behind
Of happiness forlorn
The memory of my happier days
When I was hale and young
Where still my boyish fancy strays
Corn fields and woods among

---

[1] *summat (i.e. something).*   [2] *Knight reads 'Though'.*
[3] *KT1, pp.242–4.*

It fans among the lazy weed[s]
And stirs the wild flowers leaves
Sweet is the playful noise it breeds
While the heart its joys receives
While listening to the gentle sounds
That murmur thro' the grass
And must I love the airy sounds
Of crows that o'er me pass

And larks that fly above the corn
Frit by a jilted stone
A few yards high at eve or morn
Then drop and hide alone
I love to see the breeze at eve
Go winnowing oer the land
And partridges their dwellings leave
And call on either hand

I love the all that nature loves
The water earth and sky
The greeness of the leafy groves
Brown fallows rising high
The breezes of the early morn
The early evening breeze
The Brown Larks mattin[s] in the corn
The rooks song in the trees

I love the haunts of solitude
The coverts of the free
Where man n'er ventures to intrude
And God gives peace to me
Where all I hear and all I see
In peace of freedom roam
Here shall my hearts own dwelling be
And find itself at home

Song[1]

The rushbeds touched the boiling spring
 And dipped and bowed and dipped again
The nodding flower would wabbling hing
 Till it could scarce get back again
How pleasant lay the daisey plain
 How twisting sweet the woodbine grew
Around the whitethorns in the lane[2]
Bedecked with gems of droppled dew[3]

Here Bloomfield lay beside the brook
 His memory haunts the silver flood
Musing upon the open book
 In happy and poetic mood
His fancies[4] left on every place
 The landscape seems his waking dream
Where Hannah[5] shewed her rosey face
'And leap't across the infant stream'[6]

The rush tufts touched the boiling sand
 Then wabbling nodded up anew
Then danced at every winds command
 And dipped to peirce the water through
The twisted woodbine was in flower
 And pale among the thorn leaves grew
Here Bloomfield rested many an hour
 While bees they sipped the morning dew

The little spring it boiled away
 And dancing rose the silver sand
For ever boiling night and day
 And never made an idle stand

---

[1] KT1, pp.253–4; TP2, pp.424–5. *Tibble has the sub-title:* 'On being visited by Hannah, daughter of the poet Bloomfield'.

[2] [in the rain] *This and the next rejection have been emended in pencil in KT1.*

[3] [Plashed with the rain like droppled dew]. *Tibble reads thus except for* 'drippled'.

[4] 'fancys' *TP2, p.424.*

[5] *Bloomfield's daughter.*

[6] *R. Bloomfield, Rural Tales, 1802, p.109. Tibble omits inverted commas.*

The wild flower nodded on the brink
And made its wrinkles on[1] the stream
Where Bloomfield often lay to think
And listless spend[2] his summer dream

Autumn[3]

I love the fitfull gusts that shakes
        The casement all the day
And from the mossy[4] elm tree takes
        The faded leaf[5] away
Twirling it[6] by the window pane
With thousand others down the lane

I love to see the shaking twig
        Dance till the shut of eve
The sparrow on the cottage rig
        Whose chirp would make believe
That spring was just now flirting by
In summers lap with flowers to lie

I love to see the cottage smoke
        Curl upwards through the naked[7] trees
The pigeons nestled round the coat[8]
        On dull[9] november days like these
The cock upon the dunghill crowing
The mill sails on the heath agoing

The feather from the ravens breast
        Falls on the stubble lea
The acorns near the old crows nest
        Fall[10] pattering down the tree
The grunting pigs that wait for all
Scramble and hurry where they fall

---

[1] 'in' TP2, p.425.   [2] 'spent' TP2, p.425.
[3] KT1, p.259; CL, p.215; TP2, p.412.
[4] 'glossy' CL, p.215. Tibble follows Cherry except here where he reads 'mossy'.
[5] 'leaves' CL, p.215.   [6] 'them' CL, p.215.
[7] Cherry omits 'naked' CL, p.215.   [8] cote.   [9] Cherry omits 'dull' CL, p.215.
[10] 'drop' CL, p.215.

N

Boys and Spring[1]

To see the Arum early shoot
Its cone curled leaves of green
About the white green mossy root
Where violet buds are seen

The little round hole in the roots
Looks battered hard and round
The mice come out to chimble fruits
And take hips under ground

The husks of hips and awes lie round
All chimbled seed and skin
There noses now peep from the ground
And there the tails bob in

The nettles yellow roots are bare
Where sun shine looks about
Where thin and pricked the hedges are
The leaves are sprouting out

The violets blossoms where they dwell
The childrens fingers smart
They kiss the place to make it well
And all is joy of heart

There's something yet in childhoods ways
On which I love to dwell
And oft I hunt in springs first days
The painted pooty shell

Children e'er they go to school
Hunt hedges and thorn roots
They're badgers[2] by the sedgy pool
And by the [   ][3]

---

[1] *KT1, pp.288–9.*

[2] *Knight seems to have been confused by Clare's unusual vocabulary as well as by his bad handwriting. The word 'badgers' can be identified from 'Prose', p. 183, where it means a small mottled snail shell* 'found in low places by brook sides'. *We suggest the alternative reading:*

> For badgers by the sedgy pool
> And by the willow shoots

[3] *Hiatus in Knight.*

And then they crush them nib to nib
Agen the meadow brig
And dont their little tongues run glib
At running such a rig

They call them cocks and so they fight
A little 'cocking day'
The hardest breaks the whole outright
As heroe of the day

The Shepherd Boy[1]

The fly or beetle on their track
Are things that know no sin
And when they whemble on their back
What terror they seem in
The shepherd boy wi' bits o' bents
Will turn them up again
And start them where they nimbly went
Along the grassy plain
And such the shepherd boy is found
While lying on the sun crackt ground

The lady-bird that seldom stops
From climbing all the day
Climbs up the rushes tassle tops
Spreads wings and flies away
He sees them—lying on the grass
Musing the whole day long
And clears the way to let them pass
And sings a nameless song
He watches pismires on the hill
Always busy never still

He sees the traveller beetle run
Where thick the grass wood weaves
To hide the black-snail from the sun
He props up plantain leaves

[1] *KT1, pp.329–30.*

The lady-cows have got a house
Within the cowslip pip
The spider weaving for his spouse
On threads will often slip
So looks and lyes the shepherd boy
The summer long his whole employ

The Wind[1]

The frolicksome wind [through] the trees and the bushes
Keeps sueing and sobbing and waiving all day[2]
Frighting magpies from trees and from white thorns the thrushes
And waveing the river in wrinkles and spray
The unresting wind is a frolicksome thing
O'er hedges in floods and green fields of the spring

It plays in the smoke of the chimney at morn
Curling this way and that i' the morns dewy light
It curls from the twitch heap among the green corn
Like the smoke from the cannon i' th' midst of a fight
But report there is none to create any alarm
From the smoke an old ground full hiding meadow and farm

How sweet curls the smoke oer the green o' the field
How majestic it rolls o'er the face o' the grass
And from the low cottage the elm timbers shield
In the calm o' the evening how sweet the curls pass
I' the sunset how sweet to behold the cot smoke
From the low red brick chimney beneath the dark oak

How sweet the wind wispers o' midsummers eves
And fans the winged elder leaves o'er the old pales
While the cottage smoke o'er them a bright pillar leaves
Rising up and turns clouds by the strength of the gales
O' sweet is the cot neath its colums of smoke
While dewy eve brings home the labouring folk

---

[1] *KT1, pp.347–8.*   [2] *See p.17 above.*

Song[1]

I went my Sunday mornings rounds
  One pleasant summer day
And stood i' the green meadow grounds
  'Mong cocks and swaths o' hay
Up the green rush the Lady bird
  Clomb to its very tops
And there the crickets songs were heard
  Like organs without stops

The sun was climbing up the sky
  A looking glass of gold
It melts and quivers on the eye
  And blinds us to behold
Melting and shining to its height
  It shines from pole to pole
And sliddering down at dewy night
  Goes out a dying coal

I stood among the swarths and cocks
  How sweet the light did seem
When a sweet lass with inky locks
  Came tripping by the stream
Sweet one I said I do prefer
  To ask you why you walk
'Tis merely for my pleasure sir
  As you stand there to talk

The wind came from the southern sky
  And tokened flying showers
The busy bee and butterfly
  Her ribbons took for flowers
The wasp it buzzed about her mouth
  Her lips seemed cherries red
The wind shook from the balmy south
  The curls about her head

[1] *KT1, pp.358–9.*

Young man she said you'l marry me
And waited for reply
Why yes my dear but don't you see
Love is the stronger tie
And then I kissed her lips and cheeks
And made her merry hearted
I wed[1] the maid in just three weeks
From the first day we parted

Childhood[2]

O dear to us ever the scenes of our childhood
The green spots we played in the school where we met
The heavy old desk where we thought of the wild-wood
Where we pored o'er the sums which the master had set
I loved the old church-school, both inside and outside
I loved the dear Ash trees and sycamore too
The graves where the Buttercups burning gold outvied
And the spire where pelitory dangled and grew

The bees i' the wall that were flying about
The thistles the henbane and mallows all day
And crept in their holes[3] when the sun had gone out
And the butterfly ceased on the blossoms to play
O dear[4] is the round stone upon the green hill
The pinfold hoof printed with oxen—and bare[5]
The old princess[6]-feather tree growing there still
And the swallows and martins wheeling[7] round in the air

Where the chaff whipping outwards lodges round the barn door
And the dunghill cock struts with his hens in the rear
And sings 'Cockadoodle' full twenty times oer
And then claps his wings as he'd fly in the air
And there's the old cross with its round about steps
And the weathercock creaking quite round in the wind
And theres the old hedge with its glossy red heps[8]
Where the green-linnets nest I have hurried to find—

---

[1] *Knight reads 'met'.*   [2] *KT, pp.386–8; TP2, pp.478–80.*
[3] *'the hole' TP2, p.479.*   [4]*'dear' TP2, p.479.*
[5] *Tibble's punctuation here destroys the sense. TP2, p.479.*
[6] *'prince's' TP2, p.479.*   [7] *'whirling' TP2, p.479.*   [8] *'hips' TP2, p.479.*

—To be in time for the school or before the bell rung.
Here's the odd martin's nest o'er the shoemakers door
On the shoemakers chimney the old swallows sung
That had built and sung there in the seasons[1] before
Then we went to seek pooty's among the old furze
On the heaths, in the meadows beside the deep lake
And return'd with torn cloathes all covered wi' burrs
And oh what a row my fond mother would make

Then to play boiling kettles just by the yard door
Seeking out for short sticks and a bundle of straw
Bits of pots stand for teacups after sweeping the floor
And the children are placed under school-mistress's awe
There's one set for pussy another for doll
And for butter and bread they'll each nibble an awe[2]
And on a great stone as a table they loll
The finest small teaparty ever you saw

The stiles we rode upon 'all a cock-horse'
The mile a minute swee
On creaking gates—the stools o' moss
What happy seats had we
There's nought can compare to the days of our childhood
The mole-hills like sheep in a pen
Where the clodhopper sings like the bird in the wild wood
All forget us before we are men

Oct. 15th/48

No title[3]

O could I be as I have been
  And ne'er can be no more
A harmless thing in meadows green
  Or on the wild sea shore

O could I be what once I was
  In heaths and valleys green
A dweller in the summer grass
  Green fields and places green

---

[1] *'season'* TP2, p.479. [2] *'a haw'* TP2, p.479. [3] *KT1, pp.388-9.*

A tennant of the happy fields
By grounds of wheat and beans
By gipsey's camps and milking bield
Where lussious woodbine leans

To sit on the deserted plough
Left when the corn was sown
In corn and wild weeds buried now
In quiet peace unknown

The harrows resting by the hedge
The roll within the Dyke
Hid in the Ariff and the sedge
Are things I used to like

I used to tread through fallow lands
And wade through paths of grain
When wheat ears pattered on the hands
And head-aches left a stain

I wish I was what I have been
And what I was could be
As when I roved in shadows green
And loved my willow tree

To gaze upon the starry sky
And higher fancies build
And make in solitary joy
Loves temple in the field

Love[1]

Life without the fear of death
Or dread of Lightening from above
No graves or[2] any loss of breath
Is love

---

[1] *KT1, pp.304–5. This interesting poem was left unfinished either because the transcription was not completed or because the poem was considered too obscure to bother with.*
[2] *Knight reads 'on'.*

Truth without deception this
A joy ensured above
God is the author and the bliss
    True love

Twas matchless Eve in paradise
With beauty from above
That gave to Man without Earth's vice
    Her love

Adah and Zillah next in flower
About their Adam move
They slept beside him in the bower
    In love[1]

Rachael & Rebecca next
The Scripture came to prove
Love was their God the Bible text
    Their love

Ruth and Nahoma eked the race
Of Adams hopes above
The first man shared their childrens grace
    Their love

Kessia and Icmima too
Jobs comforts from above
Gives Adams heart like Hermons dew
    Their love[2]

The Bibles race is heavens own
Turks own their God above
And Woman round Mahomets throne
    Is love

All of mankind are heavens race
From Gods own power above
And woman with Eves mother face
    Mans love[3]

---

[1] *Genesis IV; the wives of Lamech.*
[2] *The names should be Kezia and Jemima; Job, XLII. See reference to* 'Hermon dew' *in MS. 110 above, p.144.*
[3] *There is no double line after this but a half-page is left blank.*

Song[1]

Where the ash tree weaves
Shadows over the river
And the willow's grey leaves
Shake and quiver—
Meet me and talk, love,
Down the grass-hoppers baulk, love,
And then love for ever.

There meet me, and talk, love,
Of love's inward feelings
Where the clouds look like chalk, love,
And the huts and the shielings
Lie like love o'er the river
Here talk of love's feelings
And love on for ever.

Where the bee hums his ballads
By the river so near it
Round docks and wild salads
While all love to hear it,
We'll meet by the river,
And by old willow pollards
Bid love live for ever.

Jan^{ry} 13th 1848

Song[2]

The girl I love is flesh and blood
With face and form of fairest clay
Straight as the firdale in the wood
And lovely as a first spring day

The girl I love's a lovely girl
Bonny and young in every feature
Richer than flowers and strings o' pearl
A handsome and delightful creature

---

[1] KT1, p.272; GP, p.156.   [2] KT2, p.4.

She's born to grace the realms above
    Where we shall both be seen together
And sweet and fair the maid I love
    As rose trees are in summer weather

O bonny straight and fair is she
    I wish we both lived close together
Like as the acorns on the tree
    Or foxglove bell in summer weather

Come to me love and let us dwell
    Where oak trees cluster all together
I'll gaze upon thy blossoms well
    And love yes love thee then forever

Her face is like another's face
    As white another's skin may prove
But no one else could fill her place
    If banished from the maid I love

The woodland stroll[1]

Among the green bushes where primroses bloom
I sing to myself and wander alone
And by mossy roots hear the wilding bees hum
Persueing the sunbeams with wearisome drone
Stealing kisses from primroses all in their bloom

I leave the rude noise of the wearisome world
And hide me in thickets of white and black thorn
Where primroses blossom all crispy and curled
And spangled wi' dew at the breath o' the morn
O' there's ne'er such a feeling of joy in the world

---

[1] *KT2, p.5.*

I wander alone i' th' green white thorn bushes
And mock the fond whistles of glad singing birds
Where the winds oer my head like loch river rushes
And the musical bleating of heath feeding herds
And see birds building nests in the early green bushes

Among the green bushes where primroses glisten
And violets purple the mossy oak roots
Where boys creep i' the thicket to gather and listen
And fill trousers pockets with beautiful toots
While the sun o'er the trees has just risen

Among the green bushes where primroses bloom
I sing to myself as I wander alone
And among the wood flowers hear the wilding bee's hum
Persueing its ramble with wearisome drone
Stealing kisses from primroses in their first bloom[1]

The Parting[2]

O the moment was sad when I went from my true love
With her red cheeks and bright eyes blue grey
I kissed her wet cheek and ne'er sighed for a new love
And the wind sighed by us that day
I saw her heart sob wi' my arm on her shoulder
More fast than a watch while I fond did enfold her
And all the soft thoughts o' my fond heart I told her
While my cheek on her bosom did lay.

Ere the breezes of eve put the green leaves i' motion
Wi' her red rose cheek and her eyes blue grey
I left my fond lover to cross the wide ocean
And the white thorn covered with may
Wi' my arm round her waist and my cheek on her breast
It beat like a watch and its sorrows confest
I kissed that fair cheek and lull'd her to rest
Then steered for the fleet in the bay

---

[1] *This appears to be a second draft of the first stanza. Note also four eight-line stanzas printed by J. L. Cherry under the title 'Among the Green Bushes'; CL, pp.244–5, reprinted in TP2, pp.486–7.*
[2] *KT2, p.16.*

Poor girl she stood there more fixed than a statue
And white as the marble even paler than snow
At the brig foot the bramble leaved thorny and matty
As the sun on its leaves glittered golden and low
Round my neck her white arms did most fondly enfold me
I kissed her fond lips Cupid smiled to behold me
And love the most fond in my abscence he told me
Ere from her I tore me to go

The Humble bee[1]

When lifes tempests blow high
In seclusion I tread
Where the primroses lie
And the green mosses spread
Where the bottle tit hangs
At the end of a twig
Where the humble bee bangs
That is almost as big

Where I feel my heart lonely
I am solitudes own
Talking to myself only
And walking woods lone
In the wood briars and brambles
Hazel stools and oak trees
I enjoy such wood rambles
And hear the wood bees

That sing their wood journey
And stop at wood blooms
Where the primroses burn ye
And the violet perfumes
There to myself talking
I rub through the bushes
And the boughs where I'm walking
Like a sudden wind rushes

---

[1] *KT2, pp.20–1.*

The wood gate keeps creaking
Opened ever so slow
And from boughs bent to breaking
Often starts the odd crow
Right down the green riding
Gladly winds the wild bee
Then through the woodsideing[1]
He sucks flowers in glee

He flies through the stovens
Brown hazel and grey
Through fern leaves like ovens
Still singing his way
He rests on a moss bed
And perks up his heels
And strokes o'er his small head
Then hies to the fields

I enjoy these wood rambles
And the juicey wheat fields
Where the woodrose and brambles
A showers covert yields
I love the wood journey
Where the violets melt blue
And primroses burn ye
With flames the day through

No Title[2]

In the season o' swallows that brings the bright sun
And never comes nigh 'till the lammies a' run
Ever skimming[3] and crossing the gravel paved brook
While the children bright daisies and buttercups look

I courted a maid without satin or silk
That went all the week night and morning to milk
And sat on the rest harrow by the mole hill
Where I first fell in love—and I see her sit still

---

[1] *Knight reads 'woodside in'.*   [2] *KT2, pp.24–6.*
[3] 'skimming' *is written above* 'skipping'.

The sun was a setting—the cowpasture pond
Curved i' wrinkles o' gold and o' silver beyond
The molehills where[1] covered in patches o' thyme
And the season for courting was just in its prime

Her face it was lovely and so was her clothes
A hue the same colour on the sweet briar grows
Her neck and her shoulders was whiter than milk
And her lips were so soft—yes much softer than silk

Her words fell like music from those pretty lips
And her eyes—as the fly in the water pond dips
Owned two sparks of light that made the sun dim
While the dragon-fly darted about the pond brim

On the pasture I courted her both even and morn
Till the rest harrow podded and ripe was the corn
Yes I've loved her there by the side of that hill
And they tell me she blooms and is lovelier still

Thou flower of summer[2]

When in summer thou walkest
In the meads by the river
And to thyself talkest
Dost thou think of one ever
A lost and a lorn one
That adores thee and loves thee
And when happy morn's[3] gone
And natures calm moves thee
Leaving thee to thy sleep like an angel at rest
Does the one who adores thee still live in thy breast

Does nature e'er give thee
Loves past happy vision
And wrap thee [and] leave thee
In fancies elesian[4]

---

[1] *were.*   [2] *KT2, pp.47–8; TP2, pp.504–5.*
[3] *'bright days's' TP2, p.505.*   [4] *elysian TP2, p.505.*

Thy beauty I clung to
As leaves to the tree
When thou fair and young too
Looked lightly on me
'Till love came upon thee like sun to the west
And shed its perfuming and bloom on my breast

Thou flower of summers bright beaming
Thou star of the even
Thy grey eyes are beaming
Like lights of the heaven
When shall I talk to thee
In eve's dusky glooming
When shall I walk with thee
Mid summer's flowers blooming
And love thee as much as I loved thee before
And be teazed with the sighs of loves absence no more[1]

Sweet Mary o' the plough[2]

The latter end of Autum
When the trees were turning yellow
When the garden flowers were dead and gone
And all the fruit were mellow
When ponds and rivers were cram'ful
Wi' sudden showers o' rain
I went to see my true love
O'er the dirty roads again
O'er moors and mosses slups and sloughs
I went to see her many miles
The hips were scarlet awes were red
And beautiful were Marys smiles
That lonely house beside the road
I can't imagine how
But I'm always sad when I pass bye
Sweet Mary o' the plough

---

[1] *Omitted by Tibble.*
[2] *KT2, p.55. 'Hellen of the Plough' is referred to by Clare MS. 110, p.7.*

In early youth when love was sweet
So sweet no words can tell
I went far off a courting
A maiden I loved well
The woods were faded every where
And leaves began to drop
The Squirrels sputtering up the tree
And acorns from the top
Fell pattering on the dirty ground
And bursted from their cups
For which the school Boy running bye
Full very often stoops
Love urged me on my journey
Beneath each fadeing bough
That Autumn morn I went to see
Sweet Mary of the Plough

The autumn it is pleasant
Though fadeing fast away
When the lover goes a courting
Upon an autumn day
The falling leaves they littered
Every bit o' greensward round
And fell about my footsteps
Wi' many a pleasing sound
The old crows quawked for men had cut
Among the oak wood trees
While many coloured sort o' leaves
Came wailing on the breeze
The wind blew up the clouds
And I felt[1] I knew not how
When I went to see my sweetheart
Sweet Mary of the Plough

---

[1] *Knight has 'fell'.*

o

Farewell[1]

Farewell to the bushy clump Closte[2] to the river
And the flags where the butter bump hides in for ever
Farewell to the weedy nook Hemmed in by waters
Farewell to the millers brook And his three bonny daughters
Farewell to them a[ll] While in prison I lye
In the prison o thrall Seeing[3] nought but the sky

Shut out are the green fields And birds i' the bushes
I' the prison yard nothing builds
Black birds or thrushes
Farewell to the old Mill and dash o the waters
To the Miller And dearer still
To his three bonny daughters

I' the neak[4] the large burdock grows near the green willow
I' the flood round the moorcock Dashes under the billow
To the old Mill farewell
To the lock pens and water
To the Miller himself[5]
And his three bonny daughters

I met a pleasant maiden[6]

On the seventeenth of April I' the good year forty one
I met a pleasant maiden and I wished the maid was mine
She'd cowslips in her basket She'd sweet briar in her hand
Her love I would have ask'd But she would not understand

I touched her gown in passing And she looked in strange surprise
The meadow pool spread glassing In the beautiful sunrise
Her shall[7] was of the flags so green Her gown was brown and red
Her stockings white as snow was seen And lightsome was her tread

[1] KT2, p.73; TP2, pp.518–19.   [2] close.
[3] Knight has 'Seems'; Tibble: 'In the prison a thrall sees' TP2, p.518.
[4] 'nook' TP2, p.519.   [5] 'himsel' TP2, p.519.
[6] KT2, p.76.   [7] shawl.

The linnet chirrupt in the thorn the lark sung in the sky
And bonny was the sunny morn And every road was dry
I took [her] by the waist so [small] All in a pleasant place
She no denial made at all But smiled upon my face

I cuddled her in the green grass And sat among the hay
Till sunshine o'er the hill did pass And daylight went away
I kissed [her] o'er her bonny face So tender and so true
And left my blessing on the place Among the foggy dew

No title[1]

Tis now the height o summer And where so e'er I turn my eyes
The woods do naught but murmer And the hedge rows swarm wi'
    fly's
On dry banks the whasps are busy Wi' yellow jackets and sharp stings
Summer's a secret dirty hussy[2] And nothing like primrosey spring

Then leaf strewn woods are greenest And full of wild primroses
The calm green air serenest On moss nests the Bird reposes
Then by the spinny rails The violet smells so sweet
Loading with perfumes all the gales And wild bees yellow feet

Hot summer is a dirty hussey[2] Swarming o'er wi wasps and flies
That by wood sides are ever[3] busy Wi' their burning melodies
Give me the spring wi' footpaths clean The finches nest and budding
    tree
The primrose in its leaves so green And 'neath white thorn I'll happy be

The gardeners bonny daughter[4]

The chaffinch in the hedgerow sings In the brown naked thorn
And by its tail the titmouse hings Searching the buds at morn
And I'll wish dirty roads away And meadows flooded water
And court before I end the day The gardeners bonny daughter

---

[1] KT2, p.78.　　　　[2] Knight's misreading for 'hissey'?
[3] Knight has 'wood side ares are ever'.　　　　[4] KT2, pp.79–80.

She's sweeter than the first o' spring More fair than Christmas roses
When robins by the hovel sing Sweet smiles the maid discloses
Her hair so brown her eye so bright As clear as the spring water
I'll go and have a word tonight With the gardeners bonny daughter

Her cheeks are like the coloured rose A kiss would surely burn ye
Her lips are gems more red than those for love I'll go the journey
And when the white thorn comes in leaf And the chaffinch lays her
    lauter
I walk where singing birds are brief Wi' the gardeners bonny daughter

I passed the gardeners house one night My heart burnt to a cynder
When I saw her face and eyes so bright A looking through the window[1]
And when I'd passed the house agen I'd been pounded in a mortar
But she looked and smiled upon me then So I love the gardeners bonny
    daughter

Will you ever love me dearest?[2]

And will you ever love me dearest Yes by the heavens above thee
By soul breathed sighs and love sincerest I will for ever love thee
Love words will burn before they're spoken Heart thoughts no tongue
    can tell
The heart will bleed before its broken And I love Hellen well

As o'er the pebbles flows the water Gilt by the glittering beam
I love thee as earths fairest daughter In many a happy dream
I saw thee in each rushy hollow When rushes arched in dew
And then pursued thee like a swallow Far under heavens blue

And I will ever love thee dearest Now and for ever love thee
The brook below thy feet runs clearest The sun shines bright above
    thee
I'll kiss thee on thy lips one kiss That never could reprove me
And vow before I give thee this I will for ever love thee

---

[1] *Has Knight's corrected spelling destroyed the rhyme here?*
[2] *KT2, p.80.*

A fragment: no title[1]

The winter winnowed chill And fast came down the snow
T'was white on every hill In rucks the drift did blow
When a bonny Irish maiden
Came barefoot throughthe[2] snow

The evening is for love[3]

The evening is for love As the morning is for toil
Though the fire is from above The pot is got to boil
A hard days work is mine And I'll live wi' care no more
So I'll see dew come to the woodbine At Isabella's door[4]

Wi' hairy leaves and droping flowers The canterberry bell
Grows underneath [the] hazle bower By most folks favoured well
Up the bean stalks creeps the snail The moth sleeps down below
The grey mist creep along And I'll a courting go

I'll gang and Isabella see Nor more i'[5] love repine
By her yard gates the elder tree By her door the streaked woodbine
And red pink bunches on the bed And pansies blue and yellow
The west is glowering gold and red And I'll gang to Isabella

I'll court her a' the lee lang night And tomorrow being Sunday
I'll rap[6] her in my hearts delight And uggle her till Monday
Her bosom is so fair and white she never had a fellow
I'll gang and stay till broad daylight Wi' my handsome Isabella

Her love is all to me[7]

O' cold is the winter day And iron is the ground
And winters snow has found his way For fifty miles around
I turn a look to every way And nothing to be seen
The frozen clouds shuts out the day And snow hide[s] all the green

---

[1] KT2, p.83.   [2] through the.   [3] KT2, p.82.
[4] Is this the Isabella referred to on p.253?   [5] Knight reads 'I'.
[6] wrap.   [7] KT2, p.84.

The hedges all of leaves are bare my heart beats cold and chill[1]
O' once I loved a pretty girl and love her dearly still
Though love is but a frozen pearl as you may plainly see[2]
My lovely girl is handsome as any maid can be

Freeze on the bitter biteing sky Snows shade the naked tree
All desolate alone am I Yet I'll love none but thee
No tears I shed my love to show To freeze before they fall
No sighs I send along the snow But she's my all in all

The footpath leaves the ruts and carts O'er furrow and o'er rig
And my love lives at the 'White hart' a stone throw from the brig[3]
She's like a ballad sung in tune And deep in love to be
Her face is like the rose in June And her love is all to me

My bonny Jane[4]

The cows are from the pasture gone The sheep are bleating in the pen
The path they travelled one by one Is o'er the fallows beat agen
The sparrow chelps along the eaves The whasp hums in the window
pane
And I'll of labour take my leave And gang and court young bonny
Jane

The plums are misted o'er wi' dew And rosey streaks the apples wear
But Jinney's cheeks a sweeter hue Than either apple plumb or pear
The sun sinks o'er the willows grey And clammy got the fields o' grain
And at her own home ends that day I kissed the lips o bonny Jane

---

[1] *a* As any maid could be. *b* as you may plainly see.

[2] *The second half line has been erased in Clare's corrections but should remain. There follows the erased half line;* 'And my heart beats cold and chill'.

[3] *This line identifies the girl as the Mary Ludgate of the Asylum letters. Her address was* 'The White Hart Inn over Brig Northampton'. *The Northampton Directory and Almanack (1845) gives among a list of innkeepers* 'Ludgate, White Hart, Cotton End', *which is in fact a continuation of Bridge Street. See E. Robinson and G. Summerfield* 'John Clare: An Interpretation of Certain Asylum Letters', 'Review of English Studies', *N. S., XII, 50, May 1962.*

[4] *KT2, pp.84-5. Possibly Jane Wilson, MS. 10, p.78.*

Her dark [hair] hangs in parted curl Aside her forehead white as snow
She seemed a maid [of] other worlds Too fair for anything below
We stood beside the turnpike way Such meetings seldom come again
That piece of animated clay I clasped and kissed young bonny Jane

The mallow looked like satin flowers Cut by some fond and fairy
    queen
The nettle fit for garden bowers Did no where look so richly green
They cant be common nettles sure I said and stooped to look again
But love stood there blind eyes to cure My ain sweet fairy bonny Jane

The bee resumed its honey tone around And searched the alloes bloom
The windows too were open thrown For buzing whasps to leave the
    room
Her hair was lappit in a comb Then twisted glossy round again
That sweet white bosom was loves home O my ain dear bonny Jane

The hens had clockit[1] up to bed The chicks were[2] yet within the pen
The sparrows from the wheatfields sped To Jinney's mossy eaves agen
O' Jinney is the bonny flower The severest parting pain
Wi' many a vow and promise fair I kissed and left my bonny Jane

The sun set red the weary crow Flew homeward to the woods agen
The willows grey waved too and fro And dews fell like a misty rain
She threw her kerchief o'er her hair Her fond kiss cured the parting
    pain
Wi' many a vow and promise fair I kissed and left my bonny Jane

Oh! bonny is the country[3]

Tis autumn wild the swiming clouds Pass low and lowery o'er the
    green
The swopping kite peelews aloud And sparrows in the stubbs are seen
Mid hawkweed flowers on sunday's hours I lye by Besseys side
Her arm sae white her eyes sae bright Brought every joy beside

---

[1] *Knight reads 'clock it'.*
[2] *Knight reads 'where'.*   [3] *KT2, pp.99–100.*

The awe tree berries clustered brown The wilding apples green and
    sour
Her well shaped fingers pulled them down While courting in that
    autumn hour
Sparrows a crowd i' Stubbs chirped loud The partridge covey flew
O'er her bonnet crown where we sat down On the grass yet moist wi
    dew

O' bonny was the country girl While the brooklet at her feet
Curled up the pebbles white as pearl And hawthorns looked so sweet
Hung o'er its way and willows grey Swayed gently by the wind
The fetches blue and bell bind too Did in the white thorn bind

The sun it gleamed both bright and warm And sparkled in wild flowers
The gnats were dancing in a swarm And gleamy grew the hours
The butterfly and bee whissed by Loud sung the grasshopper
Save larks i' th' cloud all sang so loud As each one sung to her

I pilled the straws for want o' words And plucked up bents to plait
And thought while there the loving birds Had ne'er so sweet a mate
Her white straw hat o' smallest plait And green striped cotton gown
Her lilies bright[1] her stockings white She on the grass sat down

O' bonny Bessey wi' dark hair And face as round's a apple
Wi' lilly bosom half way bare Which blue veins richly dapple
Thy pouting[2] lips like mellow hips Thy neck hair short and curled
I clasped the[e] there so sweet and fair The angel o the world

A health to all pretty girls[3]

Here's a health to all the pretty girls that dwell about Dundee
And luck to all the spicey pearls Boys loving drops like me[4]
For priestcraft I the halter hing For freedom mints o gold
For honest men 'God save the King' May warm hearts ne'er grow cold

---

[1] *Knight has 'Her hilees white bright'. He has been unable to recognize Clare's euphemism for breasts and has not clearly indicated that Clare has preferred 'bright' to 'white' because he needs 'white' to describe the stockings later in the line.*

[2] *Knight has 'pointing'.*   [3] *KT2, pp.100–1.*

[4] *This very clumsy line seems to mean: And luck to all the spicey pearls [that is] Boys [who love] drops [of drink] like me.*

Heres a[1] the honest lasses too That round [the] wrekin be
May love be a' their lives pursue[2] There[3] persons fond and free
No matter in what Town I dwell Or what the hour I dine
I drink the 'ealth[4] to please my sell And that's to forty nine

To forty nine young happy girls I drink love peace and joy
With eyes o light and teeth o pearls May none their blooms destroy
I' rum and whiskey vats[5] o wine I' cider mead or beer
I drink to these as only mine And woman every where

Summers in its glory now[6]

Summer's in its glory now Sweet the flower and green the bough
Dry is every swamp and slough My own kind deary
Could I press thy bonny bosom Swelling like a bursting blossom
Sweetly ripe as I suppose 'em Then heaven would be near thee
Fair and buxsome bonny Lassie Let us seek for places grassy
Where the brook it dimples glassy There I'll love thee deary

On thy lilly bosom leaning View thy eyes to guess their meaning
Kiss where not a look has been in Thy lilly bosom deary
Clasp thee round thy gimpsy middle Playing loves tunes without the
    fiddle
And loves secret joys unriddle To kiss and cheer me
To throw my arms about thy shoulders And in the land o' love enfold
    us
I' these green shades where none behold us Where heaven would be
    near thee

Come my blyth and bonny deary Let me clasp thee and lie near thee
And I of love shall ne'er be weary To clasp my bonny deary
To kiss thy cheeks o' new blown roses Thy breasts where hills o' alpine
    snows is
As sweet as ever love supposes To glad and cheer me
About thy bonny arms I'll clasp thee And i' the vice o' fondness grasp
    thee
Till matrimony's charms shall hasp thee And bind thee aye my deary[7]

---

[1] *all.* [2] *pursuit.* [3] *Their.* [4] *Knight has 'thealth'.*
[5] *Knight has 'swats'.* [6] *KT2, pp.102–3.*
[7] *Followed by a letter to Patty (Letters, p.299).*

I loved the lasses dearly[1]

I loved the lasses dearly when I wadn't but a boy
They seemed angels all or nearly And everlasting joy
When I sat among the rushes By the path where maidens came
Their gowns brushed by the white thorn bushes And set my heart on flame

Their eyes looked bright and warm When warmly gleamed the weather
And each one left me such a charm I'd kissed them altogether
I sat me down where green the grass is In sunshine and the blast
And there I dearly loved the lasses Aye every one that past[2]

And when I saw the valley flower Shook by bees flying near 'em
She left her eye in that sweet hour But loves voice woudn't hear him
And when she stooped down further on for flowers love burnt to give her
I loved where the rose was gone her face was fair for ever

I dream't of Robin[3]

I opened the casement this morn at starlight And the moment I got out o' bed
The daisies were quakeing about in their white And the cowslip was nodding its head
The grass was all shivers the stars were all bright And Robin that should cam[4] at e'en
I thought that I saw him a gaist[5] by moon light Like a stalking horse stands[6] on the green

I went bed agen and did nothing but dream Of Robin and moonlight and flowers
He stood like a shawdow[7] transfixed by a Stream And I couldn't forget him for hours
I'd just dropt asleep when I dreamed Robin spoke And the casement it gave such a shake
As if every pane i' the window was broke Such a patter the gravel did make

---

[1] *KT2, p.107.*   [2] *passed.*   [3] *KT2, p.110; TP2, pp.457-8.*
[4] *come; Tibble reads 'come' TP2, p.457.*
[5] *ghost; Tibble reads 'ghost' TP2, p.457.*
[6] *'stand' TP2, p.457.*   [7] *Clare's spelling preserved.*

So I up i' the morning before the cock crew And to strike a light I
sat down
I saw from the door all his track i' the dew And I guess[1] called 'come
in and sit down'
And sure enough tramples up to the door And who but young Robin
is sen[2]
And ere the old folks were half willing to stir We met kissed and
parted agen

The daisy button tipp'd wi' dew[3]

The daisy button tipped wi' dew Green like the grass was sleeping
On every thing 'neath heaven blue In moonlight dew was weeping
In dark wood sung the Nightingale The moon shone round above me
My arms were clasped round Mary Gale[4] My dearest do you love me

Her head a woodbine wet wi' dew Held in the moonlight sleeping
And two in one together grew Wi' daisy buds a weeping
O' Mary Gale sweet Mary Gale How round and bright above thee
The moon looks down on grassy vale My dearest can you love me

How sweet the moonlight sleeps and still Firdale and hedge row brere
The mole wharps mound and distant hill Is moonlight everywhere
The totter grasses pendalums Are still as night above me
The bees are gone and nothing hums My dearest do you love me

The moonlight sleeps o'er wood and wall Sweet Mary while you'r[e]
nigh me
Can any charm o' courtship fail And any joy pass by me
The gossamer all wet wi' dew Hung on the brere above me
She leaned her cheek and said 'I do' And ever mean to love thee

---

[1] Presumably a phonetic attempt at the dialect form of 'just'.
[2] 'his sen', i.e. his self.
[3] KT2, p.111.
[4] Perhaps the sister of Susan Gale, MS. 10, p.108.

The days of April[1]

On the return of April some few days
Before it comes when everything looks new
And woods where primroses burn in a blaze
Of fire and sallows in the woods made new[2]
Seen blazeing out in blossoms not a few
But bushes smothered over what a change
Is turned upon their brightness passing by
The very birds the pies and crows and Jays
Look downward on their bloom from dark trees high
And wood larks dropping from the rich blue sky
Winner[3] and whistle to their very roots
Sitting beneath a canophy of gold
And wood anemonies the sharp air suits
Their sheltered blooms with beauties manifold

Daisies burn April grass with silver flies[4]
And pilewort in the green lane blazes out
Enough to burn the fingers neath the briars
Where village Boys will scrat dead leaves about
To look for pootys—every eye admires
The lovely pictures[5] that the spring brings out
Meadows of bowing[6] cowslips what mind tires
To see them dancing in the emerald grass
And trawling chrystal brook as clear as glass
Laughing groaning uggling[7] on for miles
That waves the silver blades of swimming grass
Upon the surface while the glad sun smiles
Such are the sights the showers and sunshine brings
To three or four bright days in[8] the first of spring

The sun shines in days heaven a bright light[9]
All gold and glorious beautiful and fair
Spanning all ether in or day all bright
With beams as glowing as an angels hair

---

[1] KT2, pp.120–1; TP2, pp.405–6.   [2] 'strange' TP2, p.405.
[3] [Warble] TP2, p.406.   [4] 'fires' TP2, p.406.   [5] 'picture' TP2, p.406.
[6] 'burning' TP2, p.406.   [7] 'guggling' TP2, p.406.
[8] Tibble omits 'in', TP2, p.406.   [9] Tibble omits this stanza.

While clouds blue ether beautiful ye are
Light spans ye like a dome without a [   ]¹
Earth ocean and the infinite blue air
Which the Almighty's presence cir[c]les round
With might immensity that knows no bound

The return of Spring²

What was expected is expected more
As the days lengthen and the sun gets warm
Wild flowers will gather to the cottage door
Daisey and pilewort—and about the farm
The young lambs skip and dance on the green floor
And pewits scream upon the neighbouring moor
Cowslips in crowds that never yet was seen
The meadows and green close is smothered o'er
And every place where winters blight hath been
Is all repaired by spring in gold and green
How lovely green and level meadows lye
Filling with flowers of spring day following day
How bright the lakes how beautifull the sky
With Harry Phillips red and fled to play
On the clear streams in the green month of May
How beautiful green golden days go by
Fish can't refuse the bait in such warm days
Such flowery meadows and so sweet a sky
And then a shower dimpling the stream melts by

The corn craiks rispy song³

The corncraik rispt her summer call Just as the sun went down
Copper red a burning ball In woods behind the town
I wandered forth a maid to meet So bonny and so fair
No other flower was half so sweet And cole black was her hair

---

¹ *Hiatus in Knight.*   ² *KT2, pp.121–2.*
³ *KT2, pp.124–5; GP, pp.183–4.*

Upon the grasses stood the dew Bead drop o' clearest pearl
Her hair was black her eyes were blue O what a lovely girl
Her neck was like the lilly white Her breast was like the swan
She was in heart and loves delight A worship for a man

The corncraiks rispy song was oer The sun had left the light [alone][1]
I love dusk kisses on the moor To lewder life unknown
Hid in the bosom of a flower Its lifetime there to dwell
Eternity would seem an hour And I'd be resting well

The wind that shakes the rushes[2]

The wind that shakes the rushes Upon the thistley crowded green
The wind that stirs the bushes Where the thrushes nest has been
That curdles o'er the water On the stone pits down the lane
There live the 'ale' wifes daughter The bonny buxsome Jane[3]

She's sweeter than the wild rose On the white thorn fence in June
Her voice more sweet and mild flows Then ballads sung in tune
The bees upon the hive stones Sing by the window pane
And sable bees the wild ones Sing pleasant songs to Jane

The skylark nauntles through the grass And startles in the air
And sings above the bonny lass His ballads sweet and fair
The sooty blackbird sings so loud Till echo sings again
And robin in the hovel proud Will sing to bonny Jane

Her wind waved gown was bonny brown Wi' wheat blade strips o
    green
A sweeter girl i' all the town Than she was never seen
The village bells o' sabbath days Sound sweetly down the lane
They seem to sing in various ways go in and marry Jane

---

[1] *Rhyme word missing in Knight, but 'alone' would make good sense.*
[2] *KT2, p.125.*
[3] *This suggests an actual person.*

Oh Sweet is the Sound[1]

O sweet is the sound o the doves clapping wings
And the sound o' the wood gate thrown open that clasps
O sweet is [the] song of the thrush where it sings
And sweet the old oak where the woodpecker taps
Where primrose and blue bell bloom littered around[2]
And the ever green Ivy feathered round the green tree
Here spoke my sweet Susan[3] there was love i' the sound
O' her voice as she stood calmly talking to me

Her hand held fine bluebells and primroses too
Ribbed leaves of the hazels were beautifully green
Anemonies too that were weeping in dew
In the white hand o' Susan that morning were seen
How sweet was her inky hair sweetened wi' dew
How sweet was her bosom more white than the snow
Her gown it was green speckled over wi blue
O' her hair was jet black like the back of a crow

Sweet looked the grey lichen upon the green oak
The violets looked rich by each root mossy green
And the raven croaked loud as a rustic had spoke
Here Susan all day wi' her lover would lean
Agen the white bark o' the oak to admire
Green mosses and wild flowers spread round at her feet
Her eyes were as bright as the suns liquid fire
And the greenwoodlands still in her absence seems sweet

Wedded Jane[4]

Is loves gold ring been broken
The twin hearts golden token
Dearest Jane,
'Truth told beside the alter
Was that e'er known to falter
Come again'

---

[1] *KT2, p.126.* [2] *Knight has 'lettered'.*
[3] *Possibly Susan Gale, MS. 10, p.108.* [4] *KT2, pp.129–30.*

I wooed thee and we wed
Bride from the alter led
The Bells rung when abed
    Wedded Jane

In summer both united
In flowers and green fields plighted
    Dearest Jane
Birds sung the truth o' nature
And thou man's sweetest creature
    Come again
The cowslips gild the morn
The chaffinch on the thorn
Sings just as when at dawn
    I courted Jane

But twenty years have braided
Loves wreaths that bloomed and faded
    Absent Jane
The chaffinch sings to morrow
None heeds if joy or sorrow
    Dearest Jane
Flowers came and none to heed
I' hedge rows and the mead
E'en the meanest weed
    Wanted Jane

Cowslips have come again
And daisy's sheet the plain
    Come again
Loves golden ties near[1] parted
Though true love has been thwarted
    Dearest Jane
I wooed thee and I wed[2] thee
And to the alter led thee
Came to love where thy head lay
    Beautiful Jane

---

[1] *ne'er.*　　　[2] *Pencil emendation to 'lov'd'.*

Come here to my heart love
And we'll never more part love
My beautiful Jane
The cowslips are growing
The broad waters are flowing
Pay debts to love owing
My beautiful Jane
'And then we'll have ease love'
'And live as we please love'
'In wedlock all freed' [love]
[My beautiful Jane]

When I was young[1]

When I was young I fell in love and got but little good on't
When she passed I turned away
At first she would then woudn't
I wished to speak and then the sigh
Came first and always stopt it
Come silence tell my wishes then
I thought so and then dropt it
And never tried to speak agen

The path that o'er the cornfield lay
I met her one day early
She turned her face another way
And I walked in the barley
A lark that moment sought the sky
Close to her gown or nearly
Her bright eye looked to see him fly
And then I loved her dearly

And turns the rosey cheek to clay
Tis beauty's face in woman's form
That steals the senses all away
That rends the bosom like a storm
Though mild as evenings sober ray
The winds they sigh the dews they weep
And on the violets bosom fall
First love and truth unriddles all

[1] *KT2, pp.133–4.*

P

Where love are you?[1]

How sweet does the hour seem When the sun's gone bed
And gay clouds soft as dreams O'er the south west spread
When the bee sleeps till morn Where thistles adorn
The lane banks by the hedges All summered wi dew
    Dragon flies on the sedges
    But where love are you

Our choice hour of meeting Youve let it go by
Me the woodbine is greeting But lonely am I
The bees on the thistle Where grass crickets whistle
And ladybirds creeping Regardless o' dew
    With nature they're keeping
    But where love are you

You promised by sunshine Where the woodbine blooms sweetly
You would come here and be mine
When the dews on the flower In this lane you would love me
Tis a beautiful hour And the moonshines above me
    You spoke not intending
    But where love are you

The dark days of Autumn[2]

The dark days of Autumn grows cloudy and rainy
The sun pales like sulphur the shadows grow long
To me the dull season the sweetest of any
I love to see yellow leaves fall in my song
The rush covered green and thistle capped mountain
The dead leaves a falling and winds singing round
The willow and ash leaves they choak up the fountain
There's health i' the strife o't and joy i' the sound

I love there to loiter wi winds blowing round me
Till the strong eddies past and the rain gust is over
Wild pigeons fly over the instance[3] looks downy
With [stunt][4] willow rows [and] pieces of clover
Brown pieces o' stubbles ground o' turnips bright green
The crows flying over the lakes silver light
Scarce a wild blossom left to enliven the scene
Rank and mist are for ever in sight

---

[1] *KT2, p.139.*   [2] *KT2, pp.146–7.*   [3] *distance?*   [4] *Hiatus in Knight.*

Winter[1]

How blasted nature is, the scene is winter
The Autumn withered every branch
Leaves drop, and turn to colourless soil
Ice shoots i' splinters at the river Bridge
And by and bye all stop—
White shines the snow upon the far hill top
Nature's all withered to the root, her printer
To decay that neer comes back
Winds burst, then drop
Flowers, leaves and colours, nothing's left to hint her
Spring, Summer, Autumn's, withered into winter

I love the blue Violet[2]

I love the blue violet that creeps on the mossy bank
And wood bell so purple wi green leaves so glossy rank
Where wild rabbits caper wi' many a tossy frank[3]
And show their white shirts to the light
I love the mossy bank by the green hazle bush
I love the early song o' the brown missle thrush
And daisy decked mole hill i' beds o the tassle rush
I' the middle o' summers delight

But better than mossy banks twenty times over
Or wind waving rush beds the form of my lover
Sweet Susan[4] as fair as the clumps o' white clover
Ever feeding the songs o' the bee
O harmless as white legged lambs round the mole hills
Wi' her beauty and truth to o'er flowing the soul fills
On Susans white bosom a beauty spot mole kills[5]
And makes her more dear to me

---

[1] *KT2, p.148.*
[2] *KT2, p.150; GP, p.187.*
[3] *'prank' GP, p.187.*
[4] *Possibly Susan Gale, MS. 10, p.108.*   [5] *hills?*

Her hair is as dark as the cloud i' the bright morn
Her bosom's as white as the flower o the white thorn
Her lips are as red as the rose bud i' light born
And dear is young Susan to me
I wooed her and won her and doatingly love her
And think her the lovliest all the world over
And sweeter than rose buds than red or white clover
Is bonny young Susan to me

The night is still[1]

The night is still dead Oak leaves strew
Dyke bottoms and the green grass too
When I came here the golden west
Wore all the daylights golden crown
The sun lay on its mottled breast
Within an hours going down
When Mary at my elbow stood
Beside the green entangled wood

I loved her there among green hues
The green white thorn i' evening dews
And loud the snort o' feeding horse
Grazeing beside that woody lane
Green bushes where we stood beneath
On green grass and beds o moss
While sweet came evenings dewey breath
Where I and Mary again met

We meet and love firm as a rock
The birds our voices seem to mock
Hedge sparrows with their eggs o blue
Sat on their green moss nest
Where Mary's smiles looked more than true
And calm her snowy breast
As by the Ivied Oak tree wood
Mary and I one evening stood

[1] *KT2, p.152.*

The Peartree Lane[1]

There's places in our village streets
Where I dearly loved to be
The round cross full o' stoney seats
At the stable end the tree
The brown bleached oaks they sit upon
Where the old roll[2] still remain
And still I love to walk alone
Down the Peartree Lane

The Elm trees o'er[3] our Garden wall
How beautiful they grew
Where ring Doves from their nest would call
And the vein leaved Ivy grew
At the old house end while one hugh Elm
That turned a whole days rain
Storms[4] roared as 'twould the town o'erwhelm
Twas shelter down the lane

The blacksmiths shed the Coblers shop
Chock holes and marble rings
By the cross steps the spinning top
Are memorable things
The schoolboys love at morn and eve'
When spring comes in again
But nought can beat the primrose leaves
Down Peartrees dirty lane

There the Bumbarrel build[5] her nest
On early green white thorn
The Chaffinch shews her ruddy breast
O'er her[6] Lichen nest at morn
The Mavis there at Christmas time
Begins his early strain
And dead Oakleaves though glazed i' rime
Look clear[7] in Peartree Lane

---

[1] *KT2, pp.155–7; TP2, pp.477–8.*   [2] *'rolls' TP2, p.477.*
[3] *'in' TP2, p.477.*   [4] *'Storm' TP2, p.477.*
[5] *'builds' TP2, p.478.*   [6] *'the' TP2, p.478.*   [7] *'dear' TP2, p.478.*

The woodland stile the broken gap
And daylights peeping moon
Where red cloaked goody fills her lap
To boil the kettle soon
Anemonies peep through the hedge
Hedgesparrows find a strain
There's nothing i' the world I pledge
Like dear old Peartree Lane

The Sweetest woman there[1]

From bank to bank the water roars Like thunder in a storm
A Sea in sight of both the shores Creating no alarm
The water birds above the flood fly o'er the foam and spray
And nature wears a gloomy hood on this October day

And there I saw a bonny maid That proved my hearts delight
All day she was a Goddess made An angel fair at night
We loved and in each others power Felt nothing to condemn
I was the leaf and she the flower And both grew on one stem

I loved her lip her cheek her eye She cheered my midnight gloom
A bonny rose neath Gods own sky in one perrenial bloom
She lives mid pastures evergreen And meadows ever fair
Each winter spring and summer scene The sweetest woman there

She lives among the meadow floods That foams and roars away
While fading hedgerows distant woods Fade off to naked spray
She lives to cherish and delight All nature with her face
She brought me joy morn noon and night In that low[2] lonely place

The evening was lovely[3]

The evening was lovely and littered wi dew
The points o' the thistle was knibbed wi a pearl
When I went i' the gloaming where bindweed bells grew
And talked to young Dinah a beautiful girl
O' bright were the ringlets adown her cheek glowing
And bright were her eyes as the dibbles o dew
That knobs all the spears o' the thistle flowers blowing
While hesperus shone like a lamp i' the blue

---

[1] KT2, p.157; GP, pp.187–8.   [2] 'too' GP, p.188.   [3] KT2, pp.162–3.

O' down i' the e'ening O' moon lighted gloaming
Among the big thistles so blooming and sweet
I' the wild flowers and rush beds were both o' us roaming
While the stars shone above us like the Lamps i' the street
I' the hollow old Ash tree the Owl hooted loud
And whewed down the hedge like a spirit i' white
The Moon for a moment popt under a cloud
And I kissed her soft cheek like a joy out o' sight

The rest-harrow trailed like small flowers o' the pea
And the dandy brow daisy-like buttoned to green
On the thistle flower stone dead asleep was the bee
That cocked up his legs when our finger was near
The moon lay like candle light on the thorn leaves
The dew glittered pearls on the bent where they hung
And O her white bosom delightfully heaves
While i the woodriding the Night[in]gale sung[1]

The crow sat on the willow[2]

The Crow sat on the willow tree
A lifting up his wings
And glossy was his coat to see
And loud the ploughman sings
I love my love because I know
The milkmaid she loves me
And hoarsely croaked the glossy crow
Upon the willow tree
I love my love the ploughman sung
And all the field wi' music rung

I love my love a bonny lass
She keeps her pails so bright
And blythe she t[r]ips the dewy grass
At morning and at night

---

[1] *Knight has 'sings', amended to 'sung'.*
[2] *KT2, pp.172–3; TP2, pp.452–3.*

A cotton drab[1] her morning gown
Her face was rosey health
She traced the pastures up and down
And nature was her wealth
He sung and turned each furrow down
His sweethearts love in cotton gown

My love is young and handsome
As any in the Town
She's worth a Ploughman's ransom
In the drab cotton gown
He sung and turned his furrows[2] o'er
And urged his Team along
While on the willow as before
The old crow croaked his song
The ploughman sung his rustic Lay
And sung of Phebe all the day

The crow was[3] in love no doubt
And wi a many things[4]
The ploughman finished many a bout
And lustily he sings
My love she is a milking maid
Wi red and rosey cheek
O' cotton drab her gown was made
I loved her many a week
His milking maid the ploughman sung
Till all the fields around him rung

In the field———[5]

In the field where the Nettle burdock and Sowthistles
Ramp up by the hovel where builds the small wren
When summer winds rustle and winter storms whistle
I gang over[6] a week to meet Katey agen

---

[1] 'dress' TP2, p.452.   [2] 'furrow' TP2, p.453.
[3] 'he was' TP2, p.453.   [4] 'And [so were] many things' TP2, p.453.
[5] KT2, pp.174–5.   [6] once?

I'm all over eager on fine Sunday mornings
To seek the old shed on the path beaten track
And I lose both my shoestrings the weeds and the corn in
Every day seems a twelvemonth e'er Sunday comes back

I love at my labour each bunch o' keen nettles
That grow where I work as the finest o' flowers
I love Kate begrimed with her black pots and kettles
And kiss her sweet face i' the shed at all hours
The milky sowthistles their pale tops I kiss
The burdocks broad leaves are my summers delight
For the good natured prickle burs Katey cant miss
They stick to her stockings both morning and night

Before me she takes up her gown in my sight
To pull the inquisitive creepers away
Her calf is so large and her stockings so white
I do nought but worship the rest o the day
O' sweet bonny Katey what maiden's so fair
The sun stops to westward the clouds come wi' night
These wind shaken cowslips I'll leave and repair
To the shed and court Katey my joy and delight

Oh come to my arms[1]

O' come to my arms i' the cool o' the day
When the veil o' the evening falls dewy and grey
O' come to me under the awthorn green
When eventide falls i' the bushes serene

O come to me under the awthorn tree
When the lark's on his nest and gone bed is the bee
When the veil of the evening falls dark on the scene
And we'll kiss love and court i' the bushes so green

O come to me dear wi' thy own maiden head
Where the wild flowers and rushes shall make thee a bed
We will lie down together in each others arms
Where the white moth flirts by and gives us alarms

---

[1] *KT2, pp.175–6.*

Where the rush bushes bend and are silvered wi' dew
Ere the sunbeam the red cloud O' morning breaks through
Thy face is so sweet and thy neck is so fair
O' come at eve dearest and live with me there

In green grassy places[1]

In the white thorn hedges the blackbird sings
Where the hedgesparrow flutters his dirty brown wings
And the skylark he trembles above the green wheat
While the thrush in the spinny is singing so sweet
So come lovely Susan we'll walk i' the fields
And meet all the pleasures the lovely spring yields
For of all they gay lasses sweet Susan I see
There's none that I fancy my sweetheart but thee

So come my dear Susan and where the thrush sings
The primrose and violets the earliest springs
The Chaffinch is building his nest on the brere
And the bottle tit hangs up his pudding bag near
I' the ribs o the hedge the hedgesparrow builds
And the brown o' his feathers the morning sun gilds
I long my dear Susan to walk out wi thee
In green grassy places thy sweetheart to be

We'll walk where the barley is hiding the clod
We'll walk where the daisy blooms stars on the sod
Where the Herrinshaw builds in the flags by the streams
There Susan we'll loiter in green summer dreams
By the side o' the river running like glass
We'll seek early cowslips that quake i' the grass
And there bonny Susan I'll love you so true
And kiss you and court you and ne'er bid adieu

---

[1] *KT2, pp.176–7.*

The Peasant Poet[1]

He loved the brook's soft sound
The swallow swimming by
He loved the daisy covered ground
The cloud bedappled sky
To him the dismal storm appeared
The very voice of God
And where[2] the Evening rock was reared
Stood Moses with his rod
And every thing his eyes surveyed
The insects i' the brake
Where[3] Creatures God almighty made
He loved them for his sake
A silent man in lifes affairs
A thinker from a Boy
A Peasant in his daily cares—
The Poet in his joy

No title[4]

And must we part that once so close
And fond where[5] knit together
Loves buds betorn by wonton force
The flowers for summer weather
And must my happy thoughts decay
And summer blossoms wither
The hope that cheered me many a day
Must now belong to neither

Yet still the Cottage chimney smokes
Beneath the spreading walnut
Though heeded not by other folks
There evil[6] can no gall put
Green grass there looks never cold
'Sward daisies none looks whiter
The willow leaves fall off like gold
In autumn and look brighter

---

[1] KT2, p.180; GP, p.194; TP2, pp.517–18; GS, p.230.   [2] 'when' GS.
[3] were.   [4] KT2, p.181; GP, p.195.   [5] were.   [6] 'evening' GP, p.195.

To Bessey I'll not say farewell
Nor trouble feel at parting
I'll love the Cottage where ye dwell
And feel one truth as certain
For natures self will dwell wi' me
To charm all sorts o' weather
And love and truth will still agree
And leave us both together

We passed by green closes[1]

The path crossed green closes and went down the lane
Where the black snail reposes and the slime marks remain
The hook prickle[2] bramble Arch's[3] over the grass
And tears in her ramble The gown o' the lass

The Wind in her ribbons green Wantoned and played
And danced round as they'd been i' love wi' the maid
Fine straw was her bonnet her cheek was the rose
Passing bee settled on it by mistake I suppose

Blue skippers in sunny hours open and shut
Where wormwood and grunsel flowers by the cart ruts
Where bees while birds whistle Sung[4] all the lane down
And passes the thistle For the flowers on her gown

The footpath all noon day We paced i' the lane
The day it was Sunday The bells rung again
The bare[5] Mare was snorting Beside of her foal
Love from that days courting Burns my heart to a coal

---

[1] *KT2, p.183; GP, pp. 195–6.*
[2] *'prickled' GP, p.195.*
[3] *arches.*
[4] *'the bee . . . sings' GP, p.196.*
[5] *'bay' GP, p.196.*

Where the hazels hing love[1]

Where the hazels hing love
Oer the Siller spring love
And their shadows fling love
O'er the mossy spring love beneath the Old Oak tree
Where the woodbines bloom so sweetly young lassie sit wi me

I' the summers sunny weather
There we'll sit and love together
Where cares no longer tether
Beside the little spring love beneath the Old Oak tree
Lucy my dearest creature come and share the day wi me

We'll gather ripe strawberries
More red than ripest Cherries
Where high the brown hawk herries
As if he'd gone to sleep i the marble coloured sky's[2]
Neer stirring wing or feather but still as a stone lies

Nature never wants to cheat love
When truth in green woods meet love
There seek wood strawberry fruit love
Where the woodbrook moists the mossy roots of old oak tree
There Lucy chuse thyself a seat and charm the world fra me

Remember dear Mary[3]

Remember dear Mary love cannot decieve
Loves truth cannot vary dear Mary believe
You may hear and believe it believe it and hear
Love could not deceive those features so dear
Believe me dear Mary to press thy soft hand
Is sweeter than riches in houses and Land

[1] *KT2, p.186.*   [2] *skies.*   [3] *KT2, p.187.*

Where I pressed thy soft hand at the dewfall o' eve
I felt the sweet tremble that cannot deceive
If love you believe in Belief is my love
As it lived once in Eden ere we fell from above
To this heartless this friendless this desolate earth
And kept in first love Immortality's birth

T'is there we last meet[1] I adore thee and love thee
Theres nothing beneath thee around thee above thee
I feel it and know it I know so and feel
If your love cannot shew it mine cannot conceal
But knowing I love I feel and adore
And the more I behold—only loves thee the more

Bonny Mary let us go[2]

Bonny Mary let us go O'er the hills of gorse and heather
Where the little harebells grow In the summers sultry weather
Where the rabbit and the hare Timid feed and hide together
Mary let us wander there O'er the hills among the heather

There the sun still rises fine O'er the golden gorse and heather
There the sunsets are divine In the summers sultry weather
See the spinners lace work shine On the bents among the heather
On the gorse from spine to spine Beaded with the dewy weather

Bonny Mary let us go o'er the wheat fields far away
Where rest harrow blossoms grow And arching brambles spread dis-
    may
Not dismay to thee and me For there's space to walk between
There blooms o' summer scenery And half the winter linger green

Dark gown and petticoat so white In hat o' straw and ribbons gay
Laced caps o'er inky curls sae bright That glitters like the milky way
Bonny Mary hither come We'll walk and sit amang the heather
The wild heath is our dearest home Where we can talk and love
    together

---

[1] *met.*   [2] *KT2, p.191.*

The wheatear on the whitethorn cheeping The furze lark whistling by
    her nest
The adder in the crimped brake sleeping But on the short sward we
    can rest
And see the dappled herd graze round us Quiet in the sultry weather
While the shade of eve surround us On the heath of gorse and heather

A wimpering brook[1]

A whimpering brook beside the path
A shady stile to cross the way
And many a hay and clover swarth
Scenting sweet the summers day
There Lucy at the shut of eve
Will[2] wander oer the grassy way
The Village cares and labour leave
Where rows of Willows waver grey

The white moth flits upon the wing
The bat has left the willow tree
In brook banks chittering crickets sing
Come Lucy dear and walk with me
We'll meet where cooling gales soft night
That flutters round the bladed wheat
As if a bird had taken flight
Or timid Leveret left his seat

The unseen shower of falling dew
Shall sprint the roses on thy face
While distant we the old oak view
Still standing in its ancient place
Come Lucy meet the evening hour
Across cornfield and grassy path
The scented bean fields are in flower
And sweetly smells the new mown swath

---

[1] *KT2, pp.192–3.*   [2] *'We'll'?*

The unseen shower of falling dew
How sweet we meet its fall at eve
When every thing perks up anew
And fancy pleasing visions wave[1]
Its eve song as[2] the cricket sung
Snug in its moss nest sleeps the bee
The ground lark broods on eggs and young
Come Lucy wander out with me

The wind sothers softly[3]

The wind suthers softly Among the green bushes
Where the wingleafed ash Hides a nest of song thrushes
The Elms green was darker The Ash shaded paler
Where I walked wi my true love And nothing did ail her

Her cheeks was the wild rose She was bonny and fat
And rainbow the ribbon On her bonny straw hat
The Elm strake was darkest The Ash trees more pale
And bonny the white thorn Shook by the gale

To and fro flew the Chaffinch Busy feeding her young
Th' spotted thrush on her blue eggs Sat brooding long
Where I went with young Dinah So bonny and fat
With the hues of the rainbow Around her straw hat

I love the flowers o' Spring[4]

The Pilewort and the daisy's I love to see them come
In sunshine and green place[s] Where Children play at home
Round cow sheds i' the homesteads Beneath the orchard trees
The double grow on some beds The wild upon the leas

They plant the double daisies The single set themsens
I' home close pilewort blazes Among the cocks and hens
And I'll gang out wi' Bessey To the bottom o' the lane
Where the water rins sae glassy And the frogs come out again

I love the flowers o' spring days Those little bits o' bloom
For they to children bring plays And happy thoughts to come
Go Bessey seek thy bonnet And wanner out wi me
The sun looks warm upon it Our happy Meadow Lea

---

[1] *weave?*   [2] *has?*   [3] *KT2, pp.194–5.*   [4] *KT2, p.195.*

I love the mossy fountain[1]

I love the mossy fountain
And the primrose by its brim
Where the silty sand keeps mounting
And the weeds with wet are dim
When hot suns drys ground starker
And morn sheds pearls o' dew
Where I sat with Mary Darker[2]
A maiden fair and true

Her bonny white straw bonnet
Was sweet and fair to see
While flowered ribbons danced upon it
Like the prissey feathered tree
Half boots her ancles hideing
The calves swelled from their tops
Spite o' her muttered chideing
The traveller nearly stops

Admiring without mention
The beautys they display
Till blushes chides attention
And bids him walk away
Her bonny neck's the lily white
Her cheeks the province rose
She's fair in every body's sight
And sweet her drapery flows

I love the fountains mossy brim
Half hid in white thorn bushes
Where splashings make the primrose dim
As from the hill it gushes
When Eve brought roses i' the West
And ground from heat got starker
There I lay on the bonny breast
Of lovely Mary Darker

[1] *KT2, pp.205–6.*
[2] *MS. 10, p.105 and MS. 110, p.18.*

Q

Wilt thou think o' me?[1]

Now the spring's coming and wild b's 'r humming
Mary think of me
When leaves come to the wild wood[2]
So loved b th n chldhd
O th'n rememb'r m
Thr think who lv'd th derst
And got wild flwrs th nrst
And clmd th kss sncrst[3]
Which Mr still ws m
O Mr n sprng wthr
Lts bth go thr tgthr
And still remember m
Where places are greenest
And summer's serenest
Wilt thou think o me

Wilt thou think o me?

[Now the spring's coming
And wild bees are humming
Mary think of me
When leaves come to the wild wood
So loved by thee in childhood
O then remember me
There think who loved thee dearest
And got wild flowers the nearest
And claimed thy kiss sincerest
Which Mary still owes me
O Mary in spring weather
Lets both go there together
And still remember me
Where places are greenest
And summer's serenest
Wilt thou think o me]

---

[1] *KT2, pp.223–4. Part of the first stanza of this interesting poem is in the code used by Clare in MS. 10. See E. Robinson and G. Summerfield, R.E.S., N.S., XIII, 50, May 1962. Our interpretation is given immediately afterwards between square brackets.*

[2] *Knight reads 'wind'—but the rhyme scheme demands 'wood'.*

[3] *Knight reads 'snerst'.*

The primrose o' the wild wood
Talk agen to thy childhood
Neath the old Ivy tree
Where the ring dove cooes lofty
And the winds flutter softly
My love think o' me
By the beds o' green mosses
That the oak root embosses
And lichens white glosses
Remember thou me
My love let's be roaming
Come to me at gloaming
I' the Lane let us be
Where the woodbine is wreathing
And dog rose is breathing
Remember thou me
The cockchaffer born
From the dewey white thorn
Is sounding his horn
Dear Mary to thee
I'll meet thee at gloaming
I' the fields to be roaming
Till then think o' me

Come the back way dear[1]

Now Granny's gone to bed Steal in the back way
Ye shall be my favoured lad I'll be your lass alway
Come in this happy night For Granny's fast asleep
And I'll put out the light Fear some should come to peep

So come the back way dear To love me ye'll be free
Should ye kick at Grannys chair Till furder ye'll find me
The fire it may be out Or they'll maybe be a spark
For theres nothing half so sweet As kisses i' the dark

---

[1] *KT2, p.228.*

Love come the back way in By the Mint and ladslove tree
And where my Grannys bin I' the next chair feel for me
The fire's upo' the hearth And there'll maybe [be] a spark
The crickets sing i' mirth And the kiss is sweet at dark

So Roger pulled the string She from the window flew
She was a Lassie sweet He was a lover true
He fell o'er Granny's chair And felt his heart delight
I' kisses sweet and fair Till morning brought a light

Song[1]

The grey green willow whispers
The prattling brook it lispers
And moths so white like specks o light
Fly round the awthorn vespers
Whose leaves are found that cool the hand
Each snow white wing flys oer the spring

Song[2]

O Liza Dadfords[3] like a pearl
A bouncing bonny lovely Girl
I loved her once and ever shall
The sweet Eliza Dadford
Her bright eyes like two Diamond drops
The maiden blushes comes and stops
From rose bush where the Linnet hops
To sweet Eliza Dadford

Her bosoms white her eyes are bright
Her face the essence of delight
The charm o day the loved o night
To be wi Liza Dadford
I loved her many years ago
Her face did like the rose bush glow
Where I kissed first she blushed and so
I loved Eliza Dadford

---

[1] *KT2, p.232.* [2] *KT2, p.235.*
[3] *See Letters, p.305. We do not agree with J. W. and Anne Tibble's note. Cf. also MS. 10, p.52 and p.100.*

Song[1]

The spring has been here just one week
These snow drops tell the time
I came here then spring flowers to seek
And now they're just in prime
My Jinney's neck's as white as they
Her cheek is much more dear
And what o love I'm going to say
Will Jinney stand to hear

Is Jinney's memory a' away
When snow drops speak so plain
She said she'd no more answer 'nay'
When spring flowers came again
And here they drop like blebs o' snow
So beautifully fair
Which Susan cropt a year ago
And wore them in her hair

The flowers are speaking Jinney's words
What she a year ago
Said to herself among these herds
When I kept teasing so
She said I teased—I only sat
And sued one kiss in vain
She said she'd grant me more than that
When snow drops came again

And they are come and Jinney's here
Bees seek their faint perfume
But Jinney nips the wild sweet brere
And wont look where they bloom
The swain got up from the molehill
Jinney nae longer teased
He caught her with his heart all chill
To court her as he pleased

Song[1]

I wish I was where I would be
With love alone to dwell
Was I but her or she but me
Then love would all be well
I wish to send my thoughts to her
As quick as thoughts can fly
But as the wind the waters stir
The mirrors change and flye

Song[2]

Twas i' the morning early
The dew was on the barley
Each hours[3] a string o' beads
Corn poppies burnt me through
Blue caps intensely blue
Seemed flowers among the weeds

Where I met young Mary Boyfield[4]
And did loves dearest joy feel
As she passed me i the corn
Her gown brushed gently by me
And love that could not flye me
Shone like the dewey morn[5]

Her cheeks the rosey breres bloom
Her eyes like ripples lately come
From gravel paving[6] Spring
She looked accross the red and blue
Each colour wore a livelier hue
While Larks popt up to sing

---

[1] *KT2, p.238; TP2. p.523; GP, p.140, prints another fragment of this song. See p.103, footnote 1 above.*
[2] *KT2, pp.240–1; TP2, pp.495–6.*
[3] *'spear' TP2, p.495.*
[4] *Mary Ann Boyfield is mentioned in MS. 10, p.101.*
[5] *J. Tibble omits this stanza.*   [6] *'paven' TP2, p.496.*

How lovely hung the barley spears
Beaded in mornings dewey tears
Rich green and grey did seem
The pea more rich than velvet glows
Sweeter than double the Dog rose
A sweet midsummer dream

The grass wi' downy tops inlaced
Where I clasped Mary round the waist
And doated on her charms
I kissed her cheek and swelling breast
That like two downy pillows prest
And held her in my arms[1]

The sun gleamed oer that waving corn
Where her I kissed one dewey morn
A shining Golden river
I clasped her in a locked embrace
And gazing on her bonny face
I loved her and for ever

Song[2]

She tied up her few things
And laced up her shoe strings
And put on her bonnet worn through at the crown
Her apron tied tighter
Than snow her caps[3] whiter
She lapt up her earnings and left our old town

The Dog barked again
All the length o' his chain
And licked her hand kindly and huffed her good bye
Old hens prated loudly
The Cock strutted proudly
And the horse at the gate turned to let her go bye

---

[1] *Tibble omits this stanza.*
[2] *KT2, pp.241–2; TP2, p.459.*   [3] *'cap' TP2, p.459.*

The Thrasher[1] man stopping
The old barn floor wopping
Wished oer the door cloth her luck and no harm
Bees hummed round the thistle
While the red Robins whistle
And she just one look on the old mossy farm

Twas Michaelmas season
They'd got corn and pears[2] in
And all the Fields cleared save some rakings and thythes[3]
Cote pregon[4] flocks muster[5]
Round beans[6] shelling cluster
And done are the whettings o reap hooks and scythes

Next years flowers a springing
Will miss Jinneys singing
She opened her Bible and turned a leaf down
In her bosoms forewarnings
She lapt up her earnings
And ere the suns set'll[7] be in her own town

Song[8]

The Daisey by the road side
It is a pretty flower
Its golden eye and silver rim
Smiles in the April shower
The pilewort on the trodden grass
Shone beautiful as gold
And there I met a lovely lass
Most handsome to behold

And there I passed a lovely lass
Eyes like ony sloes
Down her fair cheek her ringlets fell
As black as ony Crow

---

[1] *'threshing' TP2, p.459.*   [2] *peas?*   [3] *Clare's spelling of 'tythes'?*
[4] *Clare's spelling of 'pigeon'? Clare probably wrote 'piegon'.*
[5] *'Cote-pigeons muster' TP2, p.459.*   [6] *'Round the beans' TP2, p.459.*
[7] *'set will' TP2, p.459.*   [8] *KT2, pp.242–4.*

She looked down on the daiseys
A smiling i' their bloom
That told her o' the sunny days
O summer yet to come

Young Mary she was handsome
Young Mary she was fair
Soft and rosey was her cheek
And coal black was her hair
Her dress was like the country girl
A Country Girl was she
And much I wished that happy morn
Her sweet heart for to be

Good morning to you maiden fair
Good morning Sir said she
The dog rose fanned the sunny air
The ivy clasped the Tree
I placed myself behind the path
And dropt a word or two
She kind replied to all I said
And shunned the grassy dew

I clasped my arm about her neck
And looked that way and this
And while the blackcap sang aloud
I stole one happy Kiss
We stood upon the path
And shunned the grassy dew
And there I found a sweetheart where
The Gold eyed daisy's grew

Song[1]

We'll walk my love at eve unseen
By broad leaved hazel hedge
Where Anna curls like fingered glove
Dark as the ivy strakes above

---

[1] *KT2, pp.244-5.*

We'll stand on grass banks bright and dry
And count the stars all in the sky
And there we'll stand to see them shine
Till love grows fond and you divine

A kiss without thy leave I'll take
With one arm lapped round thy white neck
While curls by thy white earings
Like so many coal black rings
And loll upon thy heaving breast
And in thy secret wishes rest
My arm around thy shoulder thrown
Thy hand in mind I'd hold my own

The ash it spreads accross the leas
And bunches shake o' paler keys
We'll sit beneath or stand the while
And see the heavens burn and smile
The meadow sweets white downy tops
And round the binding wild hedge hops

Song[1]

The sulphur hued primrose
Is out i' the Lane
The morning less dim glows
The sunshine again
Gleams warmer and warmer
Down the mossy fringed lane
And the voice o' Loves charmer
Singing birds wake again

The shaded lanes dirty
The ruts dribble on
And the sludges splash spirty
Where waggons have gone
My kind love supposes
And where the Bees hum
Round the roots o' primroses
I think they might come

To see woman walking
At the spring o' the year
I the primroses talking
Is something so dear
To the joys o' the season
I think it divine
And wish with good reason
Such companion was mine

The old Cow is followed
By the maidens glad eye
Butterflyes sulphur coloured
She sees gadding bye
And the small Tortoise shell
Where the primroses bloom
By the woodside will tell
Where the warmer days come

Song[1]

Long have we parted been
Longsome and lonesome
No one to cheer the scene
None but Miss Bl–ns–me[2]
Lassie lie near me
Cuddle and cheer me
Love dont live so lonesome
But come and lie near me

I' the Bastilles o' hell
Bloody and dreary
Bloody tales captives tell
Lonely and weary
I have been where they fell
Wounded and weary
Now I wi' freedom dwell
Lassie come near me

---

[1] *KT2, pp.247–8; GP, pp.203–4.*
[2] *Miss Blunson is mentioned in MS. 10, p.51. Also see poem 'To Miss B', p.183 above.*

Kisses are sweet my Love
　　Thy cherry Lips cheer me
Sweet as one hope above
　　Heaven loves near[1] thee
Tis hell to be parted thus
　　Come love and hear me
Give me thy bosoms buss
　　Lassie lie near me

All my hearts anguish
　　And long I've endured it
In prison to languish
　　Thy smiles love has cured it
True love and lassie dear
　　Turn back and hear me
Thy white bosoms heaven near
　　Lassie come near me

Song[2]

I peeled bits o strews and I got switches too
From the grey peeling[3] Willow as Idlers do
And I switched at the flyes as I sat all alone
Till my flesh blood and marrow wasted[4] to dry bone
My illness was love though I knew not the smart
But the beauty o love was the blood o my heart

Crowded places I shunned them as noises to[o] rude
And flew to the silence of sweet solitude
Where the flower in green darkness, buds, blossoms and fades
Unseen of a shepherd and flower loving maids
The hermit bees find them but once and away
There I'll burry[5] alive and in silence decay

---

[1] *Heaven, love, is near.*
[2] *KT2, pp.249–50; see also TP2, p.512.*
[3] *Knight reads 'feeling'.*
[4] *'was turned' TP2, p.512.*　　　　[5] *bury.*

I looked on the eyes o' fair woman too long
Till silence and shame stole the use o' my tongue
When I tried to speak to her I'd nothing to say
So I turned myself round and she wandered away
When she got too far off—why I'd something to tell
So I sent sighs behind her and talked to my sell[1]

Willow switches I broke and I[2] peeled bits and straws
Ever lonely in crowds in natures own laws
My ball room the pasture my music the Bees
My drink was the fountain my church the tall trees
Whoever would love or be tied to a wife
When it makes a man mad a' the days o' his life

Song[3]

I had na been so busy
Na na indeed not I
Had I not thought the hussy
Had got tamer bye and bye
An old nag at my coat flap
A bur behind my ear
And two or three[4] banging gate claps
I heard some ither where

A nasty dirty hissy[5]
They plague me still at home
Her old rags bin too busy[6]
And so's her tuzle[7] comb
I'll name her arter horses
And rub her down i' straw
And heed no love discourses
Love's what the world neer saw

---

[1] 'walked to my cell' TP2, p.512.
[2] Tibble omits 'I' TP2, p.512.
[3] KT2, pp.250–1; TP2, p.461.
[4] 'two-three' TP2, p.461.   [5] 'hussy!' TP2, p.461.
[6] 'lousy' TP2, p.461.   [7] 'tousle' TP2, p.461.

Song[1]

Tell the wish of thy heart in flowers sweet maid
Words never speak so plain
As a dogrose cropt from the woods green bower
Or a cowslip cropt i' the rain
To stoop for't and cherish it home i thy breast
While the rain drops fall i the face
And like pearls o' joy on thy happy cheeks rest
From the bushes and green grassy place

Song. 'Bonny Mary'[2]

Dearest Mary! ever dearest!
How lovely is the morning!
All is bright when thou appearest,
Come and we'll hail days dawning.
Where the oak tree darkly shadows
O'er the dewy dasied grass
Where the song of thrushes glad us,
There I'll court[3] my bonny lass

Let me clasp thee, bonny Mary,
Underneath the dark oak bough,
Where the breeze comes light, and airy,
And quiet feeds the sheep, and cow,
Bonny Mary! let me clasp thee,
Where the ivied oak tree leans,
Oer the brambles, there I'll grasp thee,
And teach thee what true courtship means

Bonny Mary! maid the rarest!
Plump and rosy—sweetest—dearest
I'll clasp, and kiss thee as the fairest
Ever seen—With love sincerest
I'll caress thee, hear my pleading!
Thou art all the world to me:
All thy virtues I've been heeding;
Mary gi' thy hand to me.
To, 'Mary Ludgate'[4]

---

[1] KT2, p.251.   [2] KT2, p.254.   [3] [clasp].   [4] See note above, p.208.

Lines—to Helen Maria[1]

Helen Maria![2] lovely Helen!
Ere the foliage leaves the tree,
Ere the snow storm hides the dwelling,
Take a country walk with me,
In thy sunday shawl, and gown;
With thy best straw bonnet on,
Let us leave the tiresome town,
And go where love and summer's gone.

Go to the grove of willows grey,
That lean upon the rivers side,
Where the green flag's, rustling play,
And the wild duck, wanders wide:
Where the old oak, darkly green,
Shows autumn in a yellow bough;
Helen Maria seek the scene,
With health upon thy bonny brows.

And we, will mark the river run,
And fishes leap above the stream,
All golden with the Autumn sun,
How happy will the journey seem!
How happy will thy bosom be!
To feel the kiss so softly prest:
If Helen loves—walk out with me
We in each others hearts shall rest.
To 'Helen Maria Gardiner'

---

[1] *KT2, p.255.*

[2] *Helen Maria Gardiner, like Mary Ludgate, was addressed by Clare in a code letter in MS. 10. She is also listed along with Caroline Gardiner, Julia Wigginton and Mary Ludgate on page 75 of that book. In the letter she is associated with the river side as in this poem. It is possible that she was the daughter of Benjamin Close Gardiner of Help-stone (see E. Robinson and G. Summerfield, R.E.S., N.S., XIII, 50, May 1962) but we now tend to associate her with one of the mills outside Northampton.*

To Julia[1]

Dear Julia, now the new mown hay
Is littered oer the narrow path
We'll in the meadows spend the day,
And sit upon the scented swath;
We'll rest upon the fragrant hay,
Dear Julia! in the willows shade;
In fond affection spend the day:
And there I'll love my bonny maid

The knap weed falls before the scythe
And clumps of tawney meadow sweet,
Ploughmen in fallows, whistle blythe,
Where I, and bonny Julia meet,
How sweetly cool the river runs!
How richly green the flags appear!
More yellow than the brightest suns
The sweetest place in all the year

We'll gather lamb toes in the grass
Brown turned and hot as Julia's face,
And Burnet flower, a tawney lass
And rattles like a pencil case
That sound and rattles in the hand
For which the village boys will run:
For these I'll sea[r]ch about the land,
And walk with Julia in the sun.

Dear Julia! now the new mown hay
Is littered oer the narrow path,
We'll in the meadows spend the day,
And walk among the scented swath,
Dear Julia! in the willow's shade
We'll sit upon the fragrant hay,
And there I'll clasp my peerless maid,
And love, and live throughout the day.
                    To 'Julia Wiggington'[2]

---

[1] KT2, pp.256–7.
[2] *Julia Wigginton* [sic] *is listed with Mary Ludgate and Helen Maria Gardiner, MS. 10, p.75. See also p.93 and p.104.*

I'll dream about the days to come[1]

I'll lay me down on the green sward
Mid yellow cups, and speedwell blue,
And pay the world no real[2] regard,
But be to nature, leal, and true.
What breaks[3] the peace o' hapless man,
But they who truth, and nature wrong?
I'll hear na mair[4] o' evils plan,
But live wi nature, and her song.

Where natures lights, and shades are green,
Where natures peace, is strewn wi flowers,
Where strife and noise is[5] never seen.
There I'll retire to happy hours,
And stretch my body on the green,
And sleep amang her[6] flowers in bloom,
By eyes of malice, seldom seen,
And dream upon the days to come

I'll lay me by the forest green
I'll lay me on the pleasant grass,
My life shall pass away unseen,
I'll be no more the man I was,
The tawney bee upon the flower,
The butterfly upon the leaf,
Like them I'll live my happy hour
A life of sunshine, bright, and brief.

In greenwood hedges, close at hand,
Buildeth and sings[7] the little birds,
The happiest things in the green land,
While sweetly feed the lowing herds,
While softly bleat the roving sheep
Upon the green grass will I lie,
A summer day, to think, and sleep,
Or see the clouds sail down the sky

---

[1] *KT2, pp.260–1; TP2, pp.515–16.*
[2] *'more' TP2, p.515.*
[3] *'who breaks' TP2, p.515.*
[4] *'no more' TP2, p.515.*
[5] *'strife and care are' TP2, p.515.*
[6] *'the' TP2, p.515.*
[7] *'build, brood, and sing' TP2, p.516.*

R

He loved me best o' ony[1]

The path thats led across the field
Foot printed, dry, and clean,
Crept strake[2] like in its trail,
Through meadows crisp, and green;
I hung upon my sweethearts arm,
Whose face was red, and bonny,
He said, as love began to warm:
He loved me best o' ony

He said so, as he wiped away,
The hair upon his brow,
It was the happy first o' day
And I'd just milked the cow,
The rose just peeped, and on the brere,
It scented blithe, and bonny;
He softly said, my Mary dear
I love you best o' ony

He pluck'd some cowslips from the grass,
From white thorn bush, the may,
And said 'look here my bonny lass,
What hues the flowers display.'
And then I hid them in my gown,
All in my breast, so bonny,
I took them with me, to the town,
They're the sweetest flowers o' ony

The clouds hung over Lolham brigs,[3]
The sunshine glittered through the arch,
The ploughboy play'd his rustic rigs,
And cawing crows, sat on the larch.
He kiss't me on the neck, and cheek,
Wi face sae red, and bonny,
And said, 'no mair he dare to speak
But he loved me best o' ony'

To 'Mary Hobbs'[4]

---

[1] *KT2, pp.261–2.*   [2] *This could be 'snake'.*
[3] *See J. E. B. Gover, A. Mawer and F. M. Stenton, 'The Place-Names of Northamptonshire', Cambridge, 1933, p.238. 'Lolham Bridge is on Ermine Street, at the point where that road, running north from Castor, crosses the Welland.'*
[4] *Not yet identified. Should this be Mary Mobbs, MS. 10, p.88?*

To Isabel[1]

Arise, my Isabel, arise,
The sun shoots forth his early ray,
The hue of love is in the skies,
The birds are singing, come away!
Oh come! my Isabella come!
With inky tendrils, hanging low,
Thy cheeks like hedge rose, just in bloom,
That in the healthy summer glow.

That eye it turns the world away
From wanton ways, and recklessness,
That eye beams with a cheerful ray,
And smiles propitiously to bless,
O come! my Isabella dear!
Oh come! and fill these longing arms,
Come let me see thy beauty here,
And bend in worship, oer thy charms.

Oh come! my Isabella love!
My dearest Isabella come!
Thy loves affection let me prove,
And kiss thy beauty, in its bloom,
My Isabella young, and fair,
Thou darling of my home, and heart,
Come love my bosoms truth to share,
And of its being, form a part.

                    To Isabella Sharp[2]

Fragment[3]

Vetches, both yellow and blue,
Grew thick in the meadow lane,
Isabellas shawl kept off the dew
As thickly upon her it came,

---

[1] *KT2, p.267.*

[2] *Not yet identified. Ann Sharp, Flying Horse [Market Square, Northampton] is mentioned in MS. 10, p.87.*

[3] *KT2, p.270.*

R*

A thorn bush caught her umbrella
As though it would bid her to stay,
But the loving, and loved Isabella,
Went laughing, and walking away.

Song[1]

The cows they are out in the pasture
Where the maids go a milking at e'en
Untroubled by a common disaster
In every village they're seen
On the white thorn the cobweb is hinging
The knob weeds blood red on the hill
By the dyke yellow hammers are singing
Milkmaids sing more beautiful still
How sweet smells the hawthorn how lovely the scene
Where the beautiful milkmaids go milking at e'en

The cows are all out in the pasture
The Hedge sparrow chirps in the thorn
And there is the man with his master
Looking over the clover and corn
The milkmaid looks like the hedge roses
When fi[r]st they begin to unclose
Her eyes are as bright as blue posies
That all down the pasture path grows
How sweet smells the hawthorn how lovely the scene
Where the beautiful maidens go milking at e'en

The blackbird sings sweet in the vale
While the ringdove is cooing beyond
And the wagtail whose[2] wagging his tail
Catches midges that fly oer the pond
The gnats from the rushes fly up
In a column that toutches[3] the sky
At the cow pond the heifer will stop
While the swallow goes merrily by
How sweet look the maidens with aprons so clean
And their well scoured pails going milking at een

---

[1] *KT2, pp.275–6.*   [2] *who's. Knight has a cancelled reading: 'sits'.*   [3] *touches.*

Sweet Mary Beal[1]

This passion to love thee I cannot conceal
But how shall I tell thee my sweet Mary Beal
I'm sure that I love her but Mary's not here
Where the dews on the grass and the rose on the brere
But the rose on the brere and the dew on the grass
Is nothing compared to my own bonny lass
Oh the fruits of my passion I cannot conceal!
'Twas May when I first met my Sweet Mary Beal[2]

Bright daisies and Celadine starr'd the green lane
And the white thorn with blossoms was dotting again
Seeking clay from the ditches were Blackbirds and Thrushes
For the houses they're building among the green bushes
A primrose root by the waggon gate shone
As yellow as mustard or flowers o' brimstone
One Sunday in May I did silently steal
Down the green lane right happy to court Mary Beal

Her frock it was light and her kerchief was silk
And her bosom beneath it was snowwhite as milk
Her lips like twin cherries her cheeks like the rose
Which blushes so sweet down among the hedge rows
Oh sure such another could never be seen
Yet she wondereth much what my bother does mean
There are many green trees do sweet blossoms reveal
But nothing so handsome as young Mary Beal

Song[3]

How sweet the woodbines fragrant flowers
Sweet is the hum drum of the bee
But sweeter far at evening hours
The lovely smiles of Ellen Tree[4]

---

[1] KT2, p.283.
[2] Not yet identified. Mentioned in MS. 10, p.102.
[3] KT2, pp.285-6.   [4] See MS. 10, p.120.

She stood against a tree of oak
He joined her by the woodland stile
Twas just as though an Angel spoke
I heard her speak and saw her smile

Oh Ellen Tree! dear Ellen Tree
The sun is setting 'yont the hill
Walk down the white thorn lane wi me
And let us live in Eden still

White clover blooms and thistle flowers
Are lodgings for the sleepy bee
I'll worship in the evetide hours
My idol angel Ellen Tree

As none were lov'd I'll love her on
And more than happy will I be
I'll seize the moment e'er tis flown
To kiss the lips of Ellen Tree

A sad catastrophe[1]

Oh Molly Meeks! Oh Molly Meeks![2]
How can you serve me so
I' my face they say I can sow leeks
There's muck enough to grow
I dare no let the least o' drops
Of water touch my cheeks
So I must wear a dirty chops
And all through Molly Meeks

Oh Molly Meeks! Oh Molly Meeks
I'm dying—What a loss!
Children are plaguing me for weeks
By laying straws across

---

[1] *KT2, pp.289–90.*
[2] *The name here is conventional.*

And Molly Meeks when she goes by
They call a 'spotless dove'
At me they point and loudly cry
'He's crucified by love'

Oh Molly Meeks! Oh Molly Meeks!
Do let your anger stay
It's me alone your kindness seeks
To cheer my weary way
The Tom Cat mhows[1] dogs bark at me
Poor Simkin all despise
The Schoolboys let their marbles be
'Oh look at Toney's eyes!'

Young men and maids be warn'd by me
Oh be all warned in time
By Toney Simkins jeopardy
Love cut off in his prime
And all through cruel Molly Meeks
A 'Boney'[2] in her mind
Slighted I've been these fifty weeks
Nor peace nor rest can find.

The gown o' green[3]

The Spring is come and winters gone
And nature all ears tingle
Sweet Mammy's put her bonnet on
For flowers wild i' the pingle
The birds are building everywhere
Wi hair and bents and mosses
On white thorn, blackthorn, dog rose **brere**
Mid sheep and cows and horses

My love is in her gown o' green
Walking and talking still
Among the hills and hollows seen
By the old water mill
Her face is comely as a queen
Her auburn curls hang down
Oer shoulders white as snow I ween
Set off by her green gown

---

[1] *miaouws.*   [2] *Presumably a 'Bonaparte', i.e. a bogey-man.*   [3] *KT2, pp.290–1*

She's tight and jimpsey in her stays
Her bosom soft and round
Her Sunday clothes on common days
She wears the whole year round
My love she is a handsome thing
Travel the country oer
I'll buy my love a wedding ring
And love her evermore

Mary Collingwood[1]

Oh Mary gentle Mary[2] let us not disagree
I took thee for my true love to share thy company
Relentless fate pursued me and sent me cross the sea
But there sweet Mary Collingwood was all the world to me
At last when I came back again after staying months away
Her absence was made up to me by the pleasure of that day
To look upon that sweet face where fell the silent tear
Recompenced the absence I'd been away a year

The Yellowhammer[3]

When shall I see the white thorn leaves agen
And Yellowhammers gath'ring the dry bents
By the Dyke side on stilly moor or fen
Feathered wi love and natures good intents
Rude is the nest this architect invents
Rural the place wi cartruts by dyke side
Dead grass, horse hair and downy headed bents
Tied to dead thistles she doth well provide
Close to a hill o' ants where cowslips bloom
And shed o'er meadows far their sweet perfume
In early Spring when winds blow chilly cold
The yellow hammer trailing grass will come
To fix a place and choose an early home
With yellow breast and head of solid gold

---

[1] *KT2, p.291. This is the first of three stanzas—the other two are doggerel.*
[2] *Not yet identified, but see Letters, p.304, and MS. 10, pp.52, 100 and 112, where her name is always next to Eliza Dadford.*
[3] *KT2, p.303; TP2, p.445.*

Primroses[1]

I love the rath primroses pale brimstone primroses
  That bloom in the thick wood and i' the green closes
I love the primroses whenever they come
  Where the blue fly sits pensive and humble bees hum
The pale brimstone primroses come at the spring
  Swept over and fann'd by the wild thrushes wing
Bow'd down to the leaf cover'd ground by the bees
  Who sing their spring ballads thro bushes and trees

Like patches o' flame i' the Ivy so green
  And dark green oak leaves where the Autumn has been
Put on thy straw hat love and russet stuff gown
  And see the pale primroses grow up and down
The pale brimstone primroses wild wood primroses
  Which maids i' the dark woods make into posies
Put on thy stuff gown love and off let us be
  To seek brimstone primroses neath the Oak tree

Spring time is come love primroses bloom fair
  The sun o' the morning shines in thy bright hair
The ancient wood shadows are bonny dark green
  That throw out like giants the stovens between
While brimstone primroses like patches o' flame
  Blaze through the dead leaves making Ivy look tame
I love the rath primrose in hedgerows and closes
  Together lets wander to gather primroses

Meet me my own pretty dove[2]

O come i' the evening my own pretty dove
  When the dews o' the Heaven cool the fever o' love
When the day stars o' daiseys shut up in green buds
  And the eyes o' Anemones close i' the woods—

---

[1] *KT2, pp.304–5.*   [2] *KT2, pp.305–6.*

Come love in thy airy straw hat and new gown
And we'll ramble at even away from the town
We'll ramble away by the hawthorn and briar
Where the waggon ruts lead to the woods free from mire

And we'll kiss by the oak and the hazel boughs hid
When the Owl hurries out as though he knew what he did
Yes we'll kiss by the light o' the silvery moon
When the stars will na tell what two lovers ha done

So come out and meet me my own pretty dove
The stars are all sleepy and blinking above
The moon who is silent tells not what we do
So come love and meet me nor fear the mild dew

The Fitting Place[1]

The day was cold and rawkin
    Though 'twas April of the year
And the cows they fell a gawkin
    As if enemies were near
Winds blew about the rushes
    The Finch built on the brere
And chirp'd in white thorn bushes
    In the April of the year

The flying showers went over
    Like large birds upon the wing
Silver drops were on the clover
    Pearl beds o' early spring
There a bonny maid was weeding
    The thistles from the wheat
And the Partridges were breeding
    Little Birdies at their feet

Oh! I eyed the maid all over
    As I pass'd her in the grain
Then I hasten'd through the clover
    And the Heav'n was dropping rain

---

[1] *KT2, pp.307–8.*

I kisst her on the cheek so red
  Her neck was soft and white
She heeded every word I said
  And felt that it was right

We lay[1] together side by side
  Around us grew the wheat
She'd make a bonny winsome bride
  The woodbines wer'nt so sweet
We saw the sun drop in the woods
  The stars light up the eve
The moon got up wi' dewy hoods
  Before we took our leave

There's pleasure in the sweet greenwood
  Wi a sweet girl by ones side
To think of it it does one good
  And fills our heart wi pride
To walk amang the silken grass
  To kiss her rosy face
Courting till eve the bonny lass
  In such a fitting place

Angels of earth[2]

Love is the immortal souls delight
  For 'God is love' we see
I love his seasons day and night
  His world so fair and free
The evening breeze and morning gale
  And Gods own masterpiece
Woman! Thy joys can never fail
  Our pleasures to increase

I loved sweet woman from a boy
  They are Gods types o' love
Wi' bosoms white all full o' joy
  Wafting our thoughts above

---

[1] *Knight has substituted 'walk'd'.*   [2] *KT2, pp.310–11.*

Angels o' earth though made wi clay
Love clippit o' the wing
To them I sang my early lay
Continue still to sing

Their soft eyes tell o' bliss in heaven
Sweet are the words they say
In their sweet smile the power is given
To cheer our lonely way
Their rosy cheeks and lips I loved
Their diamond eyes I sung
My songs of love by them approved
By them my harp was strung

Creations masterpiece is woman!
Of lifes dark sphere the soul
Queen o' every blossom bloomin'
A light to charm the whole
Angels of earth tho' made of clay
Loves type without a wing
My first and last immortal lay
Is woman when I sing

Early Morning[1]

Primroses are in hedge rows peeping
Neath white thorn roots violets are sleeping
Dew bespangled they seem weeping
In the early pleasant morning

The Primrose peeps aneath the thorn
By woodland hedges newly born
Shows sulpher bosom in the morn
The calm and tranquil morning—

The violets blooming neath the hedge
Peeping in clumps thro wither'd sedge
Of Spring the sweet and early pledge
Sweet scenting early morning

---

[1] KT2, pp.325-7.

By Hazel Stulps and mossy green
Where the bubbling brook is seen
Oft you and I, in Spring have been
    Walking at early morning

The Lark is cheeping to the sky
A bursting flood of melody
Till clouds conceal him from the eye
    In the mild and early morning

The crow is on the furrow'd field
The Blackbird in the spinney shield
They in the Quick set hedges build
    Singing sweet at early morning

The hanging mist the blebs of dew
That makes the early pasture blue
As if the Heaven was looking through
    To welcome early morning

In such a place 'tis hard to sever
We met and could have talked for ever
In meadows by that winding river
    On that lovely early morning

There then a bonny maiden fair
As sweet a flower as any there
Went forth to take the healthy air
    I' the quiet early morning

Blessings attend thy leisure hours
May happiness descend in showers
When Spring revives those fragrant bowers
    On a joyous April morning—

Spring[1]

In every step we tread appears fresh spring
Hedge weeds all juicy run up tall and flowers
Birds near their nests in early morning sing
By yonder Chaffinch there the Leveret cowers
Unseen and nestles through the days warm hours
Then plays at eve tide in the grass and dews
The old field barn is based with wild spring flowers
The old cart wheel agen the hovel threw
Leans neath the thatch where last year robins flew

The summers messenger the sooty swallow
On level meadows like a shadow swims
Then darts with nimbler speed oer the brown fallow
On o'er the farm within a minute skims
His flight to mark the keenest vision dims
Now o'er the green wheat field it playful springs
Then oer the meadow field its flight begins
There drops and drinks and twitters round and sings
The happiest welcomer of early spring

The children shout to see a swallow fly
When they come first where the bow'd cowslips bloom
Down valleys where lone lodge and hamlets lie
They eager bawl and halloo 'Here they come'
'And there they go' as thoughts do to their home
They hasten quickly to warm chimney pots[2]
Day after day the Children watch them come
The sight of swallows their flower gathring stops
Skimming the valley, brooks, through woods he pops

Above the Quick set blooms 'Jack by the hedge'
His white flowers shine all down the narrow lane
In April sunshine still a welcome pledge
To show warm weather brings wild flowers again
Primrose to woods and cowslips to the plain
The Arum red or white their flower shows
The grass gets darker with the run and rain
The yellow rocket by the dyke side grows
And every wild weed in perfection glows

[1] *KT2, pp.327–8.*   [2] [tops].

Acrostic[1]

Jane[2] Summer is with thee thy fancy may chuse
Any amusement with thy sister the muse
Nor meet dissappointment in walking the fields
Endearing the pleasure that innocence yields

Where wild flowers are blossoming sweet in their joy
In Natures own scene where pleasures neer cloy
Light as a summer day softly your tread
Silent as evening o'er the daisey's bed
Oer meadows by Woodside by Brooklets she speeds
Neer gathering one of vain follys weeds

Country Courtship[3]

It was on a Summers morning
Nigh the middle of the day
When dewy pearls the Breres adorning
Shone on the hedge rows spray
Just while a getting oer the stile
And the green bank stepping down
I met a maiden wi sunny smile
A coming from the town

The roses blush'd upon the Brere
Her cheek flush'd wi the heat
'Good morning to your Smiles my dear
Good morn said she so sweet
The wheat stalk showed its milky ear
And bowd down heavy oer the baulk
The birds they whistled full and clear
The Jays they almost seem'd to talk

I said 'my pretty maiden fair
Excuse a strangers first love token
I wiped aside her curling hair
And kiss'd her cheek before twas spoken

---

[1] *KT2, p.329.*   [2] *The name 'Jane Wilson' appears, MS. 10, p.78.*
[3] *KT2, pp.322-3.*

We pass'd o'er grounds and crossed the lane
Her gown was brushd by milky ear
I saw her home and back again
Went every sunday all the year

I went while wheat grounds turn'd to brown
I went till[1] stouks were standing there
Head aches where[2] blushing up and down
And blue caps blossom'd late and fair
I went till Bean fields were turn'd black
And Barley shocks where[2] clear'd away
Saw Rickyards fill'd wi many a stack
And then we had our Wedding day

The rawk o' the Autumn[3]

The rawk o' the Autumn hangs over the woodlands
Like smoke from a city dismember'd and pale
The sun without beams burns dim[4] o'er the floodlands
Where white Cawdymaws slow swiver and sail
The flood froths away like a fathomless ocean
The wind winnows chill like a breeze from the sea
And thoughts of my Susan give the[5] heart an emotion
To think does she e'er waste a thought upon me

Full oft I think so on the banks of the meadows
While the pale Cawdywundy[6] flies swooping all day
I think of our true love where grass[7] and flowers hid us
As by the dyke side o' the meadows we lay
The seasons have chang'd since I sat wi my true love
Now the flood roars and raves o'er the bed where we lay
There the bees kiss'd the flowers—Has she got a new love
I feel like a wreck of the flood cast away

---

[1] *Knight has 'when till'.*
[2] *were.*   [3] *KT2, pp.342–3; TP2, p.506.*
[4] *[dead].*   [5] *'my' TP2, p.506.*
[6] *'cawdy-mawdy' TP2, p.506.*   [7] *Knight reads 'glass'.*

The rawk of the Autumn hangs over the woodlands
Like smoke from a City sulphurously grey
The Heronshaw lonely hangs over the floodland
And cranks its lone story throughout the dull day
There's no green on the hedges no leaves on the darkwood
No cows on the pasture or sheep on the lea
The Linnets cheep[1] still and how happy the lark would
Sing songs to sweet Susan to remind her of me

An anecdote of love[2]

When April dew brings primroses here
I think love of you at the spring o' the year
Did I harbour bad words when your garter fell off
I to stoop was deterred but I stood not to scoff
A bitt of brown list of small value must be
But as it lay there 'twas a diamond to me

Ere back you turned to pick it up
I noticed well the place
For children there for violets stoop
With many a rosey face
I fain would stoop myself you see
But dare not well presume
The blackbird sung out let it be
The maid was in her bloom

How beautiful that ancle was
From which that garter fell
And lusty was the bonny lass
Whose name I dare not tell
I know the colour of her gown
Her bonnet Ribbon too
The fairest maiden in the town
Is she that wears the blue

---

[1] *'chirp'* TP2, p.506.   [2] *KT2, pp.356–7.*

Though years have gone but when I see
The green spot where it fell
The stitchwort flower delighteth me
There blooming in the dell
And years may come no winter seers
The green haunts of the Dove
Those wild flowers stand the blight of years
Sweet anecdote of love

Roses[1]

Go rose my Chloes bosom grace
   How happy should I prove
Could I supply that envied place
   With never fading love

Accept dear Maid now Summer glows
   This pure unsullied gem
Loves Emblem in a full blown rose
   Just broken from the stem

Accept it tis[2] a favoured flower
   For thy soft breast to wear
Twill blossom there its transient hour
   A favourite of the fair

Upon thy cheek its blossom glows
   As from a mirror clear
Making thyself a living rose
   In blossom all the year

It is a sweet and favorite flower
   To grace a maidens brow
Emblem of Love without its power
   A sweeter rose art thou

---

[1] *KT2, pp.360–1; CL, pp.184–5.*   [2] '*as*' *CL, p.184.*

The rose like hues of insects wing
  May perish in an hour
Tis but at best a fading thing
  But thou'rt a living flower

The roses steep'd in morning dews
  Holds every eye in thrall[1]
But woman she alone subdues
  Her beauty conquers all

Woman had we never met[2]

Woman had we never met
I nor thou had felt regret
Never had a cause to sigh
Never had a wish to die
    To[3] part and cease to love thee

Had I shared the smallest part
Of friendship from a womans heart
Never had I felt the pains
Of these ever galling chains
    Or ever ceased to love thee

And never on my burning brow
Felt the cain[4] curses[5] I do now
That withers up the anxious brain
Blighting what never blooms again
    When woman ceased to love me

The Spring may come the sun may shine
The earth may send forth sweets divine
What pain I've felt have still to throw[6]
The[7] nought in Nature e'er to show
    Since woman ceased to love me

---

[1] *'Would every eye enthrall'* CL, p.185.
[2] *KT2, pp.366–7; TP2, pp.521–2.*
[3] *'I' TP2, p.521.*
[4] *Cain.*   [5] *'curse' TP2, p.521.*   [6] *'know' TP2, p.522.*
[7] *'There's' TP2, p.522.*

Woman had we never met
Love had witnessed no regret
Never left us cause to sigh
Or me a vainer wish to die
To part[1] and cease to love thee

The Maple Tree[2]

The Maple with its tassell flowers of green
That turns to red a stag horn shaped seed
Just spreading out its scallopped leaves is seen
Of yellowish hue yet beautifully green
Bark[3] ribb'd like corderoy in seamy screed
That farther up the stem is smoother seen
Where the white hemlock with white umbel flowers
Up each spread stoven to the branches towers
And mossy[4] round the stoven spread dark green
And blotched leaved orchis and the blue bell flowers
Thickly they grow and neath the leaves are seen
I love to see them gemm'd with morning hours
I love the lone green places where they lean[5]
And the sweet clothing of the Maple tree

Sonnet[6]

I love to see the summer beaming forth
And white wool sack[7] clouds sailing to the north
I love to see the wild flowers come again
And Mare blobs[8] stain with gold the meadow drain
And water lilies whiten on the floods[9]
Where reed clumps rustle[10] like a wind shook wood
Where from her hiding place the Moor Hen pushes
And seeks her flag nest floating in bull rushes
I like the willow leaning half way o'er
The clear deep lake to stand upon its shore

---

[1] 'hate' TP2, p.522. [2] KT2, p.371; TP2, p.435.
[3] Knight reads 'Burk'. [4] 'moss' TP2, p.435.
[5] 'be' TP2, p.435. [6] KT2, p.370; TP2, p.410.
[7] Knight reads 'rock'; Tibble, 'pack', TP2, p.410.
[8] blebs? Tibble: 'horse-blobs', TP2, p.410.
[9] 'flood', TP2, p.410.   [10] 'nestle' TP2, p.410.

I love the hay grass when the flower head swings
To summer winds and insects happy wings
That sport about the meadow the bright day
And see bright beetles[1] in the clear lake play

Along the willow banks of Nen[2]

Along the willow banks of Nen
Where bows the bullrush tall
I wander from the ways of men
And get released from thrall
Winds rustling in the flags and sedge
That pucker o'er the stream
In ruffles to the waters edge
How beautiful they seem
Cool and refreshing is the flood
It does the weary spirits good

Theres nought so sweet as summer winds
Their soft and perfumed wings
That every wild flowers dwelling finds
And to their blossom clings
That nothing half so soft or sweet
It helps the busy bee
Trees, bushes dance where'er they meet
Its rural minstrelsy
They bend and bow and then are still
As summer winds their mins[t]rels will

How beautiful the river glides
And wanders at its will
What plashing ripples wash its tides
And crinkle further still
How beautiful the gurgling noise
The shingly pebbles make
The fish leap up as many boys
Are playing 'Duck and Drake'
Fish leap in rings and rush and sedge
Conveys them to the waters edge

---

[1] [*fishes*] *TP2, p.410.*   [2] *KT2, pp.381–2.*

s

Here could I but my Hannah see
The winds play in her Auburn hair
On the green bank beside o' me
Her red rose cheek so plump and fair
How beautiful the place would be
How brighter far the flowing stream
Millions of suns in spangles flee
Tis doubly happy so to dream
And this green place secure from ill
Makes Hannahs memory dearer still

An angel in the summer hours[1]

In the bloom of June arrayed
When the grass is fit to mow
Barley spindling in the blade
And the turnips on the grow
Beside the meadow bank
I lay gazing at the sky
The cows stared round and drank
When a maiden passed me by
In hat of straw and ribbons gay
Her face like roses all the way

The thistle flowers with prickles burred
The blue caps in the corn so blue
Hot headaches like a fire new stirred
Nigh burnt the lookers through
So burnt her cheek aneath the sun
Her dark brown hair was hung in curls
She stood where meadow waters run
And deeply rolled with frothy swirls
Through flag clumps full o yellow flowers
An angel in the summer hours

---

[1] *KT2, pp.384–5.*

I said some words and she replied
And pauzeing[1] tied her hat anew
Red hot grew poppies by her side
And blue caps most divinely blue
I would have kissed her on the cheek
Her gimpsy[2] waist I long'd to span
But purling like a silver streak
Between us both the waters ran
A lone and undivided lot
Soft words and looks were all I got

I saw her in the meadow lake
In every flower the maid appear'd
The lark seem'd singing for her sake
And every bloom the maid endeared
In fancys ear she spoke as plain
And soft and lovely as before
My eyes looked after her in vain
And saw the meadow as before
Yet till the mirk eve lowered the sky
Her spirit seem'd as lingering nigh

Mary Helen from the hill[3]

The flaggy wheat is in the ear
At the low end of the town
And the barley horns begin to spear
Fine[4] the spindle through the crown
The black snail he has crept abroad
In dangers ways to run
And midges oer the road
Are dancing in the sun
When firdales darkest shadows leave
Sweet Mary Hellen walks at eve[5]

---

[1] *pausing.* [2] *Knight reads 'disnsey'.*
[3] *KT2, pp.387–8; TP2, pp.421–2.*
[4] *Tibble omits 'Fine'.*
[5] *The association of Mary Hellen with the firdales suggests that she is in fact Helen Maria Gardiner.*

In the deep dyke grows the reed
The bullrush wabbles deeper still
And oval leaves of water weed
The dangerous deeper places fill
The river winds and feels no ill
How lovely sinks the setting sun
The fish leaps up with trembling trill
Grasshoppers chirrup on the reed
The mead so green the air so still
Evening assembles sweet indeed
With Mary Hellen from the Hill
Who wanders by that rivers brim
In dewy flowers and shadows dim

Right merrily the midges dance
Above the river stream
Their wings like silver atoms glance
In evenings golden beam
The boat track by the rivers side
Where Mary Hellen roves
The cloud sky when the river wide[1]
The banks o willow[2] groves
And Mary Hellen in young pride
Rambling by the river side

Flow on winding river[3]

Flow on winding river in silence for ever
The sedge and flags rustle about in a bustle
You are dear to my fancy thou smooth flowing river
The bullrush bows calm and theres peace in the hustle
    As the boat gently glides
    Oer thy soft flowing tides
As the young maidens sail on a sweet summer day

---

[1] 'where the river's wide' TP2, p.422.
[2] 'yellow' TP2, p.422.
[3] KT2, pp.411–12; GP, pp.219–20; GS, pp.233–4.

The wavelets in ridges by osiers through bridges
Neath the grey willows shade and the rustling reeds made
Vere[1] dear to my fancy as onward they sail
The osiers they dip in the rings lilys made
    And the maiden look'd red
    As the corn poppy bed
Or dog rose that blushed in the shade

The day was delightful where[2] but gadflies where[3] spiteful
The hum of the Bee carolled merrily there
The Butterflies danced round the wild flowers delightful
And the old willows toss'd their grey locks in the air
    The boat softly rippled
    Suspended oars drippled
While the maidens were lovely and beauteously fair

The boat gently pushes aside the bullrushes
All gilt by the water and summer sunbeams
How soft the oar dashes the stream as it splashes[4]
By the side of the boat wi its burden o' dreams[5]
    The rushing of waters
    The songs o' earths daughters
How sweetly they sound in the plash of the streams

What beauties the Summer discloses[6]

What beauties the summer discloses
How sweet are the banks o' the Nen
How lusciously sweet the dog roses
Hang over the old Otters den
The fish they leap up in the stream
The flags they look green by its side
The flowers up and down like a dream
And the insects are glancing wi pride

---

[1] *Veer.*   [2] *'when' GP, p.219; 'when' GS, p.234.*
[3] *were.*   [4] *'plashes' GS, p.234.*
[5] *'burdens and dreams' GS, p.234.*
[6] *KT2, pp.414–15; GP, pp.220–1.*

The birds are all out in the sun
And they build in the flags o the stream
From the reeds how the water rats run
While sun rays on wave ridges gleam
Come hither my Hellen Maria[1]
The Meadow pink[2] blossoms for thee
The top of the rivers on fire
How green is the bush and the tree

The hemlocks and keksies and Rue[3]
Grow[4] rank by the side of the flood
And the reed clumps a' simmer wi dew
Would hide the Coots nest if they could
What beauties doth summer disclose
How sweet are the banks o' the Nen
Goats beard meadows sweet[5] and wild rose
And the larks o'er the wheat i the glen

Come here sweet Maria oh come
To the banks and green spots o' the Nen
Where the Coot in the reeds builds a home
And where all the year hides the Moor hen
Come Hellen Maria here live
Like the Bee in the flowers and the dew
And the pleasures which nature will give
Is love ever faithful and true

Above the brook the midges play[6]

Above the bruik the midges play
The Stickleback below
Glides like a nimble shade away
Home flops the weary crow
To neighbouring woods and hedgerow trees
And milkmaids that scarce bruize the grass
With Kerchief open to the breeze
Along the pastures pass

---

[1] *Helen Maria Gardiner.*   [2] *'meadow's pink' GP, p.220.*
[3] *'pue' GP, p.220.*   [4] *'grows' GP, p.220.*
[5] *meadow-sweet.*   [6] *KT2, pp.429–30; GP, pp.221–2.*

Her bosom bare her cap untied
She's like a wilding rose
That grows agen the pasture side
And like the sunset glows
Merriest sounds at close of day
Come fra[1] her cherry lips
The crickets stop their evening lay
As light the maiden trips

The dews are mizzling on her cheek
Like smallest kind of rain
The woodbine with its ruddy streak
Smells half as sweet again
The kingcups growing on the green
Spangle like sparks o' fire
And like to blinking stars are seen
As days last shades retire

The swallow tumbles o'er the bush
A moment and is lost
Then through the pasture gateways rush
As though they'd hit the post
Their wings of sooty eve the hues
Like a dark spot he seems
They whisk along through evening dews
Like one o evening dreams

The bramble bushes and sheep tracks
Of milk and water flowers
Their hue is neither white or black
As they bluim in dusky hours
Oh Lucy with thy bonnet on
Were thou but standing here
I would not envy any one
This evetide would be dear

---

[1] 'from' GP, p.221.

Glossary

Aizle. A hot cinder (*Burns*, p.481).

bell bind. Var. of *bell-binder*.
a benting. Bents are twigs or pieces of grass. *Benty* (Scots)—*To take to the bent* = to fly to the moors, to escape from some danger by flight. Cf. *benting-time*, the time when pigeons, etc., are reduced to feeding on bents.
birkenshaw. A small wood (*Burns*, p.483).
blackstock. *blackstonea?*
bleb. A bubble. Clares uses it also as a verb. (*Glossary*, I, 55, where three examples are given from Clare's poems).
blue skippers. Butterflies—perhaps *Carterocephalus Palaemon*, 'Checkered Skipper', which is rather limited to the Peterborough area, being found among other places on Castor Hanglands.
bumbarrel. The British Long-tailed Titmouse (*Acredula rosea*).

cauf. A calf.
chelp. To chirp as a young bird (*Glossary*, I, 110).
chimble. To nibble (*Glossary*, I, 112).
chock hole. A game at marbles played by *chocking* or pitching marbles into a hole made for the purpose, instead of shooting at a ring (*Glossary*, I, 116).
clomb. Preterite of *climb*.
clumb. Var. of *clomb*. Grigson confuses these, *GP*, p. 74.

dandybrow. Dandelion?
drebbles. Var. of *dribbles*.

elting. Moist, damp.
erie. Var. of *eery*, timid.

frit. Frightened.
furder. Var. of *further*.

gadder. A beast being tormented, e.g. by gad-flies, and running about wildly (cf. *Glossary*, I, 362).
gaist. Ghost.
gilafer. Gillyflower.
gimpsy. Var. (diminutive?) of *gimp*, neat or slender.
goud spink. Goldfinch.

Harry Phillips. Var. of *hariff*.
hen and chickens. A children's game.

hermit bee. A female bee which separates itself from the hive and lays eggs in an old post.

herrinshaw. Var. of *Heronshaw.*

herry. To hover with very little movement.

hing. To hang. Cherry, *CL*, *p.xiii*, incorrectly defined it as the preterite of hang.

hissy. Var. of hussy.

hugh. Clare's almost consistent spelling of *huge*. John Taylor had difficulty with this word when editing *The Shepherd's Calendar.*

hurd up. To hoard or store.

jilt. To throw, to fling (*Glossary*, I, 357).

knibbed. Capped or topped.

knobweed. Var. of *knapweed.*

lamb toe. *Lotus corniculatus.*

lauter. Var. of *laughter*, a sitting of eggs.

lisper. Var. of *lisp.*

lowery. Louring. Possibly Knight's misreading of *lowering.*

matty. Matted (*Glossary*, II, 10.)

mole wharp. Var. of *mouldwarp*, the mole or earth-thrower.

nauntle. To elevate, to hold yourself erect (*Glossary*, II, 46-7: 'Clare who is my only authority for this word, makes frequent use of it, both verbally and adjectivally').

neak. Nook.

palm grass. *Poa aquatica.*

pink. The chaffinch, *Fringilla coelebs.*

princess feather tree. Var. of *Prince's feather tree*—lilac.

printer. Privet, or prim print.

prissey feathered tree. Var. of *Prince's feather tree*—lilac.

quawk. *Glossary*, II, 150 gives 'Quawing' and Quawking'—the noise of crows croaking or cawing.

risp. To make a grating sound.

rispy. Grating, rasping.

siller. Silver.

slup. Wet, slippery ground. Cf. *slub.*

sprint. To sprinkle or moisten.

starnel. The starling.

stoven. The stump of a tree (*Glossary*, II, 302).

stulp. The stump of a tree.

sturnel. Var. of *starnel.*

sueing. Sometimes pronounced *suffing* but more commonly *sooing*. A rushing, murmuring, melancholy sound, as the whistling wind among trees (*Glossary*, II, 308).

suther. To sigh heavily (*Glossary*, II, 311).

swee. To rock or swing.

swopping. Pouncing, as a bird upon its prey (*Glossary*, II, 320).

thurrow. Furrow (*Glossary*, II, 337).

tossy. Agitated. Cf. *toss*, a state of agitation, and *to tussy*, to jump about, to struggle.

uggle. To cuddle.

uggling. Gurgling.

wanner. To wander.

whemble. To turn over, to turn upside down.

whew. To call, as an owl.

whiss. Var. of *whizz*, its effect being lighter and more delicate.

winner. Var. of *winnow*, to beat the air.

wopping. Beating. Cf. *wapping*, *Glossary*, II, 382.

Index of First Lines

Note: this index includes the first lines of the songs and ballads which are to be found in *Child Harold*, *Don Juan*, and MS. 110, but does not include the first lines of the nine-line stanzas in these poems. We have included the first lines of songs and ballads in order to facilitate cross-reference and comparison with other editions.

A charm is thrown oer Olney plains   116
A whimpering brook beside the path   233
Above the bruik the midges play   276
Along the willow banks of Nen   271
Among the green bushes where primroses bloom   197
And in the maple bush there hides the style   97
And must we part that once so close   229
And will you ever love me dearest   206
Arise, my Isabel, arise   253

Beautiful Sorrow in thy silence thou   120
Bonny Mary let us go   232

Come dwell with me   128

Dear Julia, now the new mown hay   250
Dearest Mary! ever dearest   248
Did I know where to meet thee   54
Dying gales of sweet even   50

Eliza now the summer tells   88

Farewell to the bushy clump Closte to the river   204
Flow on winding river in silence for ever   274
From bank to bank the water roars   224

Go rose my Chloes bosom grace   268

He loved the brook's soft sound   229
Helen Maria! lovely Helen   249
Her cheeks are like roses   61
Here's a health to all the pretty girls   210

Heres a health unto thee bonny lassie O   60
Heres where Mary loved to be   39
How blasted nature is, the scene is winter   221
How hot the sun rushes   180
How silent comes this gentle wind   184
How sweet does the hour seem   220
How sweet the happy evening hails   118
How sweet the woodbines fragrant flowers   255

I had na been so busy   247
I'll come to thee at even tide   155
I'll lay me down on the green sward   251
I long to think of thee in lonely midnight   147
I love the awthorn well   127
I love the blue violet that creeps on the mossy bank   221
I love the fitfull gusts that shakes   187
I love the mossy fountain   235
I love the rath primroses pale brimstone primroses   259
I love to see the summer beaming forth   270
I loved the lasses dearly   212
I opened the casement this morn at starlight   212
I peeled bits o strews and got switches to[o]   246
I saw her in my springs young choice   78
I sit upo' a simmer bank   99
I think of thee at early day   64
I've wandered many a weary mile   38
I went my Sunday mornings rounds   191
I wish I was where I would be   103
I wish I was where I would be   240
In every step we tread appears fresh spring   264
In the bloom of June arrayed   272
In the field where the Nettle burdock and Sowthistles   226
In the season o' swallows that brings the bright sun   200
In the white thorn hedges the blackbird sings   228
In this cold world without a home   67
Is loves gold ring been broken   217
It was on a Summers morning   265

Jane Summer is with thee thy fancy may chuse   265

Let us go in the fields love and see the green tree   168
Life without the fear of death   194
Long have we parted been   244
Lord hear my prayer when trouble glooms   160

Love is the immortal souls delight 261
Lovely Mary when we parted 46

Many are poets—though they use no pen 35
Mary Ann Abbot 143
My bonny Ann Sharp 140
My bonny blooming Oundle Lassie 119
My bonny Mary Ann 112
My old Lover left me I knew not for why 160
My thoughts are of thee Love 149

No single hour can stand for nought 51
Now Granny's gone to bed 237
Now the spring's coming 236

O a' the flowers o' scottish land 131
O aince I loved the lily 123
O beautifull Sorrow 120
O' cold is the winter day 207
O come i' the evening my own pretty dove 259
O come to my arms i' the cool o' the day 227
O could I be as I have been 193
O dear to us ever the scenes of our childhood 192
O Edinburough Katys a beautifull girl 152
O Liza Dadfords like a pearl 238
O Love is so decieving 157
O Loves bonny Mary Green 142
O Mary dear three springs have been 56
O Mary sing thy songs to me 45
O Nelly Giles o Nelly Giles 138
O once I loved a pretty girl 158
O sweet is the sound o the doves clapping wings 217
O the moment was sad when I went from my true love 198
O wert thou in the storm 165
Odd rot it what a shame it is 183
Oh Mary gentle Mary let us not disagree 258
Oh Molly Meeks! Oh Molly Meeks 256
On the return of April some few days 214
On the seventeenth of April 204

Pale sun beams gleam 129
'Poets are born'—and so are whores—the trade is 83
Primroses are in hedge rows peeping 262

Remember dear Mary love cannot decieve   231

Sally Frisbys fair and bonny   117
Say What Is Love—To Live In Vain   70
She tied up her few things   241
She's like the daisey on the hill   100
Spring comes and it is may—white as are sheets   157
Summer morning is risen   35
Summer's in its glory now   211
Sweet days while God your blessings send   48
Sweet Susan Chaplin was a maid   124
Sweet twilight, nurse of dews   176

Tell the wish of thy heart in flowers sweet maid   248
The Apple top't oak in the old narrow lane   175
The bird cherrys white in the dews o' the morning   115
The Blackbird Has Built In The Pasture Agen   73
The chaffinch in the hedgerow sings   205
The corncraik rispt her summer call   215
The cows are from the pasture gone   208
The cows they are out in the pasture   254
The crow sat on the willow tree   225
The Daisey by the road side it is a pretty flower   242
The daisy button tipped wi' dew   213
The dark days of Autumn grows cloudy and rainy   220
The day was cold and rawkin   260
The evening is for love   207
The evening was lovely and littered wi dew   224
The flag top quivers in the breeze   167
The flaggy wheat is in the ear   273
The floods come oer the meadow leas   63
The fly or beetle on their track   189
The frolicksome wind [through] the trees and the bushes   190
The Fruit is fair to luik upo'   97
The girl I love is flesh and blood   196
The grey green willow whispers   238
The heavens are wrath—the thunders rattling peal   42
The Land it is a dangerous strand   150
The lark's in the sky love   178
The Larks in the sky love   113
The latter end of Autumn   202
The Maple with its tassell flowers of green   270
The may bush smells sae very sweet   141
The meadows fill with cow slips   156

The morning comes—the drops of dew   167
The night is still dead Oak leaves strew   222
The path crossed green closes and went down the lane   230
The path thats led across the field   252
The Pilewort and the daisy's   234
The rawk o' the Autumn hangs over the woodlands   266
The Rose Of The World Was Dear Mary To Me   74
The ruin of a ruin—man of mirth   101
The rushbeds touched the boiling spring   186
The skylark mounts up with the morn   181
The spring has been here just one week   239
The spring is come and winters gone   257
The spring is come forth, but no spring is for me 169
The spring may forget that he reigns in the sky   51
The sulphur hued primrose   244
The sun has gone down with a veil on her brow   36
The sunny end of March is nigh   179
The sweet spring now is coming   105
The wind suthers softly   234
The wind that shakes the rushes   216
The winter stays till e'en the spring it canna cum 125
The winter time is over love   102
The winter winnowed chill   207
The wood anemonie through dead oak leaves   180
There is a day a dreadfull day   108
There is a feeling nought can calm   121
There is a Star I know it well   132
There's a gladness of heart in the first days of Spring 171
There's a little odd house by the side of the Lane 127
Theres beauty in the summer flower   159
There's places in our village streets   223
Theres pleasure on the pasture lea   114
They near read the heart   53
This passion to love thee I cannot conceal   255
Thourt dearest to my bosom   66
Tis autumn now and natures scenes   57
Tis autumn wild the swiming clouds   209
'Tis evening the black snail has got on his track 166
Tis martinmass from rig to rig   162
Tis now the height o summer   205
Tis spring my love tis spring   111
To see the Arum early shoot   188
Twas i the morning early   240
Twas just when early springs begin   135

Twilight meek nurse of dews 134

Vetches, both yellow and blue 253

We never know the sweets o' joy 146
We'll walk my love at eve unseen 243
What beauties the summer discloses 275
What was expected is expected more 215
When April dew brings primroses here 267
When I was young I fell in love and got but little good on't ... 219
When in summer thou walkest 201
When lifes tempests blow high 199
When shall I see the white thorn leaves agen 258
Where last years leaves and weeds decay 148
Where the ash tree weaves 196
Where the hazels hing love 231
Wing-winnowing lark with speckled breast 172
Woman had we never met 269